More Praise for *What I Learned from Sam Walton*

"The secret's out. Now we know how Sam was so successful. The best thing about this book is that pharmacies around the country can use this as a resource guide to overcome the "Wal-Mart" effect."

> —Sharlea Leatherwood
> Independent Pharmacist, President,
> National Community Pharmacists Association

"The integration of storytelling, facts and suggestions makes *What I Learned from Sam Walton* both informative and a "how to" primer regarding competing with Wal-Mart or any powerful competitor."

> —Kerley LaBoeuf
> President and CEO
> National Association of Convenience Stores

"Michael Bergdahl's personal experience, extensive research and knowledge of the retail industry will not fail to give readers a "bushel basket" full of great ideas. His "inside-out"–"outside-in" analysis of Wal-Mart provides much to consider from the competitive view. Bergdahl pulls all the pieces together."

> —John F. Morrison
> Missouri State Director
> National Grocers Association

"A very readable summary of a charismatic and innovative entrepreneur and the firm and the culture that he created. Bergdahl provides insights and recommendations so that other retailers will not be crushed by this eight ton steamroller."

> —Robert Z. Aliber
> Professor of International Economics and Finance
> University of Chicago
> Graduate School of Business

"Learn the details 'secrets' of Walt-Mart's success. A must read for any business person! Bergdahl's energy as a speaker shines through this book!"

> —Rich Tiller
> President www.ProfessionalSpeakersNetwork.com
> Past President, International Assoc. Speakers Bureau

"I like the retail lessons about operations, culture and expense control so much I decided to make Bergdahl's book required reading for all of the managers in our 400 stores!"

—Chester Cadieux
Chairman of the Board
QuikTrip Corporation

"Competition with Wal-Mart is not a death sentence for retailers. Michael Bergdahl's insightful book bridges fundamental theory with practical examples to help companies of any size meet the challenges they face. Applying these concepts at any retailer will provide a firm foundation to distinguish your business from competitors, delight your customers and keep your cash registers ringing."

—William S. Cody
Managing Director, Jay H. Baker Retailing Initiative
Lecturer, Marketing Department
The Wharton Business School,
University of Pennsylvania

"Michael Bergdahl reveals the secrets of what produced Wal-Mart's success. This is a terrific book! It can be used as a guide for helping your organization to seize new opportunites."

—Somers H. White CPAE, FIMC
President, Somers White Company, Inc.
Marketing, Management, Coaching
and Financial Consultants

"Michael Bergdahl's new book is neither another homage to the world's largest retailer, nor another attack on Wal-Mart's influence and power over the consumer market. Instead, it is a practical guide that shows retailers and suppliers that they can indeed survive and thrive in a post-Wal-Mart world. Peppered with a liberal dose of actual anecdotes from his experiences working at Wal-Mart, Bergdahl has composed an easy-to-digest manual of strategies and tactics for retailers of any size."

—Don Longo
Publisher and Editorial Director,
Retail Merchandiser Magazine

"Michael Bergdahl's first hand experiences at Wal-Mart's Headquarters in Bentonville, Arkansas, along wth his personal stories of working with and around Sam Walton, provides useful insights into the company's day to day operations. His discussion of Wal-Mart's methods of operation is enhanced by his background working on the supplier side at Frito-Lay and as a business turnaround expert. Grocers will benefit greatly by reading Bergdahl's analysis of how to pick Wal-Mart's POCKETS."

—Wes Ball
President, Tennessee Grocers Association
Past President, Food Industry Associaton Executives

"A great story—some very powerful insights The summaries and suggestions at the end of each chapter represent a focused set of lessons valuable for anyone in marketing—especially anyone going up against one of the "big guns." College students, professors and business leaders, studing Wal-Mart, will all benefit from Bergdahl's experiences."

—Ralph A. Oliva
Executive Director,
Institute for the Study of Business Markets (ISBM)
Professor of Marketing,
Smeal College of Business, Penn State

"Bergdahl's book gives a fascinating insider's view of the world's most successful retailer. At the same time he provides a vital check list for any retailer faced with seemingly unequal competition from a much larger rival."

—David Rae
Chief Executive
Association of Convenience Stores, England

"This book provides a unique perspective on Wal-Mart's business philosophies and competitive methods and details how they permeate the entire community and ultimately all businesses! This compelling story makes this one of the few books I have read in one sitting!"

—Helen Gordon
Chairman and CEO, GREENSHEET,
Advertising Publications
Houston, Dallas, Ft Worth, Austin and Phoenix

What I Learned from Sam Walton

How to Compete and Thrive in a Wal-Mart World

Michael Bergdahl

WILEY

John Wiley & Sons, Inc.

To the inspirational leaders in my life,

My wife, Sheryl

My daughter, Heather

and

My son, Paul

Contents

Foreword

Retailing is a brutal business. Over the past thirty years, few industries have undergone the level of change that retailing has. Even if you've developed the "perfect" retail concept, the minute you open your doors to the public, you're providing a living laboratory of your "perfect" concept to your competition. Every merchandising, pricing and promotion decision is visible to your competition and, for the most part, can be easily replicated. By anticipating and reacting to changes in consumer shopping behavior, competitive economics and technological innovation, 'upstart' retailers such as Best Buy, Kohl's and Wal-Mart sit at the top of their industries, while the former innovators of retail's past such as E.J. Korvette and Woolworth's are relegated to history books and nostalgia items on eBay.

The success of Wal-Mart Stores is unparalleled. Wal-Mart accounts for almost nine cents of every non-auto retail dollar spent in the United States and register tape from one day's sales at Wal-Mart would stretch almost 2,700 miles, or from Philadelphia to Los Angeles. In fact, Wal-Mart's day-after-Thanksgiving sales in 2003 of $1.5 billion were larger than the gross domestic product of 36 countries. Fortunately, the almost 5,000 Wal-Mart stores worldwide provide a living laboratory for all retailers to shamelessly borrow from the most successful retailer in history.

Competing in the same markets as large, well-capitalized retailers such as Wal-Mart takes a well-crafted strategy to meet the challenge. In this book, Michael Bergdahl details the key factors that have guided Wal-Mart's rise to the top of the Fortune 500. By distilling the elements of their retail strategy into pockets of information that are controllable, and more importantly, actionable, Bergdahl provides a tactical plan that retailers large and small can employ to survive and thrive in the shadow of Wal-Mart.

Wal-Mart has been called many things, but complacent is not among them. As shown by the rollout of their 'Neighborhood Markets' format,

Wal-Mart continues to experiment with new businesses and formats in an effort to meet more of the needs of its core customers, gain more share of wallet, and attract potential new shoppers. This book will not provide the magic elixir for beating Wal-Mart at their game. However, this book provides invaluable insights from a Wal-Mart insider that will help any retailer construct the right mix of products and services that both satisfies the target customer and produces the projected sales and profit. By leveraging the same battle-tested techniques of Wal-Mart, you can build a profitable retail business that continually "turns on" your customers. The alternative is much less attractive.

William S. Cody
Managing Director, Jay H. Baker Retailing Initiative
Lecturer, Marketing Department
The Wharton School, University of Pennsylvania

Preface

In 1862, a pivotal Civil War battle called the Battle of Pea Ridge was fought in Northwest Arkansas. The fighting took place in Benton County, just outside of Bentonville, Arkansas, today the home of Wal-Mart Stores. In that battle, the Union soldiers defeated the Confederates soundly. But as the saying goes, "the South shall rise again." A century later, in 1962, Sam Walton opened his first Wal-Mart store in Benton County, starting his own retailing civil war. He began his march toward retailing supremacy by building stores in rural areas across the southern USA. Eventually, after establishing himself and gaining momentum in the Confederate states, he began his expansion campaign in the west, southwest, north, and northeast, pummeling hapless American competitors. With the domestic markets rapidly coming under his control he set his sights on dominating an even bigger retail battlefield . . . the world!

How has Wal-Mart accomplished so much in such a short period of time? How important is the influence of its founder, Sam Walton, to the ongoing success of the company? What do competitors, domestic and international, both small and large, need to know about the world's largest retailer in order to compete effectively? What is the importance of its culture to the success of the company? In this book, I will answer these questions as I provide you with an insider's perspective on what you are up against as you try to compete in a Wal-Mart world and survive.

The idea behind this book evolved over a period of years. After leaving Wal-Mart I became a business turnaround specialist. In that role I often find myself drawing upon my experiences at the world's largest retailer. I learned that many of the basic business strategies and tactics utilized by Wal-Mart are lessons from which any company could benefit. Along the way I've found some of its simplest concepts, though easy to understand, are often extremely difficult for other companies to implement.

Another experience spurring me to write this book came out of my speaking experiences. As a keynote speaker I have presented at companies and conferences all over the country. On one of these occasions, I had the chance to speak at the National Retail Federation's Store Works Conference, held in San Diego, California. In my keynote speech I talked about my experiences working with and around Sam Walton and specifically about competing with Wal-Mart. At that time, it became apparent to me there was tremendous interest in the retailing world, domestically, in gaining a better understanding of the inner workings of the company. The seed had been planted but I still hadn't made the decision yet to capture my experiences on paper.

I gained the final commitment and motivation to write this book in an interesting and unusual way. Michael Menchel and Tony D'Amelio at the Washington Speakers Bureau scheduled me as the keynote speaker at an international retail conference in Cologne, Germany. Over 600 retailers from across Europe were in attendance. The topic I was asked to present was "How to Compete with Wal-Mart and Survive." The questions I received from audience members following my presentation made me realize how concerned international competitors are when Wal-Mart is expanding into their backyards. At the same time, it became very apparent to me just how little domestic and international competitors knew about the inner workings of the world's largest retailer.

The combination of my turnaround experiences and the San Diego and Cologne speeches finally convinced me there was an important story to tell, it needed to be put in writing, and I was the one to do it. The more I talked to my literary agent Sam Fleischman (Literary Artist Representatives) the more excited I became about crafting an insider's competitive perspective for readers around the world. It was my wife, Sheryl, who actually inspired me to action by directing me to stop talking about writing a book and start writing!

In writing *What I Learned from Sam Walton: How to Compete and Thrive in a Wal-Mart World,* I want current and future competitors to gain a better understanding of what they are up against when a Wal-Mart Discount Store, Supercenter or Neighborhood Market comes to town. The messages, in the book, are equally applicable to retailers, suppliers, college educators, students and main street merchant organizations. Domestic and international businesses in retailing, non-retailers, manufacturers and suppliers will benefit from the glimpse inside the world's most successful company. I wrote the book from an "outside-in" perspective with the reader in mind. Multi-store retail chains, single site operators, international competitors and their suppliers will find the information I have provided of particular interest.

In order to accurately portray the strategies and tactics I'm recommending, I've extensively researched Wal-Mart. I've quoted retail analysts, newspaper and magazine articles, book authors and studies related to retail competition. I interviewed retail industry professionals, company CEO's and Association Executives, who compete in the trenches with Wal-Mart every day. By blending my experiences as a retailer, along with those of retail industry experts, my goal is to provide the reader with focused competitive insights which can be tactically implemented immediately.

In sharing my inside experiences, I will uncover and unravel the principles, myth, culture, mystery and secrets behind Wal-Mart's success, based upon my firsthand observations of the company, Sam Walton and its executive team. You don't have to be a retailer to enjoy the insights I have provided. The lessons are just as valuable for any business, domestic or international, competing for market share. I will say, even though I provide readers with the chance to "pick Wal-Mart's pockets" the cultural lessons they will learn are easy to understand in concept yet at the same time they are extremely hard to duplicate. You'll find in practice many of Wal-Mart's strategies and tactics require an unusually high degree of operational discipline to implement. Some organizations will find the cultural changes required to replicate some of the Wal-Mart's best practices painfully uncomfortable for their managers and employees to accept.

In the appendix of this book, I have included two useful tools to help companies develop competitive strategies and tactics. The first is a Competitive Self-Assessment and the second is a thought provoking questionnaire for focusing your strategy. At the end of each chapter is a checklist to help stimulate ideas you can use in your business. If I were to come to your company as a business coach, to help you focus your strategy and tactics, these are the tools I would use to guide our discussion.

Acknowledgments

Sam Fleischman, Literary Artist Representatives
David Pugh, editor, John Wiley & Sons, Inc., Publishers
Todd Tedesco, senior production editor,
   John Wiley & Sons, Inc., Publishers
Elsie Lampl, line editor, CMU, MA in Professional Writing
Heather Bergdahl, final manuscript proofreader
Dick Wood, chairman, Wawa Convenience Stores
Steve Sheetz, chairman, Sheetz Convenience Stores
Chester Cadieux, chairman, QuikTrip Convenience Stores
Stan Fortune, former Wal-Mart manager
John Morrison, director, Missouri Grocers Association
Wes Ball, director, Tennessee Grocers Association
Kerley LeBoeuf, president and CEO of
   National Convenience Store Association
Stephen Giroux, board member, National Community Pharmacy
   Association (NCPA)
John Musil, president, Arizona Pharmacy Association, NCPA
Al Norman, Sprawlbusters
Fred Martels, president, People Solution Strategies
Tony D'Amelio, Washington Speakers Bureau
Michael Menchel, Washington Speakers Bureau
Somers White, president, Somers White Company
Mike Kleinfelder, financial advisor, UBS PaineWebber
David Herdlinger, business coach, Resource Associates Corporation

INTRODUCTION

Picking Wal-Mart's POCKETS—
Strategies and Tactics I Learned From Sam Walton

"Wal-Mart's success strategies and tactics are easy to understand yet hard to duplicate."

Would you willingly bet your hard-earned money on a direct competition against an opponent who is stronger and faster, and who can jump higher than you? Against a competitor with a proven track record of victory against seasoned veterans and promising upstarts alike? An Olympic-caliber team whose world-class athletes have set the record in virtually every event they have entered? That's the sort of Herculean task retailers take on when they attempt to go toe-to-toe in competition with Wal-Mart. They go for the gold and are hard to beat in all ten events in the "retail decathlon:" Price, operations, culture, key-item promotion, product selection, expenses, talent, service, technology, and distribution/fleet logistics.

Wal-Mart sets the standards and controls its own destiny in every retail area. It makes the retail competition rules, and can change them whenever it likes. And what everyone else is learning is that it's virtually impossible to hold your own in a competition when the rules of engagement are set by the largest, strongest, and fastest competitor. If you think Wal-Mart is simply K-Mart on steroids, think again. Wal-Mart is a race-fit competitor with little credible competition. Clearly it is in a league of its own.

The company is loved by its millions of customers, but ofttimes is despised by competitors and special-interest groups who have given the company a variety of nicknames including the Beast from Bentonville, World-Mart, the 800-Pound Gorilla, Weed-Mart, the Giant, the Evil Empire, the Bentonville Colossus, the Retail Juggernaut, Godzilla-Mart, and Big Brother Wally.

Not all communities have welcomed Wal-Mart's arrival. Some fight the construction of Supercenters in their backyards. Take the example of Inglewood, California, a Los Angeles suburb, fighting the proposed construction of a Supercenter. California has become a battleground ever since Wal-Mart announced its intent to open 40 Supercenters in the state. Some communities in California have actually introduced zoning regulations prohibiting retail store construction exceeding 100,000 square feet.

In early 2004, Wal-Mart invested over a million dollars to get the 10,000 signatures required for a ballot measure in Inglewood so residents, not local politicians and a vocal minority, would decide the fate of a proposed store. Using TV and radio, Wal-Mart heavily advertised the virtues of a Supercenter for the local community. The debate pitted religious leaders, community activists, business owners, local politicians and unions against the world's largest retailer. Describing Wal-Mart's efforts in Inglewood, UFCW International President Joe Hansen stated, " Wal-Mart is undermining living standards across the country and tried to undermine the democratic process itself." The final outcome was a "no vote" in April 2004 against Wal-Mart as residents drove a stake in the ground declaring "not in my neighborhood!" I talked to Al Norman, a nationally recognized expert on big box sprawl. He runs a consulting firm that helps community coalitions fight the expansion of big box retailers. Norman said he led a successful 1993 campaign to keep Wal-Mart out of his hometown of Greenfield, Mass. Since then, he said, more than 215 communities, like Inglewood, have successfully opposed Wal-Mart and other big-box retailers.

Sam Walton always insisted that his goal for Wal-Mart was never to be the biggest retailer in the world; it was simply to be the best. When I think about Sam's success I'm reminded of something the late Earl Nightingale, one of the world's foremost experts on success, once said: "What you think about most of the time is what you become." Sam Walton, in his obsession with becoming the best in retail, was entrepreneurial focus personified. He spent his every waking moment trying to improve Wal-Mart. He did it by outthinking, outworking, and outperforming his competition. He did it the old-fashioned way—by visiting stores, talking with associates, and listening to customers. He had a vision to which he was steadfast, even when his suppliers and competitors told him his rural-retailing discount strategy wouldn't work.

He was determined to prove them wrong and in the process he forever changed industry beliefs about the historical product and pricing approach, with his low price, stack it high, and let it fly merchandising tactics. Contrary to Sam's insistence he didn't want to be the biggest, in

1991 Wal-Mart surpassed Sears to become just that; the biggest retailer in America. Today, just 13 years later, Wal-Mart's sales are 6 times the sales of Sears!

His singularity of focus also led Wal-Mart to become the biggest retailer on Earth, named by *Fortune* in 2003 the most admired company in the world—a distinction it continues to hold in 2004. Wal-Mart is in good company as the top ten most admired companies in 2004 includes: 2. Berkshire Hathaway, 3. Southwest Airlines, 4. General Electric (GE), 5. Dell, 6. Microsoft, 7. Johnson and Johnson, 8. Starbucks, 9. Fed Ex and 10. IBM. Until Wal-Mart took over the number one spot GE had held that position for 5 years straight from 1998–2002. Coca-Cola lead the others for two years, 1996 and 1997. Rubbermaid was number one for 2 years, 1994–1995. Merck was in the top spot for 7 years in a row from 1987–1993 and IBM was number one for four years straight from 1983–1986.

Over the past 10 years, Wal-Mart's company's stock has increased in value by 300%. Competitors, on the other hand, have seen their stocks negatively impacted in recent years as Wal-Mart continues to gobble up an ever increasing share of consumer purchases. That said, several competitors have continued to see their stocks performing admirably, bucking the downward retail trend, including: Target, Wawa, Sears, Walgreens, Costco, QuikTrip, Fred's Stores, Supervalu, Sheetz, Dick's Sporting Goods and Weis Markets, proving it is possible to compete successfully with Wal-Mart.

What Sam Walton thought about most of the time was making Wal-Mart the best retailer in the world, and that is exactly what it has become. In fact, in 1999 Wal-Mart was recognized as Retailer of the Century by *Discount Store News*. Whether Wal-Mart executives like it or not, Wal-Mart has also become the biggest and most visible company in the world, with sales exceeding 260 billion dollars a year. In 2002, *Fortune* magazine crowned Wal-Mart the number-one company on the *Fortune* 500 list, a distinction it will hold for many years to come.

In my research for this book I found that Wal-Mart executives still regularly quote from Sam's book, *Sam Walton: Made in America,* and his teachings remain an integral part of Wal-Mart's corporate culture. His values—treat the customer right, take care of your people, be honest in your dealings, pass savings along to the customer, keep things simple, think small, control costs, and constantly improve operations—remain to this day the focus of company literature and web-site communiqués designed to teach employees and outsiders about the company. So revered is his memory that a decade after his death company leaders still refer to him as "Mr. Sam."

When I first met Sam Walton he was no longer in his prime; he was in the twilight of his career and his life, yet he still projected the energy of a much younger man. He wasn't a big man, but he cast a huge shadow. On one hand he was humble and God-fearing, and on the other he was as aggressively competitive as any business leader I have ever met. I have always been a "student of human behavior" so I quickly became a student of Sam Walton's philosophies and of Wal-Mart. It was Sam who gave me the nickname "Bird Dawg." Like an embedded reporter following a presidential candidate, I watched his every move when he led a Saturday morning meeting or when he and I attended the same business meeting. I will also never forget the one-on-one meetings I had with the world's greatest merchant.

Sam was directly involved in interviewing me and offering me an executive position at Wal-Mart. At the time I was working for Frito-Lay in Dallas, Texas and it was because of Sam Walton that my wife Sheryl and I decided to move to Bentonville. Under different circumstances I would never have moved my family to the middle of the Ozark Mountains but the chance to work with Sam in his final years was an experience I couldn't pass up. Bentonville is in the middle of nowhere. It's 116 miles east of Tulsa, 212 miles north of Little Rock, 215 miles south of Kansas City, and 334 miles southwest of St. Louis. We ended up buying a 17-acre horse farm off a dirt road in Cave Springs, Arkansas with money we borrowed from a Bentonville Bank owned by Sam Walton. For my wife and me the Ozark Mountains conjured up thoughts of hillbillies, poverty, and unsophistication. Nothing could have been further from the truth when I met the people at the Wal-Mart headquarters itself.

Sam was a true charismatic leader and a teacher. He was comfortable in his own skin and for that reason he was readily approachable. I found he spent most of his time instilling his personal values into the leaders and associates of the company. To that end, like a politician, he always seemed to be on a soapbox preaching and teaching using rhetoric, humor, stories, and folklore to drive his messages and beliefs into the hearts and minds of his employees. He used live satellite broadcasts, the company radio and TV station, the company web site, prerecorded video, written correspondence, and in-person speeches to get his message out. Sam was always visible and always available; his leadership example was emulated by company executives and managers. There was little doubt he cared about the people around him and they cared about him. It was very apparent to me nobody wanted to let him down.

As you read about my impression of Sam Walton you'll sense the respect I had for him and all that he accomplished. Like many people, I too am in awe of Wal-Mart's incredible success both domestically and internationally. You'll begin to understand there is clearly something different about the "Wal-Mart Way" of doing things compared to the way other companies approach business. Much of that difference is directly attributable to Mr. Sam.

The impact of Sam's teachings has led Wal-Mart to become a force to be reckoned with across the globe. Economists say Wal-Mart single-handedly lowers U.S. inflation by constantly driving down prices at its stores.[1] It raises the standard of living of customers around the world by saving consumers billions of dollars. Its competitive efforts also force other retailers to improve their product selections, pricing, and service. When this happens the ultimate winner is the consumer. Sam once said, "We'll lower the cost of living for everyone, not just in America, but we'll give the world an opportunity to see what it's like to save and have a better lifestyle.[2]

Visionary, transformational leaders are few and far between. But when they surface, they achieve remarkable things. Take the examples of Andrew Carnegie and Sam Walton, who have much in common. Both were confident, ambitious innovators—risk-takers with a singularity of focus. Carnegie made the Bessemer method of producing steel economical by producing on a massive scale. And Sam Walton's rural retailing and Every Day Low Price (EDLP) strategy created a monumental shift in consumer buying preferences. These two leaders, with their different ideas, transformed their respective industries, and in the process their companies also became the biggest in the world. US Steel's sales in 1917 represented 2.8 percent of the U.S. gross national product (GNP); in 2002, Wal-Mart's sales represented 2.3 percent of the GNP. These men are proof that an individual can make a difference. Innovative ideas backed by visionary leadership and hard work can lead to transformational changes in the world we live in. True leaders influence organizations in ways that outlive those leaders. In debates about who is the most influential business leader of the twentieth century Sam Walton's name is always among the finalists.

Sam Walton died of bone cancer in April of 1992, but his philosophies and beliefs remain alive, intertwined with the cultural DNA of Wal-Mart. Read any of the annual reports since his death, or surf the company web site, and you'd believe the man is still alive. This book, drawing on my personal insights into the impact of Walton's leadership—then and now—will provide you with an understanding of the effects of culture on the consistency of standards which are pivotal to Wal-Mart's success as it expands across the globe, and in so doing, will help you to adapt Wal-Mart's best practices and principles to apply to your own organization and retailing vision and mission.

How fast do you read? Depending on your answer, by the time you finish this book, Wal-Mart will have opened one, two, three or more stores. (As a writer, I have chosen to risk committing to paper numbers that are changing even as I write, so that I can give you a sense of scope). Sam's retailing empire has grown to become the largest private-sector employer and the largest company in the world.

A direct comparison of Wal-Mart's annual dollar volume, with its USA competitors, indicates the retail giant is fully 4 times the size of Home Depot, 5 times the size of Target, 5 times the size of Kroger, 6 times the size of Sears, 6 times the size of Costco, 7 times the size of Safeway, 7 times the size of Albertson's, 8 times the size of JC Penney, 8 times the size of Walgreen's, 8 times the size of Lowe's and 9 times the size of K-Mart! In fact, if you were to combine the annual sales of Home Depot, Kroger, Target, Costco and Sears the total would be less than Wal-Mart's 259 billion dollars of annual volume. But these are hardly the most interesting big facts about the world of Wal-Mart. Consider these:

- In 2004, it plans to open a new store each and every day of the year.
- Wal-Mart employs more people in the U.S. than any organization other than the federal government.
- 1.3 million associates worldwide make Wal-Mart the largest employer on earth.
- Over two million associates will work for Wal-Mart worldwide by 2005.
- Over 100 million customers per week cross Wal-Mart thresholds in the U.S.
- The company operates distribution centers in 120 communities across the country.
- In the near future the company plans to increase its annual sales to close to $500 billion.

Wal-Mart achieved this stature through a combination of innovation and adaptability. And as it reaches market saturation domestically through existing strategies, the ever-present pressures of Wall Street are pushing company leaders toward creative new ideas around which to expand the company. Being the pioneers, Wal-Mart leaders must blaze trails into uncharted lands. One example of their competitive innovation is a new concept store called the Neighborhood Market. Says retail analyst Burt Flickinger, "Wal-Mart's strategy is very similar to Mao Zedong's. Conquer the countryside first and take the cities second. If this sounds alarmist, consider the Neighborhood Market. It's a prototype grocery store roughly the size of sixteen 7-Elevens."[3] Now that Wal-Mart is close to saturating the rural landscape it will be moving into your urban neighborhood, and soon. That is especially true in places like Europe where large parcels of land conducive to building a Supercenter are hard to find.

According to Bill Saporito, Wal-Mart is aiming for the top 20 European markets, which account for 60 percent of all retail activity. "I'm not trying to be flippant," remarked Lee Scott, Wal-Mart's third CEO, to Saporito, "but simply put, our long-term strategy is to be where we're not." Now the leading retailer in Mexico, it has also bought a 34 percent stake in Seiyu, a leading Japanese retailer with 400 stores, acquiring its tenth international market, and currently has the vast part of Europe, Asia, and South America in its sights. But lest you consider this expansion to be indiscriminate gorging, consider this: The successful $10.7 billion acquisition of Asda (UK) in 1999, where "it discovered a company almost perfectly in tune with its Every Day Low Price (EDLP) culture,"[4] demonstrating Wal-Mart has learned the lessons of necessary cultural compatibility that have eluded so many other would-be colossi and doomed them to the fate of dinosaurs.

Wal-Mart is rapidly becoming one of the biggest players in the grocery business in Europe. According to Corinne Millar (M+M Planet Retail, 2003), the following are the European rankings: 1. Carrefour (France), 2. Metro Group (Germany), 3. Tesco (UK), 4. Rewe (Germany), 5. ITM (France), 6. Aldi (Germany) 7. Edeka (Germany), 8. Auchan (France), 9. LeClerc (France), 10. Sainsbury (UK), 11. Schwarz (Germany) and 12. Wal-Mart (USA). If you are thinking Wal-Mart's interest in international expansion is simply meant to gain a toehold on other continents, think again. Their goal is to literally crush retail competitors across the globe. Wal-Mart's president and CEO, David Glass (now retired) told *USA Today* business reporter Lorrie Grant "Our priorities are that we want to dominate North America first, then South America, and then Asia and then Europe."[5] I guess having achieved Sam's goal to be the best retailer in the world makes it natural for Wal-Mart's executives to now strive to be the biggest, most dominant player everywhere. Is world retail domination possible? I've always heard that "it ain't braggin if you can do it" and it is the only company out there with the potential for world dominance. If Wal-Mart has set dominance as a goal, watch out international competitors because there is no reason to believe it won't pull it off. Wal-Mart's leaders are world-class competitors who play the retail game to win.

With its southern roots extending deep into small-town American soil, and spreading like weeds, Wal-Mart a.k.a. Weed-Mart is increasingly dependent on foreign expansion as it runs out of room at home. According to AP business writer Traci Carl[6] (though, remember, the numbers change even as you read this book), Wal-Mart has 597 stores, and restaurants in 58 Mexican cities and, along with its familiar U.S. brand names, Wal-Mart and Sam's Club, in Mexico operates Bodega, a SAM'S-like bulk store; VIPS, "diners that serve everything from cheeseburgers to chicken enchiladas"; the supermarket chain Superama; and Suburbia, which offers clothing and home goods. Of Wal-Mart's 1,288 foreign stores as of the time of this writing, 40 percent were in Mexico. Put in perspective, if Wal-Mart's operations *outside* the U.S. were a stand-alone company, it would rank number 33 on last year's *Fortune* 500 list, based on its $41 billion in sales.

This is not to say it has all gone perfectly smoothly. Discussing Wal-Mart's international ventures, BBC business reporter Danielle Rossingh notes, "From the beginning, Wal-Mart faced stiff competition from well-established German chains, and German shoppers were put off by Wal-Mart's friendly—or sickening, depending on your perspective—door greeters. After a difficult start-up period, Wal-Mart turned things around in Canada, while its acquisition of Britain's Asda in 1999 has been branded a success. Wal-Mart's roll-out into China and Korea seems to be proceeding well, although Argentina and Brazil have remained difficult markets."[7] Time will tell how Wal-Mart can adapt to the more challenging international expansion, and whether the culture some think is a cult is open enough to accommodate the behavioral norms of foreign markets. But the smart money seems to be betting on across-the-board wins. And there's a good reason for this; in Wal-Mart's case past success is an excellent predictor of future success.

Sam Walton the innovator used to say, "If everybody else is doing it *this* way, why don't we try doing it *that* way." He eschewed the well-traveled path in favor of the road not taken. As a lifelong learner, he was always eager to pick up new ideas and figure out how to use them. Using the total-quality principles of continuous learning and continuous improvement, Wal-Mart leaders constantly challenge the status quo, embracing change as a fond companion. If as a competitor of Wal-Mart you feel like you're playing on an uneven playing field, that's probably because you are. As a competitor, the reason you feel as though you're always on your heels is because you're trying to hit a target that's quickly moving past you. By the time competitors have a chance to address one competitive strategy, Wal-Mart has already moved on to the next— as Wal-Mart innovates others try to imitate. They are a fast adapter to changes in the market. If something works they stick to it and continuously work to improve it. If something isn't working they change it.

They aren't sentimental about decision-making, and anyone in the company who has a good idea has a right to challenge the status quo. It's tough to compete with over one million of Sam's empowered disciples who are constantly thinking of ways to improve the business, help the customer, and beat the competition. They don't just talk a good game, they go out and play to win; racking up points and putting the ball in the end zone, over and over again at their competitor's expense. They win, their competitors lose, and the game is over. From Wal-Mart's Darwinian, capitalistic perspective, survival of the fittest is the natural order of things.

Many competitors who have failed over the years either refused to change or just could not change. There's a natural tendency to stick to what made you successful in the first place. In some instances, this is a result of foolish entrepreneurial pride and stubbornness. But for competitors believing past success will lead to future success is antiquated. The competitive rules have changed and so have the expectations of consumers. If you don't adapt and change you will fail. So even if you think you're standing still you really aren't because you'll quickly find your competition has passed you by as they quickly watch you disappear in their rearview mirror. Legendary Ohio State football coach, Woody Hayes, said it best, "You're either getting better or you're getting worse." In business, as in sports, you can't maintain the status quo and expect to compete effectively.

To that point, the corporate junkyard is heaped high with companies either too exclusively inward looking, too enamored with their own historical success or too rigid to change. Whatever the reason, like Edsel, which was produced using an "inside out" approach to product development, many retailers who have failed, offered products and services that didn't take into account their customers' current wants and needs. They failed to keep their finger on the pulse of their target customer as product preferences and customer tastes evolved and changed. Sam Walton learned that lesson long ago as he made staying close to the customer a priority. An "outside in" approach to understanding customers' preferences remains one of the strengths of Wal-Mart's buyers and store managers to this day.

Internationally, more and more small and large competitors are discovering the power of Wal-Mart's low-price philosophies. It doesn't matter whether you run a convenience store, grocery store, discount store, pharmacy, restaurant, or gas station: Wal-Mart wants to "pick your pockets" and steal your market share. I think part of the attraction of Wal-Mart, in other countries, is its American roots; people view it as representing American tastes and values. By opening a store in their backyard they bring a slice of the American lifestyle into their locale.

In the "Wal-Martization of the world" process, Wal-Mart in some ways is actually leveraging the power and influence of products, services, tastes, and lifestyle of the "United States of America brand" as perceived by international customers. Even though the majority of the products it sells are manufactured in third-world countries the perception of Wal-Mart itself is America personified. By buying at Wal-Mart, international customers are buying a slice of the American culture and Western lifestyle. In the process the Arkansas retailer is improving the cost of living for consumers everywhere and distrupting the entire economies of individual cities, countries and continents.

Do you sell eyeglasses? Photo services? Jewelry? Fashion apparel? Footwear? Tires and batteries? Car accessories? Plants? Toys? Paint? Hardware? Sporting goods? Crafts? Health and beauty aids? Food? Office supplies? Candy? Books and magazines? Office furniture? Cleaning supplies? Televisions? Stereo equipment? DVDs? Compact discs? Paper products? Telephones? Tropical fish? If you do, you're vulnerable. Can you name a retail business Wal-Mart doesn't touch? When it comes to competition, Wal-Mart, the retail predator, is like a one-eyed cat watching 100 rat holes, constantly hunting for new competitive opportunities and new products. Wal-Mart is everywhere and they are into all kinds of businesses and they are serious about all of them. By the way, if you were wondering whether or not you are one of Wal-Mart's direct competitors, according to David Glass, former CEO, "Anyone that sells anything that we do is a competitor."

Local competitors have felt the sting of Wal-Mart coming to town from Tokyo to Toronto, London to Lexington and from Sao Paulo to Shenzhen. Canadian reporter Kevin Potvin explains: "The power of large retail chain operations with their economies of scale and purchasing clout to wipe out local independent competition is well documented. Starbucks ended the era of the neighbourhood coffee shop, 7-Eleven put the kibosh to the corner store, and Chapters oversaw the systematic liquidation of the community bookshop."[8] And while Potvin suggests these larger, cookie-cutter operations actually damage quality of life for consumers by depersonalizing the neighborhoods, customers, despite lamenting the loss of their corner stores, continue to frequent the national chains because they appreciate the selection of branded merchandise and the convenience these chains provide. It's painfully obvious: If consumers were choosing Ye Olde Corner Bookshoppe over Wal-Mart, that bookshop would not be closing its doors.

While some of our more reserved and formal European counterparts may be put off initially by the door-greeters, Wal-Mart's everyday-low-price philosophy translates easily around the world. As of this writing, the countries in which it has opened stores include: Mexico, since 1991 (597 stores); Puerto Rico, since 1992 (52); Canada, since 1994 (213); Argentina, since 1995 (11); Brazil, since 1995 (22); China, since 1996 (26); Korea, since 1998 (15); Germany, since 1998 (94) (Interspar and Wertkauf); United Kingdom, since 1999 (258); and Japan, since 2002 (participation in Seiyu, 400). This foreign expansion of "World-Mart" is only the beginning.

International retailing is going through the same metamorphosis, caused by Wal-Mart, that has occurred in the U.S. over the past forty years. Further global expansion is inevitable as only 16 percent of total company sales come from the 1288 stores in those ten countries. Wal-Mart is changing the shopping culture as it rapidly expands around the world. It won't be long before Wal-Mart people greeters are saying "g'day" to customers in Australia and New Zealand.

Competitors need to understand change is inevitable in the world of business. "Of the 100 largest U.S. companies in 1917, we count only 15 companies surviving today. Besides 6 oil companies, there are 2 automakers and these 7 others: AT&T, Citicorp, Du Pont, General Electric, Kodak, Procter & Gamble and Sears. The other 85 went bankrupt, were liquidated, were acquired or were left behind."[9]

Many of Wal-Mart's competitors have faced a similar fate. There is a long and growing list of failed companies left in the wake of Wal-Mart's intrusion into markets around the world. Department stores, grocery stores, pharmacies, convenience stores, specialty stores, main street merchants, and discount competitors are all vulnerable. A case in point is the list of discount retailers who started the same year Sam founded Wal-Mart. In 1962, Target, Woolworth (Woolco), and K-Mart also opened their "big-box" discounting doors. Woolworth failed in the United States outright and K-Mart had to declare chapter 11 bankruptcy. Through differentiation and attracting a unique customer, Target has been able to compete successfully and thrive in the shadow of Wal-Mart.

Discount big-box retailers are typically defined as stores in excess of 50,000 square feet; some have more than 200,000 square feet of space. A true big-box retailer is a discounter deriving its profits from high sales volume as opposed to marking up its prices. The buildings are windowless cookie-cuter designs. The lots have acres of asphalt that provide free parking for customers willing to commute long distances to take advantage of low prices.

In the world of big-box discount competition you have to change and adapt—or face extinction. The unfortunate reality is the retail graveyard is filled to capacity with competitors both small and large who have failed to make the adjustments necessary to remain competitive. Some competitors have been so slow to change that they seem almost to embrace the definition of business insanity: doing things the way they have always done them while expecting a better result. But the competitive rules have changed. Those still playing by the old rules are either lucky to still be in business or are in a niche currently untouched by the likes of Wal-Mart. The lesson many have learned the hard way is that past successes have proved to be no guarantee of present or future success.

Who would have thought Sam's vision of backwoods, country retailing would be so wildly successful? While everyone else in retail concentrated on urban America, Sam saw the opportunities in rural America. With K-Mart as his primary competitor in some small towns, and in some cases no competition to speak of, Wal-Mart refined its strategies and tactics in the hinterlands in preparation for the inevitable onslaught upon urban markets. By the time Wal-Mart was ready to move into urban areas the momentum was already behind them to clobber the competition. In many cases the competitors, small and large, didn't even see them coming. It turned out the strategy of everyday low prices has universal appeal whether the customer is rural or urban or even U.S. or international. Everybody loves low prices.

In the '70s, '80s and '90s Wal-Mart focused on saturating U.S. markets. In recent years it has formed strategic alliances or partnerships in countries around the world creating toeholds on several continents. As Wal-Mart quickly exhausts domestic expansion possibilities, the new millennium is providing it with new growth challenges, forcing it to aggressively pursue international expansion. The Wal-Martization of the world is the only way company leaders can continue to enlarge the company and satisfy its investors. Wal-Mart's 2003 Annual Report boasts, "Wal-Mart participates in the most attractive retail space, discount retailing, which continues to take market share from both department stores and specialty retailers. By way of Wal-Mart Discount Stores, Supercenters, Neighborhood Markets, and Sam's Club's, Wal-Mart is the world's premier retailer in terms of size, market share growth, and consistency of sales and profits."

Confirming its claim about the most attractive retail space is this list of the top ten global retailers in rank order by sales volume: 1. Wal-Mart (Bentonville), 2. Carrefour (France), 3. Ahold (Netherlands), 4. Home Depot (Atlanta), 5. Kroger (Cincinnati), 6. Metro (Germany), 7. Sears (Chicago), 8. Target (Minneapolis), 9. Albertsons (Boise, Idaho), and 10. K-Mart (Troy, Michigan). To put its international growth in perspective, Wal-Mart is bigger than European competitors Carrefour, Ahold, and

Metro combined, and fully three times the size of its nearest dollar-volume competitor, the French retail company Carrefour. With 9,774 stores worldwide, Carrefour is the largest retailer in Europe. It also has retailing operations in 30 countries and employs almost 400,000 employees across the globe.

Although Wal-Mart has thrown down the gauntlet as it has stepped onto Carrefour's European home turf, symbolically crying "en garde," its French competitor, if it is anything like its U.S. counterparts, is probably unaware that meeting Wal-Mart in Europe will be like fencing with Zorro. Not that competition in Europe is easy, but over time Wal-Mart will solve cultural and logistical problems and eventually achieve the same success it has in the U.S., Mexico, and Canada. Just as U.S. competitors failed to see the giant discounter coming, you can bet European competitors are underestimating the appeal of Wal-Mart's folksy culture and small-town values. And in the end, low prices will win customers over across the world.

It's hard to fathom a company of the size and reach of Wal-Mart, but let me try to capture the massive scope of the big discounter for you. If Wal-Mart were a country, according to the 2001 CIA World Factbook, Wal-Mart would rank twenty-seventh on the GNP list of 197 countries based on company sales. That means Wal-Mart's total sales are larger than the GNP of entire countries. Said another way, it takes the combined GNP's of the lowest 70 countries on the global GNP ranking list to equal the total sales of Wal-Mart. If you are a competitor trying to comprehend the nature of the beast with whom you are competing, these facts may be both scary and sobering.

In this book, with these staggering statistics in mind, I will discuss the realities associated with direct competition with Wal-Mart. I've chosen the acronym P.O.C.K.E.T.S. because I know that for you to compete effectively you have to carve out a niche or business pocket in order to be successful. Each of the letters in the acronym represents a chapter in the book as follows: **P.**—Price, **O.**—Operations, **C.**—Culture, **K.**—Key Item Promotion/Product, **E.**—Expenses, **T.**—Talent, **S.**—Service. In each chapter I will address some of the inside strategies and tactics utilized by Sam Walton and Wal-Mart that make competition with them so difficult.

My goal in this endeavor has been to write an insightful book of my perceptions of what it takes to be successful in a Wal-Mart world. I wrote this book with the intention of uncovering the secrets of Wal-Mart's strategies and demonstrating HOW competitors can compete with Wal-

Mart and survive, but it became clear to me it would be easier to write a book about WHY it is difficult to compete with Wal-Mart and survive. My goal is not to discourage you and convince you to give up hope. Rather, I want to encourage you and help you find and implement the right strategy for your business. I have tried to offer a realistic portrayal of what you're up against when you face the largest and most powerful retailer in the world and to provide immediately implementable strategies, tactics and ideas enabling you to compete. Having been an insider, I'll peel back the cultural layers of the Wal-Mart onion and give you a glimpse into the competitive mind of the founder of the world's largest retailer and in that endeavor I'll share with you what I believe are the seven secret success strategies of Sam Walton.

Why not pick Wal-Mart's pockets? What better way to improve your game than to learn from the strongest, fastest, and toughest competitor? I'll discuss what I perceive to be its various areas of competitive advantage but at the same time I'll tell you why you'll have difficulty duplicating some of the simplest things it does. The insights provided include the point of view of industry experts who currently compete with Wal-Mart and who have adapted in order to compete successfully. Don't be surprised if some of the things you learn are "tantamount to the discovery of fire." My hope is that the ideas and strategies included will help you to not only survive in the shadow of the biggest of the big-box stores, but also to thrive.

1

Pricing Strategies and Tactics

"Differentiate your products, provide great service and don't even think about trying to compete with Wal-Mart on price."

If it seems impossible to compete directly with big-box retailers like Wal-Mart on price, the unvarnished truth is, that it is! The combination of their buying power of big brands, private-label programs, off-shore manufacturing, distribution efficiencies, incredible technology, culture, expense structure, company-owned truck fleet, and low paying non-union jobs provide a vise-like grip on costs no competitor can match. By putting all of these competitive advantages together, Wal-Mart is able to roll back its prices to the lowest possible levels.

A 200-plus-billion-dollar company, which also focuses on squeezing a nickel, gains considerable leverage from its economies of scale and by doing so creates still another competitive advantage. By consciously and culturally focusing on cutting costs and slashing expenses, Wal-Mart is able to rain cost saving dollars to the bottom line. Whoever said that in business you can't save your way to prosperity never met the likes of Wal-Mart.

I can't think of any industry over my lifetime that has been so dominated by one company without the Federal Trade Commission's antitrust laws kicking in. I guess if you build a company from scratch and develop it primarily through internal expansion and new concept stores, rather than through acquisition, you avoid the Fed's involvement. It also doesn't hurt that Wal-Mart's overriding and advertised goal is to charge consumers as little as possible for their products. If consumers were complaining en masse the story would be different. The fact that competitors are the only ones who are upset about alleged unfair trade practices falls on deaf ears. There isn't a politician in his or her right mind who would risk upsetting the ranks of middle America, who most benefit from the low-priced product offerings of Wal-Mart. That's what the American free-enterprise system is all about, isn't it?

So retailers small and large need to suck it up and develop strategies to compete the best way they can. Inefficient retailers with high prices, who have taken their customers for granted, have learned some tough free-enterprise lessons of their own as Wal-Mart has crushed them with the powerful one-two punch of their "smiley-faced" customer service and great prices. Contrary to conventional wisdom and everything I've read, Wal-Mart's competitors still attempt to go toe-to-toe with the 800-pound gorilla on price. That's not the right strategy. The key to price competition with Wal-Mart is to attempt to avoid it altogether, if you possibly can.

Let me illustrate the power of Wal-Mart's low prices on consumers. Several years ago, one of the TV news exposé programs did a feature on Wal-Mart and sweatshops. I remember seeing David Glass, the CEO of Wal-Mart at the time, being bushwhacked by the interviewer concerning child labor in a third-world country. He was asked to watch a videotape of a child manufacturing a shirt while the camera zoomed in on his face capturing his reaction. At the end of the video, the news reporter handed David the actual shirt made by the child with one of Wal-Mart's labels in it and challenged him to explain Wal-Mart's stance on child labor. Cool as a cucumber, David explained that Wal-Mart had strict manufacturing guidelines against the use of child labor and the company did not knowingly work with manufacturers who employed children.

As a Wal-Mart home office employee at the time, I remember being worried about the potentially negative change of perception of customers as a result of this story. Wal-Mart was in the middle of its "Buy American" promotion at the time and this type of negative publicity could have had a devastating impact on sales. The story aired with customer reactions included. They asked customers what they thought about the use of child labor to manufacture products for American companies at a cheaper price. Customers responded that they were appalled children were working in manufacturing facilities overseas but they would not change their shopping patterns as a result of those concerns. They preferred to purchase cheaper, comparable quality items manufactured offshore, rather than purchasing the same quality goods manufactured in the USA, if this choice meant cheaper prices at the register.

I thought customers would vote with their feet following that story and they did. But interestingly enough, not the way I thought they would. Not only did sales not go down following the broadcast, they went up! More customers were attracted to Wal-Mart stores as a result of the free advertising provided by the news story. What consumers heard was that Wal-Mart has low prices. They did vote with their feet and their checkbooks. It seems low prices are more important to the consumer than a perceived child labor problem in a third-world country. Any concerns, on my part, about the negative impact of this story on company sales, was much ado about nothing.

I've worked directly for several public companies in my career. I don't believe there is another Fortune 1000 Company in America which would allow a nationally televised interview of their CEO without meticulous preparation and a copy of the interview questions in advance. David Glass did not rehearse and he was candid when confronted with the information for the first time. I'll never forget how David Glass conducted himself in that interview. He had to know what the interviewer was about to do and he had no fear.

David Glass had used an old-fashioned Wal-Mart strategy called *telling the truth!* I was told by Don Soderquist, the former COO, Wal-Mart never rehearses anything. They don't rehearse Saturday morning meetings, stockholder meetings, analyst calls, or press interviews. Although that's shocking in this day and age, I think that makes them better able to move more quickly than their competitors, who get bogged down in "posturing, positioning or spinning" stories to respond to questions from the media, customers, shareholders, or even their own employees. In his book entitled *Leadership*, Rudy Giullani said it best, "A leader who fails to act until every group has been heard from, every concern addressed, every lawsuit resolved, is a leader who's abdicating their responsibility."[1] That's exactly what happens to many executives when they are faced with scrutiny by the media. By being refreshingly unrehearsed Wal-Mart is able to concentrate on "substance" rather than "form." It would appear our litigious American society has forced companies to choose their words carefully out of fear their own openness and honesty will be used against them in a court of law.

Wal-Mart's straightforward way of dealing with customers, employees and the news media is seldom seen in our society today. I have to say it is a refreshing approach and at least at Wal-Mart it works! Employees, customers, and the public in general really respond to open and honest communication! On the other hand, when you spin stories it's easy to get caught telling half truths. Who would have thought by being honest Wal-Mart would create a "new wave" and "cutting edge" concept in business called "telling the truth"!

We sell for less" is one of the guiding principles of Wal-Mart. This philosophy involves buying low and, in the end, providing customers with the lowest possible prices. The question at Wal-Mart isn't how much it can get for an individual product, but how little. They don't use sales gimmicks to draw customers into the store. With respect to product pricing, I heard one of the Wal-Mart executives say, "Our merchandise is on sale every day." Wal-Mart works diligently to find great deals and then to pass the savings on to their customers. Thanks to Sam Walton's Philosophies, Wal-Mart is a customer-focused store in which consumers can count on value for their hard-earned dollars. The goal is to never be undersold by a competitor.

In the article *Wal-Mart, After Remaking Discount Retailing, Now Nation's Largest Grocery Chain*, the authors talk about the radical changes occurring in the grocery business because of Wal-Mart:

> The fight for the carts an d minds of customers is already having an impact. Shoppers in competitive markets are seeing prices fall as Wal-Mart pushes rivals to match its low costs. Among the tactics the chains are using: improving their inventory-tracking systems, doubling or tripling discount coupons, and boosting customer loyalty with discount-card plans. Grocery chains are feeling the pinch of low prices and are enacting strategies as best they can in order to try to survive.[2] Wes Ball, the President of the Tennessee Grocers Association said grocers need to, "Be lean and mean and believe there is life after Wal-Mart."

Unlike K-Mart and other competitors, which put items on sale constantly, Wal-Mart lets its everyday low prices speak for themselves. Recently, its national advertising campaign has focused on its price roll-back strategy—sending the consumer a clear message Wal-Mart is doing everything possible to keep prices low, always. It even has a low-price guarantee. To the consumer, the bottom line is the bottom line. Over 100 million customers a week prove that low prices are king by shopping at their local Wal-Mart stores. According to the Seifert Group at Barrett Associates, "Wal-Mart's prices are the lowest amongst all discount retailers, yet operating margin is the highest at around 6 percent, proving they are the lowest cost operator in retail." Compete with Wal-Mart on price? As my New York friends say, "Fughedaboutit!"

So if you can't compete on price, what is the answer? The key is to find a niche or what I call a "pocket" within your area of expertise, with products and services not offered by Wal-Mart. In a study called *Small-Town Merchants are Not Using the Recommended Strategies to Compete Against*

National Discount Chains: A Prescriptive Versus Descriptive Study, the author discusses retail pricing strategies to use when big-box retailers come to town:

> In the middle of this price war among national chains are smaller independent retailers. Typically unable to purchase in large quantities to receive lower prices like their larger competitors, ma-and-pa retailers have either learned to use other strategies to compete or gone out of business. For instance, to compete with Wal-Mart's low prices, small retailers have developed niche strategies by providing a broader assortment of merchandise within a given product category and better service. Wal-Mart may have the lowest average price on the few athletics shoes and clothing that it carries. A good sporting goods specialty store, however, might have a larger assortment than Wal-Mart and would be willing to special-order merchandise so that its customers could get exactly the shoes they're looking for."[3]

Some companies are able to carve out a niche by providing unique products and services not offered by Wal-Mart. I spoke to John Musil who is the president and owner of 10 community-based independent pharmacies in Scottsdale, Phoenix, and Payson, Arizona. Musil, who is also the president of the Arizona Pharmacy Association, a state chapter of the National Community Pharmacists Association, has 17 pharmacists employed by his company, Apothecary Shops. Arizona is a chain-dominated pharmacy market and Dr. Musil has been able to compete successfully by developing a successful niche strategy.

Approximately 50 percent of his business is generated through specialized compounding of medications. His pharmacies routinely receive referrals from area Wal-Mart Pharmacies because they don't offer services which he provides. Musil's pharmacies specialize in infertility treatment, natural hormone consultations and pain management, with an emphasis on providing traditional personalized service to his "customers."

Musil talked about his views on customer service stating, "I don't have any customers, everybody who comes to me is a patient because they require my services as a health care professional. More and more independent pharmacies are realizing we serve a specific need in the community and people rely on us for expertise as health care professionals. Wal-Mart has customers, we have patients."

The idea behind Wal-Mart's pricing strategy is startlingly simple to understand. In Sam's autobiography, *Made in America*, he describes Wal-Mart's discount pricing philosophy, he said:

Here's the simple lesson we learned . . . say I bought an item for 80 cents. I found that by pricing it at $1.00, I could sell three times more of it than by pricing it at $1.20. I might make only half the profit per item, but because I was selling three times as many, the overall profit was much greater. Simple enough. But this is really the essence of discounting: by cutting your price, you can boost your sales to a point where you earn far more at the cheaper retail than you would have by selling the item at the higher price. In retailer language, you can lower your markup but earn more because of the increased volume.[4]

Sam Walton's discounting principle is that the less you are able to charge, the more you'll sell and in the end the more you'll earn. This is the "stack-it-high-and-let-it-fly" philosophy, which, at the time it was introduced, challenged the existing product-pricing and merchandising beliefs of retailers and wholesalers alike. Historically, product was sold with supply-and-demand philosophies at whatever price the market would bear. This pricing strategy alone has turned Wal-Mart into a destination store by creating the perception in the mind of the retail consumer of significant value. It is for this reason that millions of consumers flock to Wal-Mart every day. Pricing is one of Wal-Mart's many towering strengths and has to be considered its single most important competitive advantage.

Wal-Mart has three pricing strategies: Everyday low prices (EDLP), rollback, and special buy. Here is how Wal-Mart describes them on its corporate web site:

- Every Day Low Price (EDLP). Because you work hard for every dollar, you deserve the lowest price we can offer every time you make a purchase. You deserve our Every Day Low Price. It's not a sale; it's a great price you can count on every day to make your dollar go further at Wal-Mart.
- Rollback. This is our ongoing commitment to pass even more savings on to you by lowering our Every Day Low Prices whenever we can. When our costs get rolled back, it allows us to lower our prices for you. Just look for the Rollback smiley face throughout the store. You'll smile too.
- Special Buy. When you see items with the Special Buy logo, you'll know you're getting an exceptional value. It may be an item we carry every day that includes an additional amount of the same product or another product for a limited time. Or, it could be an item we carry while supplies last, at a very special price.

Pricing is instrumental in the creation of an exciting low-price shopping experience for the consumer. Everyday low pricing of groceries and general merchandise makes the Supercenter a unique and attractive one-stop shopping experience for consumers.

Wal-Mart's pricing strategies provide customers with an incentive to drive long distances to shop. This can help retailers in proximity to Wal-Mart but may hurt retailers in surrounding towns. In a story entitled, "Category Killers Stalk Small Towns," Editor Jim Cullen wrote:

> Wal-Mart moved into Storm Lake, Iowa, a county seat of approximately 8,500 population in northwest Iowa, in 1990. A music store, a variety store and two smaller discount stores have gone out of business in Storm Lake since then, but many local merchants report that their businesses are doing well. In fact, local business operators say the impact is probably greater on smaller businesses in surrounding communities as residents of nearby Sioux Rapids or Rembrandt drive to Storm Lake rather than shop at local stores.[5]

A well known study, *The Impact of Wal-Mart Stores* by Kenneth Stone found the opening of a discount store in small to medium-sized towns may help to expand local retail trade because it reduces the amount of "outshopping" by local consumers and brings more shoppers from the surrounding areas. "Unfortunately, the discounters usually saturate the market with their stores, which causes some towns' trade areas to shrink to a smaller size than before," he wrote. Nearby towns without a discount store suffer sales losses and shopping habits change, as consumers buy more from discount mass merchandisers and less from local merchants."[6]

Cullen goes on to say:

> Wal-Mart has not run any of the five independent pharmacies in Storm Lake out of business. "Ever since they've moved in our business has gone up," said pharmacist Tony Bedel, whose father opened the drive-in pharmacy in 1955. "Once people figured out that they (Wal-Mart) don't do after-hours prescriptions, they don't deliver and they don't let you charge, they came back to us. If an independent pharmacy still keeps full service, it can make it. [7]

Pharmacies are a good example of a retail specialty that feels the pinch when a Wal-Mart store opens in town. Many experience soft sales of their front-end general merchandise items. Fortunately, independent and chain drug stores for the most part have been able to maintain strong sales of prescription drugs due to the convenience of their locations, personalized service, and low consumer price sensitivity. Stephen L. Giroux, R.Ph., a board member of the National Community Pharmacists Association

(NCPA) and an owner of five independent pharmacies, stated, "In 80 to 90% of the pharmaceutical marketplace the price is controlled by an outside force, i.e. third-party insurance, so 80% to 90% of the people walking in have a prescription card dictating what they will pay in terms of co-pay. Therefore the price competition is a bit removed from the market place and we are more focused on service. An independently owned business can survive and in fact thrive in a service environment where you are only competing on the basis of service level and you can compete against the big boxes very, very effectively."

The good news is that successful competition with Wal-Mart is not only possible, it is highly probable if your store is more convenient, and you provide good old-fashioned service. You may also be able to increase your business by attracting new customers to your store by siphoning off some of the additional customer traffic coming into town. For this reason, some retailers even look forward to Wal-Mart's entry into the market.

The bad news is that internationally, competitors are forced into the realization that their past success in dealing with their own customers isn't necessarily going to allow them to hold on to all of their previously loyal customers. When the market conditions have changed and products are available at lower prices elsewhere people aren't going to be sentimental or blindly loyal to a local business if they have the option to save money shopping elsewhere. Unfortunately, some of the businesses in towns around the world that are affected by Wal-Mart's arrival the most are family owned and have been in business for generations. Many have failed and will fail under the pressure of everyday low prices.

Like a moth to a flame some businesses actually set up shop in the shadow of Wal-Mart Supercenters. Tempting fate they attempt to compete in close proximity to the big box in order to take advantage of their drive-by traffic. As one example, I've noticed "dollar" stores opening just off the parking lots of Wal-Mart Supercenters. In visiting these stores, my wife has pointed out many of the items offered for a dollar are available at a Wal-Mart Supercenter for 79 or 89 cents. Trust me when I tell you this is not going unnoticed by the Wal-Mart buying team. There will come a point in time when a section of a Supercenter will be devoted to similar items in order to tap into this market. The lesson is: Even if you think you've found a niche, don't ever become complacent.

Some retailers can not only survive the onslaught of Wal-Mart's entry into the market but even thrive during downturns in the economy. Stephen L. Giroux stated, "We have 5 independent drug stores with large front ends with general merchandise. Our biggest store is about 7,500 square feet and our smallest store is about 3,500 square feet. We have traditional front ends with card and gift shops. In a bad economy, because of a lot of factors, we tend to do well, if not better than normal. We are in a climate presently where prescription volumes are exploding exponentially. They predict the number of prescriptions to double in the next five years with the aging of the baby boomers. From that perspective our business tends to succeed in tough economic times and one would potentially argue that when the economy is bad, people are stressed out so they need more stuff to help them deal with it. In a bad economic climate people tend to not necessarily go big ticket at the malls, but they still need to give gifts, so they are more apt to come to a lower end gift retailer such as a drug store for the card and gift because they still need to give everybody a gift; it's just that they can't spend as much money as they might have otherwise. Our business model with a strong front end, with lower ticket items serving a niche need, tends to survive and thrive. The real big thing is service, I know practically everyone who walks in the door, by first name, that's pretty difficult to compete with on any level including price." Even though every Wal-Mart has its own pharmacy, many local drugstores have been able to compete successfully by offering superior personalized service.

I asked a former Wal-Mart manager about the flexibility each store manager has regarding the setting of prices locally and he said, "They have what they call the Wal-Mart Sale Price. As an example they would work out a deal to buy Scope mouthwash at a certain cost, put a markup on it they wanted and set the Wal-Mart Price on it at say, $4.97 a bottle. The store could never sell it above $4.97 because the computer will not allow you at the store level with that bar code to go above $4.97. If one of the competitors was pricing less than that you had the ability to drop it down below that. If they were running it at $4.50 you could go to $4.50 regardless of whether or not you were still making money on it."

As described in this example, pricing below cost is sometimes referred to as "predatory pricing." Wes Ball, president of the Tennessee Grocers Association, describes predatory pricing as "the practice of coming into a market and losing money in the location that you are low-balling [prices] to run competition out. Say I have six locations around town and I lower all my prices at all six locations until the other folks fold up. The competition bankrupts themselves trying to meet that price. The way you recover is to charge anything you want to afterwards. It's a variation of a monopoly. When you have umpteen stores around the country, that allows you to operate in that manner. If the last company standing is a single company, they can charge anything they want. Our friends from Wal-Mart are extremely competitive when they come into town. Three years later you're not going to find anything like the disparity [in prices] you did when they came in."

John Morrison, the state director of the Missouri Grocers Association, said, "Wal-Mart is our next-door neighbor here in southern Missouri, we are basically at ground zero. David Glass comes from this area and managed a chain of local grocery stores prior to his Wal-Mart employment. Wal-Mart's competitive strategy comes in many shapes and sizes from EDLP (Every Day Low Prices), to potentially "over storing" the marketplace, in which case the deepest pockets usually win. We have witnessed severe erosion in some of our business communities. Within the Supercenter, our local town's main-street business area has been recreated and departmentalized under one roof. The synergism of this marketing approach has both positive and negative consumer appeal. Many consumers just aren't into buying a gallon of motor oil and then running across several hundred feet to buy a gallon of milk. Obviously others do not feel this way."

I asked Morrison what type of grocery store was most vulnerable to the entry of a Wal-Mart Supercenter into the area and he answered, "Many independent neighborhood grocers have survived several generations and some pretty bleak times. True, they are not accustomed to this type of completion, but don't sell them short. When a new Supercenter rolls in some businesses quit without a fight and others have done an excellent job in evaluating how to compete. The impact of a Supercenter is different in every town. In some, Wal-Mart has dominated, and in others the fight is on! Our job must be to educate our consumers on the value of the shopping experience, products, promotion, service and convenience we offer. The historic problem, or opportunity, as the case may be, with many companies like Wal-Mart, is the bigger they get the less flexible they become, a true advantage for the hands-on local merchant who can successfully take advantage of it."

You may or may not consider Wal-Mart a direct competitor. If you are a retailer fortunate enough to not be in direct competition, thank your lucky stars! But remember, that could change. It wasn't that long ago Wal-Mart wasn't in the gasoline, banking, or grocery businesses.

Steve Sheetz, chairman of Sheetz Convenience Stores, discussed with me the changing world of gasoline retailing as more and more grocery stores, Sam's Club, and Wal-Mart Supercenters are getting into the gasoline business. He said, "In the '70s we began to see a switch from gasoline retailing from the service station to the convenience store and now we're seeing a huge segment of gas purchasing change moving from convenience stores over to the so-called big box or supermarkets and Wal-Mart who have a different model. They all of a sudden see the combined purchase potential of gasoline. In essence they are subsidizing that to increase the inside. I don't know that it is predatory pricing, it's more of a different model.

"On the inside of our store we really don't have much in the way of economies of scale because our volumes per location are so small on a lot of those items compared to Wal-Mart that none of us really on the inside can compete with their pricing. They're geared more towards the restocking of home and we're geared more to an on-the-go customer. The only real significant price-sensitive items to us, in the convenience-store business, are gasoline and cigarettes, the two commodities that are really price-driven more than the rest of our offer. We know we can't compete on the inside with them and we don't attempt to."

Convenience stores have been able to thrive in the curl of the Wal-Mart wave until recently. The introduction of gasoline at Wal-Mart stores has changed everything. According to the National Association of Convenience Stores, 75 percent of its membership is single-location retailers. Mom and pop stores have no leverage in purchasing fuel. Sheetz says, "With gasoline there is a purchasing advantage: As you get bigger and buy more gallons, then you can begin to go under contract with refiners and that offers obviously some competitive advantage on purchasing." Unfortunately, the vast majority of convenience-store operators aren't large enough to take advantage of volume discounts. Adding insult to injury, Wal-Mart promotes low-cost cigarettes at their fuel pumps, directly affecting both of the convenience store's two primary business drivers. The resulting tsunami is having a devastating affect on the convenience-store industry as a whole.

Kerley LeBoeuf who is the president and CEO of the National Association of Convenience Stores said, "We do a statistical report for the convenience-store industry and if you take the top quartile, the top performers in the channel trade, they on average have less gasoline margin percentages and a higher proportion of their margins from merchandise sales from food service. The signal that sends is that those operators in the top quartile are relying less on cents per gallon for their basic profitability and they are relying more on the higher-margin food-service products."

Sheetz says, "If you segment the convenience-store industry, I think the bottom 25 percent of the convenience stores need 12 cents or more a gallon just to survive and we're saying you're not destined to be here, that's an old model and you've got to have a stronger inside offer because this gasoline retail environment is going to dictate over time that everybody moves to a much lesser margin. It's a different model and you better have a strong business outside of gasoline in order to make it. The bottom 25 percent is going to go away, I think the next 25 percent may take a little longer, they need up to 10 cents per gallon, but they are going to go away too."

It's not just Wal-Mart affecting convenience stores by selling gasoline and cigarettes out on their parking lot. Many grocery stores are getting into the business as well. It's service they can provide viewed as a convenience for their customers. Wal-Mart uses gasoline as a way to expand its customer-service concept of one-stop shopping. It also prices gasoline in keeping with its every-day-low-prices strategy.

I asked Kerley LeBoeuf why Wal-Mart hasn't aggressively gone directly into the convenience-store business and here is his response, "I'm not really sure that is their core competency. If you think about their core competency it seems to me it is to be able to purchase products for resale pretty much cheaper than anybody based on their enormous clout and buying power. They deal in extremely high volumes and convenience stores tend to not do that, they tend to deal in lower volumes. It seems their whole concept is designed for low price and is generally 'pile 'em high and sell 'em cheap.' Convenience stores have a whole different business philosophy and business model." Wal-Mart may yet enter the convenience-store business in the future and in the process could reinvent convenience-store retailing as we know it.

Wal-Mart has experience turning other retail markets upside down. Look at the impact they've had on college bookstores. Local bookstores, on or near college campuses, used to be the only source of college textbooks for students. They had a virtual monopoly on setting prices, because there was no competition. This led the small campus bookstore to have complete pricing freedom and market dominance, but not anymore. Wal-Mart as well as other web-based book sellers have aggressively moved into the college textbook market via the Internet in a big way. Students can buy brand-new college textbooks on the Internet, from the comfort of their dorm rooms, at the same price charged for used books in the campus bookstore. It seems no market is considered safe from potential competition with the world's largest retailer.

Not only does Wal-Mart compete in selling pharmaceuticals, automotive, books, jewelry, garden, groceries, toys, sporting goods, clothes, candy, magazines, crafts, pet, flowers, office supplies, swimming-pool accessories, paint, video equipment and DVDs, etc., it owns many of these markets, having garnered huge market shares. The logistics of running so many diverse businesses under one roof and doing them well is mind-boggling. All of these unique businesses have to be executed in a 24/7/365 business environment while utilizing average people interchangeably to achieve above average sales results. It seems logistically impossible to perform such a diverse and difficult task so well but Wal-Mart does it around the world every day.

To begin to understand the purchasing power and price advantage provided by big-box retailers like Wal-Mart, we need to explore how they do it. Let's go back to Purchasing 101. The vast majority of retail companies are forced to purchase the goods they sell from wholesalers or distributors of their specific line of products. The wholesaler or distributor, in turn, acting as a "middleman," buys product directly from the manufacturer in larger quantities than an individual retailer could handle and this process enables it to negotiate a better price. The wholesaler/distributor then sells the product to a variety of retailers in the quantities they demand, at a marked-up price. Historically, this symbiotic relationship has served the retailer and the wholesaler/distributor well. The retailer was able to take advantage of the buying power of the wholesaler/distributor and both benefited handsomely. Over the years, this process has kept the retail-purchasing playing field level among competitors. This purchasing balance worked just fine until Wal-Mart came along and changed all the retailing rules.

I remember hearing discussions about eliminating the third party in the purchasing process when I worked at Wal-Mart. As the company was getting larger and larger it was becoming more critical to expedite direct communication between Wal-Mart and its vendors for automatic-replenishment purposes. Elimination of third-party intermediaries was also a way of reducing cost. Wholesaler commissions sometimes added as much as three percent to the cost of goods with little perceived value added. Wal-Mart decided to buy directly from the manufacturer wherever possible. Because of the sales volume generated through its stores Wal-Mart sometimes purchases all the products some of its manufacturers can produce. In most cases, Wal-Mart buys even more products than a single large wholesaler/distributor can buy. This allows it to pay even less for its product than a manufacturer would charge its existing wholesaler/distributor network.

Because of its buying power, Wal-Mart can sell product at retail for less than the price at which most wholesaler/distributors can buy the same product from the same manufacturer. Talk about a competitive advantage in the marketplace. Other retailers can and do buy products at Wal-Mart for resale in their stores for that reason. Therein lies the problem for competitors. Retailers who are trying to compete with Wal-Mart by selling the same merchandise get blown away on pricing. It's scary to think small retailers might get better prices by purchasing directly from a Wal-Mart store than it can from its own distributor/wholesaler network. Not exactly a level, competitive playing field.

One example of this phenomenon involves small independent bookstores located in a shopping mall or a downtown area. When a new hot-selling book comes out, a small store may order a few dozen copies while Wal-Mart will buy many thousands of copies of the same book. Because of its buying power Wal-Mart can then sell the books at retail for a lower price than that at which the small store can purchase them from the publisher. Once local customers figure out how inexpensive books are at Wal-Mart they simply stop shopping at the small independent bookstore altogether. At that point Wal-Mart becomes the only source of books in town, supply and demand takes over and consumers may ultimately be forced to pay higher prices for books. With little or no competition left, Wal-Mart is able to raise the price on the books it sells due to lack of local competition. This same aggressive pricing scenario plays out in every retail category in a Wal-Mart store. This phenomenon forces all kinds of local retailers out of business due to their loss of customer traffic.

There are variations of this scenario, but the bottom line remains the same because regardless of what Wal-Mart sells, you can bet it sells it cheaper than any other local retailer in the immediate market area. Everything from gasoline, flowers magazines, candy, jewelry, plants, tires, shoes, paint...well, you get the message. No matter what the product line, its pricing power puts its competitors at a distinct disadvantage. That is a direct result of the way it buys and its pricing philosophy. Sam Walton always told the buyers, "You're not negotiating for Wal-Mart, you're negotiating for your customer, and your customer deserves the best price you can get. Don't feel sorry for a vendor...he knows what he can sell for and we want his bottom price."[8]

In the study *Small-Town Merchants are Not Using the Recommended Strategies to Compete Against National Discount Chains: A Prescriptive Versus Descriptive Study*, author Christopher Achua surveyed small-town merchants to identify retail-pricing strategy changes they had made when big-box discounters arrived on the scene:

> To determine how local merchants were dealing with intense price competition from the discount chains such as Wal-Mart, K-mart, and Lowe's respondents from the local market area were asked to describe what actions, if any, they had employed to stay competitive. Responses are as follows:
>
> No change in pricing strategy 42%
> Lowered price to match discount chains 37%
> Did not make major changes in original pricing strategy 16%
> Consciously moved away from price competition 3%
> Brought in new product lines for price conscious consumers 2%

Interestingly enough, contrary to the common-sense notion that small retailers need to promote product and change their merchandising

mix and avoid direct-price competition a full 79 percent of those participating in this study either didn't change prices at all or lowered their
prices to match the discounters'. The study also noted that a high percentage of retailers who attempt to engage directly in price competition
end up paying the ultimate price, which is the failure of their business.[9]

When Wal-Mart's company-owned prop planes were not available, I
would fly on commercial flights packed with vendors flying in or out of
the Fayetteville, Arkansas airport who were coming from or going to
Wal-Mart. In those days you had to fly through Memphis, Kansas City,
Dallas, or Tulsa to get to northwest Arkansas. I remember overhearing
conversations between vendors complaining about their experiences
with Wal-Mart buyers or simply grousing about the crummy flights and
low-end hotels, or the fact that Bentonville was located in a dry county. I
had heard some of Wal-Mart's vendors traded dollars selling to Wal-Mart
and in some cases even lost money. The reason they continued to sell to
Wal-Mart was because it provided a tremendous showcase for their
brands and kept their manufacturing facilities operating at full capacity.

I'll never forget seeing the New York apparel merchants setting up
their wares in the Wal-Mart parking lot. They would ship their samples
ahead and then fly to Fayetteville and rent a car for the 25 mile trip to
Bentonville. Early in the morning, the vendors put clothes on their
clothing racks out in the middle of the parking lot, steaming out the
wrinkles, and then rolling the racks into the main lobby of the Home
Office building.

Those vendors that sold gas grills, picnic tables or swing sets were out
there too, with their screw drivers and socket sets assembling their samples. I can still picture them, wearing their suits and ties while building
their samples, and to me, they looked out of place and unhappy. Sometimes Wal-Mart's buyer would have to go outside to look at the larger
product samples out on the parking lot. I guess some of the unhappiness I
sensed from the manufacturer's sales representatives stemmed from the
fact that every other company's retail buying team went to the show rooms
of manufacturers to see products displayed, but not the Wal-Mart buyers.

Adding insult to injury, when suppliers entered the Sam's Club buying area, their neckties were unceremoniously cut off with scissors by
company buyers, knot and all. On a wall near the plywood vendor-
negotiation cubes, just off the lobby in the Sam's Club headquarters, is a
permanent display of hundreds of neckties removed from the necks of
vendors who were not in touch with the company's informal dress code
and values. I always thought the display had to be a bit intimidating to
their suppliers and manufacturer's sales people.

The wall of ties and the Sam's Club plywood negotiating cubicles symbolized and reinforced the casual culture of the warehouse-store environment and the low-price cost structure. Sam's Club and Wal-Mart had two distinctly different cultures. Historically, they intentionally operated out of separate headquarters buildings and had separate buying staffs to insure each brand stood on its own merit. Although neckties were taboo at Sam's Club, they were commonplace at the Wal-Mart Home Office just across the parking lot. Recently the two buying teams have started working together to take advantage of the negotiating power provided by combining their purchases.

The negotiating prowess of Wal-Mart buyers is renowned in buying/vendor circles. They are trained to be tightfisted hardnosed negotiators known in industry buying circles for not leaving money on the table. Wal-Mart buyers are not allowed to take gratuities from the vendors such as free meals, or even a free baseball cap. The business is set up strictly on volume, timely delivery and price. Vendor relationships are important but the only guarantee of product continuity for vendors is to sharpen their pencils and to provide the best price, the first time it is requested. Failing to do so will lead to replacement in favor of a lower-cost provider. Competitive bids are encouraged and it is normal operating procedure for vendors to be pitted against one another.

We negotiated everything in every department. We were trained to negotiate by the famous negotiating-skills expert, Chester Karass, who taught us, "In business, you don't get what you deserve; you get what you negotiate." With the negotiation training we received, no one was embarrassed to push back on suppliers' published, advertised, or quoted prices. That included things like health- and welfare-benefit suppliers, temporary-employment services, office supplies, and even drug-screening services. Company pricing contracts were in place for travel expenses like rental cars, hotels and airlines. When I worked for Wal-Mart, I can't remember a time that I questioned a proposed price for anything and didn't immediately get a price reduction. We didn't care what everyone else in the business world was paying for a product or service, we demanded the lowest possible *Wal-Mart* price.

Being a present supplier of products or services to Wal-Mart is no guarantee of future business. The best advice I have to suppliers is to offer your best and lowest price the first time it is requested. Game-playing, posturing, and positioning is not only frowned upon, it is viewed as at least a lack of integrity and at worst out-and-out dishonesty. For those vendors not used to honest and open communication, operating with integrity was a real challenge. Dishonesty is the fastest way to have your products pulled from Wal-Mart's stores. Lacking integrity or being dishonest will also prevent you from getting your products into their stores in the first place.

Understanding this total integrity standard is critical to the success of vendors and Wal-Mart associates alike. Situational integrity or ethics are not tolerated. I once heard Sam Walton say he would walk a million miles with someone who had a job-performance problem but he wouldn't take the first step with someone with an integrity problem. Good old-fashioned integrity, honesty, and business ethics are required if a vendor wants to do business with Wal-Mart or if a job applicant wants to work there. Employees are held to the highest ethical standards and anything less is unacceptable.

Rob Walton, son of the founder and chairman of the board since 1992, talked about ethics and integrity in Wal-Mart's 2003 annual report. "First and foremost, a culture of ethical behavior underlies all that we do at Wal-Mart. All of us who worked with my father remember the many talks he gave stressing the importance of honesty, integrity, and fairness in our dealings with our customers, suppliers, associates and the communities in which we operate. David Glass, your former chief executive officer, and Lee Scott, your current chief executive officer, have continued that commitment. Setting the right ethical tone at the top is the first step towards good corporate governance at Wal-Mart." Whether you are a buyer, a job applicant, or an associate, operating with honesty, ethics, and integrity is a condition of employment at Wal-Mart. It's also a requirement if you want to be a supplier of products for their stores.

Wal-Mart gets better pricing from vendors than its competitors do. This won't change unless a competitor buys more product from that vendor then Wal-Mart does. This is rarely the case. Wal-Mart's lower purchase prices lead to higher sales and higher profitability. Other retailers are truly at a competitive disadvantage in buying from their own vendors when Wal-Mart purchases from them also. This is the capitalist system at its best if you are Wal-Mart and at its worst if you are anybody else trying to compete and survive.

Grocery retailers have really felt the pinch of Wal-Mart's buying power and incredible expense control in its aggressive pricing. Those who compete in the grocery or convenience-store businesses must diligently track how they compare in shopping-cart comparisons of staples like milk, eggs, bread, coffee, soft drinks, ketchup, mustard, motor oil, cigarettes, and gasoline. Consumers have excellent pricing intuition when it comes to staple items and for this reason pricing them competitively is critical. Grocery store staple items include bread, ice cream/cones, chips, baby food, baking powder, candy, cereal, cocoa, chocolate, coffee, cornstarch, crackers, cookies, ketchup, mustard, eggs, flour, bananas, apples, oranges, lettuce, honey, jams, orange juice, pasta, hamburger, fryer chicken, milk, peanut butter, pickles, popcorn, rice, salt, tuna fish, vegetable oil, baking soda, soft drinks, soup, sugar, maple syrup, tea, canned vegetables, vinegar, yeast, motor oil, gasoline, and cigarettes.

A general rule of thumb is to always price staples within ten to 15 percent of Wal-Mart's price structure, if you possibly can. Retailers have to do what they can to remain as competitive as their cost structures will allow on staple items, without giving away the store. John Morrison said, "An average supermarket will carry around 25,000 items and at any time I can select a cart full of products that we are at a price advantage over Wal-Mart on and at the same time I am sure Wal-Mart can make that same statement. It all depends who is doing the shopping cart comparison. Wal-Mart appears to move from the "lowest price" to "lower price" in their advertising message, based on those comparisons. If you check your best food day ad prices, with your local grocer, against Wal-Mart's every day low price, you will see what I mean. They spend an awful lot of time in our stores checking prices for some reason. The truth is on some products we are lower and on others they are." His point is that Wal-Mart doesn't have the lowest prices on everything, unfortunately, because of Wal-Mart's extensive EDLP (Every Day Low Prices) advertising, consumers perceive their prices are the lowest on everything.

One of Wal-Mart's former managers shared this insight with me regarding shopping-cart comparisons. "If we went into a town and opened a store or in the case of a Supercenter expansion, you went in to start competing with the grocery stores. You pick the top 30 or 50 items in a department or a category and you'd go to the competitors and find out what they were selling it for and you'd price it at Wal-Mart for 10 percent less. In some cases they would even price it less than that.

"In a shopping-cart comparison of 50 or 60 top items you'd then want to be 15 to 20 percent below what your competitors were. You were able to do that better at Wal-Mart, even on the general-merchandise side of it, because you were making more money than the other stores were and you could absorb some of the extra costs of the markdown. When you get into that situation, a grocery store is doing good to run a two- to three-percent profit, where now all of a sudden you're throwing in a combined store like Wal-Mart with general merchandise and groceries where as a store manager if you weren't running eight- to nine-percent profit margins you weren't doing your job. That gives you an awful lot of money to play with to drop prices on the grocery side to knock your competitors out of business.

"That's what I considered more of a predatory-pricing thing, where you'd go in and use the fact that you're the biggest company in the world and can absorb some losses temporarily. As soon as these other stores go out of business Wal-Mart actually has a plan of how to raise prices back up to the Wal-Mart retail or up to wherever they want them over a 90-day or 120-day time frame so the public won't really notice what is going on.

"If we were selling that Scope mouthwash for $4.50 and all of a sudden that store closes we wouldn't just all of a sudden bring that price up to $4.97, we would do it in three or four increments over a period of time. Predatory pricing is just a way to put the other company out of business or it's a way for your customer to discover it is cheaper here.

"The store managers were under constant pressure and scrutiny by upper managers to keep prices low. One of the district managers or regional vice presidents would come in, and there were some who would just go to the local Target and buy 30 or 40 items and bring them over to your store and ring them up and if you weren't priced less than what your competitors were, if there was very much difference at all, you'd be in trouble. This was one of the biggest things they did. We were supposed to send our department managers, in every department, out once a week to check prices."

Local grocers have the advantage of catering to local tastes and preferences in selecting products for their customers. They also have a better handle on catering to ethnic customers in the local area. Knowledge of the local market is a competitive advantage for the local merchant in the selection of products and services desired by local consumers. Private-label offerings are clearly another way to provide low-price alternatives to price-conscious consumers while at the same time improving margins. Customer-loyalty programs, product sampling, and double-couponing are additional strategies for retaining existing customers and attracting new ones. Wes Ball stated, "When you're looking at a grocery store, as much as anybody would like to believe differently, you have to have cleanliness, friendliness, and variety, all of which precede price as a reason for someone buying from you. If you're in your store, you're keeping it stocked, you're speaking to the people, you are relating to the community, and you are keeping your product fresh, you are very likely to survive."

If you compete with Wal-Mart on the general-merchandise side of the store, be aware of the price structure offered in the categories within which you compete. Intimately understand their product mix versus yours. Develop within your assortment some products at higher quality and price points to clearly differentiate your store from Wal-Mart. You can also cater to local preferences and tastes. The good news is not every consumer wants the cheapest-quality item at the lowest price. There is a wide array of customers out there, many of whom are interested in higher-quality products and willing to pay a higher price for them. Find that niche and cater to it.

Remember, your vendors have a vested interest in your success. Partner with them in developing your strategy to compete. Leverage their experience and knowledge of the marketplace. They understand as well as you do consumers are savvy and have an excellent feel for how your products compare on both quality and value. Ask your vendors to help you compete as best you can on price and everybody wins. You don't have to match or equal Wal-Mart's prices, just be in the ball park.

Webster's Dictionary defines juggernaut as "a massive inexorable force that crushes whatever is in its path." Using that definition Wal-Mart truly is a "retail juggernaut" on the offensive when it opens a new store in an area previously devoid of big-box competition. Stories abound of small retailers who simply close their shops and go out of business when Wal-Mart comes to town. Lacking a clearly defined game plan, some competitors look like a deer in the headlights. Some competitors appear confused as to whether the best defense is a good offense or the best offense is a good defense! Undoubtedly, one way or the other, you have to have a strategy to compete and survive. Unfortunately, in the "ready, shoot, aim" world of retailing the term "retail strategy" is almost an oxymoron. Most retailers err on the side of tactical activity, rarely stepping back to evaluate that activity against a predetermined plan of action. When price is the perceived driver of consumer purchasing preference and Wal-Mart is the destination of choice, it may seem futile to some to develop competitive strategies they perceive are destined for failure regardless of the quality of execution. "Oh woe is me" is not a strategy and that attitude will surely lead to a retailer's demise against the onslaught of the Beast from Bentonville.

Strategy for most retailers begins with the realization you can't compete directly with Wal-Mart on price. The list of those who have tried is long and their demise was painfully slow and tortured in some cases. Because of its size and the leverage it has with its suppliers, Wal-Mart has the ability to sell its product at retail for less than you pay wholesale. So don't try to compete on price. Some retailers, believe it or not, still foolishly believe they can. As Mark Twain once said, "Denial ain't just a river in Egypt."

When Wal-Mart enters the picture it only takes one trip to the Supercenter to prove Wal-Mart's prices on the same items are lower. When that discovery is made, loyalty may rapidly become a secondary consideration for the consumer interested in saving a buck. It's easy enough to run your own price comparisons in your community. Interestingly enough, your shopping-cart comparisons will prove Wal-Mart's prices are not the lowest on all items. There is, however, a perception in the mind of the consumer that they are. This perception has been strategically planted there by targeted advertising and marketing messages focused on Wal-Mart's "everyday low prices" campaign. Consumers begin to believe that Wal-Mart has the lowest prices on everything, so they stop doing comparison shopping.

The simplified retail-pricing formula has always been *Price = Cost + Markup*. Traditionally the one-size-fits-all approach to pricing may have worked when competition was minimal. According to basic economics, if there is demand for a product and you are a single source of supply, prices can be set based on what the market will bear. In a big-box world everything is different and low prices drive the shopping patterns of the masses. Pricing strategies are instrumental to maintaining an existing customer base and attracting new customers. If individual prices aren't set appropriately price-sensitive, consumers will shop elsewhere. For grocers, I believe the best pricing strategy for competing in a big-box world focuses on developing price formulas for individual products based on solid market intelligence, varied assortment, private label products, and courage and commitment to buy enough inventory.

For retailers that sell general merchandise, pricing strategy begins with differentiating your product selection. Don't be afraid to purchase higher-quality merchandise to sell at higher price points. Customers are willing to pay a premium for product of higher perceived quality. Depth of quantity of that product purchased allows you to merchandise as if you are serious about your business. To determine the appropriate markup, a competitive pricing analysis of the same or similar products in the local market area will give you the confidence of knowing that the prices of your products are positioned properly in the marketplace. Unlike in the past when prices were set based on "cost plus," in this day and age appropriate prices are market-driven.

Competitors are clearly at a disadvantage with big-box retailers when it comes to price. You will lose if you try to square up on the likes of Wal-Mart by selling the same products at the same prices. Price war in this context isn't a fair fight; it's more of a lopsided aerial dogfight ending predictably for you in a self-inflicted death spiral. So don't go there, you can't win. Remind your vendors in price negotiations partnering with you is in their best interest. By keeping you in business, with the best possible prices for your customers, everybody wins. Don't be blindly loyal to your vendors. If your suppliers won't work with you then negotiate prices with two or more suppliers to ensure you are always getting the best prices possible. Give your business to the supplier who acts like a true business partner.

The success of your business is directly related to the tailoring of the products and services you offer to the interests of your targeted customer. You need to recognize that to one customer a product may be a convenience, to another a necessity, and to another a potential impulse buy. All customers aren't motivated to buy for the same reasons. Ask your customers what they like about the items they buy and why they don't buy other items in your assortment. The differences in what people look for in products and services, and the insights they provide you, represent an opportunity for your business to tailor its product selection.

Your pricing strategy will depend on numerous factors including target market, location, competition, expense structure, and the types of products/services you offer. The key to setting your prices correctly is striking a balance between price and quality that creates a perceived value in the mind of your customer. The bottom line on pricing is that it ultimately leads to profitability.

Many retailers use a cost-based approach to pricing their products. The simple formula they use is cost of goods plus some percentage of that cost. It is important to remember a one-size-fits-all pricing strategy won't work. Individual products need to be competitively priced within the market where you do business. In other words, markup on individual products will be affected by the price structure of your competitors as well as what the market will allow. One strategy for pricing is to price items that are the same as or similar to those of your competitors comparably. This will require you to periodically shop competitors' stores for the items you sell to stay on top of changes in their strategies. For those items unique to your store, pricing may be established by what the market will bear.

You may be surprised to find your prices on certain merchandise are actually lower than those offered at Wal-Mart. That's because in the Wal-Mart assortment, certain price-sensitive items will always be priced the lowest. Wal-Mart checks its competitors' ads and shops their stores, and store managers are directed to always have the lowest prices on those products. Ask most Wal-Mart shoppers about prices and they'll tell you Wal-Mart has the lowest prices on everything. They have stopped comparison shopping and simply load their shopping carts to the brim with all types and varieties of items, confident they're getting the best possible prices. Wal-Mart's marketing and advertisement of low prices have been very effective in that regard.

By leveraging what you do best, differentiating your product selection, and delivering knock-your-socks off service, you will create a niche within which to compete. As a discounter, Wal-Mart isn't able to do what you can do on a local level. You know your community and your customers better than it does, and you know the kinds of products and services that appeal to local tastes and preferences. Have the courage to buy to those local tastes and preferences. With a differentiated merchandise assortment you can survive and thrive in the shadow of big-box retailers.

Hand-to-hand combat with an 800-pound gorilla may seem like an exciting and challenging exercise, but unless you are a thousand-pound gorilla, the outcome of the confrontation is absolutely predictable. Those with delusions of grandeur who knowingly choose to compete directly with Wal-Mart on price, as they say in Arkansas, "ain't thinkin' quite right." In the end, you're only fooling yourself with the mistaken perception you are that thousand-pound gorilla. When and if you do attempt that kind of competition, you've chosen a path that will surely lead to financial disaster and the demise of your business. Remember the path to success: "In niches there are riches."

Pricing Checklist

Review this pricing checklist of success strategies and tactics designed to help you compete with big-box retailers like Wal-Mart and not only survive, but thrive.

✓ Avoid selling the same products Wal-Mart sells
✓ Don't try to match Wal-Mart's prices
✓ Ask your vendors for competitive product/pricing ideas
✓ Provide higher-quality products at higher price points
✓ Price a consumer shopping cart of comparison staples competitively (within 10 to 15 percent)
✓ Broaden your overall selection of price/product choices: good, better, and best
✓ Talk to your vendors about partnering with you on lowering their prices
✓ Shop competitors' stores for ideas and an understanding of their price strategy
✓ Ask your suppliers for special-buy and sale merchandise for your customers
✓ Make certain shelves or inventory are clearly marked with accurate prices
✓ Advertise product guarantees and service after the sale

2

Operational Strategies and Tactics

"The key to operations at Wal-Mart is its ability to maintain the highest standards while at the same time getting things done with lockstep execution."

Part of the myth and folklore of the Sam's Club organization was the use of an associate performance motivation technique called "HEATKTE," a pseudo-American Indian word. HEATKTE was used as a focal point for internally campaigning the importance of individuals and work groups achieving targeted results. There was a HEATKTE song and a HEATKTE dance accompanied by a classic, stereotypical, politically incorrect American Indian drumbeat, BOOM-boom-boom-boom, BOOM-boom-boom-boom, BOOM-boom-boom-boom! Well, you get the idea.

The result of the song and dance was to drive individuals and departments to higher levels of performance through the creation of a self-fulfilling prophecy. You see, HEATKTE is an acronym for High Expectations Are The Key To Everything. Communicated to supervisors and employees alike, HEATKTE is literally a company rallying cry for higher levels of performance.

This philosophy that high expectations are the key to everything forms a large part of the foundation of Wal-Mart's achievement of standards of operational excellence. High expectations lead to higher productivity, which reduces costs. Lower costs allow for lower prices, which in turn build sales and profitability. Greater sales and profitability finance the opening of more stores. More stores enable greater economies of scale. Greater economies of scale leads to lower costs. It is a never-ending mission to drive costs out of the system, which in turn allows the company to pass the savings along to the customer.

In his autobiography, Sam Walton stated, "None of our competitors has been able to operate on the volume that we do as efficiently as we do. They haven't been able to get their expense structure as low as ours and they haven't been able to get their associates to do all the extra things for their customers that ours do routinely: Greeting them, smiling at them, helping them, thanking them and they haven't been able to move their merchandise as efficiently or keep it in stock as efficiently as we do."[1] By focusing constantly on trying to become more operationally efficient, Wal-Mart sets itself apart from its competitors.

One of the first secrets of survival in the world of Wal-Mart is to look for opportunities to improve through change and to embrace that change—and rapidly. The lessons Wal-Mart has learned have evolved over four decades of trial and error. According to John Morrison, the state director of the Missouri Grocers Association, "We (grocers) have to understand what our strengths and weaknesses are and we must play to those. One retailer alone cannot successfully compete with a competitor like Wal-Mart. What can be done, and is being done, is that our wholesalers and chains are helping their stores come together in order to reach a new level of technology, quantity buying, product selection, advertising, information, and community presence. We must reestablish our importance within our communities and become brilliant in our competitive efforts. Many of us became dull, listless, and believing that it was a sure thing that we will be in business forever."

Healthy competition brings out the best in companies; the lack of competition leads to complacency. Often when big-box retailers come to town many existing retailers expect to rely on their reputations and current customer loyalty in order to survive. That sounds like a good strategy in concept but reputation quickly becomes ancient history and customer loyalty rapidly dissolves under the weight of the attraction of everyday low prices. A change of business and product strategies is pivotal in order to compete with a rival as powerful as the Bentonville Colossus.

There are companies that view the creation of a strategy as an end in itself. Some leaders get so enamored with its development they forget why they need it: to drive execution. Wal-Mart isn't successful because of its strategies so much as because of its lockstep tactical execution of those strategies. Ideas are the easy part of strategic planning; it is the implementation of the tactics that is tough. I remember hearing company leaders constantly telling us to simplify everything. At Wal-Mart, if you couldn't explain an idea or a concept in simple terms on one piece of paper it was too complicated to implement in the stores. We were taught to use the KISS principle: Keep It Simple, Stupid! If you think about it, retailing is actually a simple business most companies end up over-complicating.

There are several different important facets to Wal-Mart's operational competitive advantage. One of the most important of these is its part-nership with vendors for purposes of inventory replenishment. This is one of the reasons Wal-Mart cannot afford to work through distributors, wholesalers or manufacturer's reps. Wal-Mart's appetite for product, because of the velocity of product sell-through, is insatiable. For this rea-son, the logistics of timely replenishment are absolutely critical for retail-ers to achieve the operational goal of always being in stock in their stores. The fact that Wal-Mart owns its own fleet of over 5,000 tractors and 23,000 trailers also helps makes just-in-time replenishment possible.

Wal-Mart's hub-and-spoke distribution strategy is one of the key operational competitive advantages of the organization. In *Made in America*, Sam described it this way: "Each store has to be within a day's drive of a distribution center. So we would go as far as we could from a warehouse and put in a store. Then we would fill in a map of that territory, state by state, county seat by county seat, until we had saturated that market."[2] By designing its operations in this manner, Wal-Mart has been able to maximize efficiency and lower the cost of sales for warehousing, distri-bution and logistics. Through the strategic location of distribution centers and cross-docking, the company is actually able to lower the amount of square footage in the store devoted to the storage and staging of inven-tory to only 10 percent as compared with competitors, who must allow as much as 25 percent of their space for storing inventory. This increases the efficiency of Wal-Mart's sales floor by increasing the amount of square footage devoted to the merchandising of products, and at the same time lowers inventory costs.

On the importance of distribution to Wal-Mart's success, Sam says, "We were forced to be ahead of our time in distribution and in commu-nication because our stores were sitting out there in tiny little towns and we had to stay in touch and keep them supplied. Ron [Mayer] took over distribution and began to design and build a system that would enable us to grow as fast as we could come up with the money. He was the main force that moved us away from the old drop shipment method, in which a store ordered directly from the manufacturer and had the merchandise delivered directly to the store by common carrier. He pushed us in some new directions, such as merchandise assembly, in which we would order centrally for every store and then assemble their orders at the distribution center, and also cross-docking, in which preassembled orders for individual stores would be received on one side of our warehouse and leave out the other."[3]

Cross-docking is a way to receive products from manufacturers at the distribution center and deliver that product directly to the customer with little or no handling in between. The goal is to reduce the costs associated with merchandise handling and warehousing by minimizing or eliminating the storing of inventory. Cross-docking virtually eliminates the storage of goods as products are received on one side of the warehouse and leave out the other side. Sam believed, "The efficiencies and economies of scale we realize from our distribution system give us one of our greatest competitive advantages."[4]

Wal-Mart has pummeled its U.S. competitors by creating tight links with its vendor partners, fine-tuning its distribution and fleet-management systems, minimizing costs and passing the savings along to customers with lower prices. "The misconception is that we're in the retail business," said Jay Fitzsimmons, a Wal-Mart senior VP and treasurer; but in reality, "we're in the distribution business. It's Wal-Mart's job to bring product from the dock to the customer's trunks in as little as 72 hours."[5]

Located in about 120 communities, Wal-Mart distribution centers are big—really big. Their footprint can gobble up 500,000 to over a million square feet. Fred Edmonds, the Wal-Mart distribution center general manager in Wintersville, Ohio, offers perspective: "The 880,000-square-foot facility is so big that it could fit 18 Steeler football fields in it. Or 181 University of Pittsburgh basketball courts. Or 271 3,000-square-foot homes."[6]

With miles of high-speed conveyor belts and state-of-the-art technology, these huge facilities, some employing over a thousand people, move millions of units of product to Wal-Mart stores across the country every day. The distribution centers are geographically dispersed across the country in keeping with Sam's spoke-and-hub strategy.

It's no wonder Wal-Mart is one of the most high-tech companies around. As geographically dispersed as its stores are, Wal-Mart operations would break down without state-of-the-art distribution technology. Walking in the front door of the store and finding yourself greeted in that folksy manner, you'd never guess behind it all Wal-Mart has one of the largest private-sector IT organizations in the world. Inventory management, satellite technology and point-of-sale systems place Wal-Mart on the leading edge of retail technology. A good example of the far-reaching impact of Wal-Mart's state of the art technology is the fact that the temperature of every one of its stores in the United States is centrally controlled from its headquarters in Arkansas. More impressive than its technology is its ability to process and integrate the information into its strategic decision-making and tactical execution.

According to Abbie Lundberg, "To understand just how big [Wal-Mart is], consider that on Nov. 23, 2001, the 40-year-old retailer sold more than $1.25 billion worth of goods in a single day. The company has 4,457 stores, 30,000 suppliers, annual sales of more than $217 billion—and one information system. According to CIO Kevin Turner, running centralized IS with homegrown, common-source code gives Wal-Mart a competitive advantage and helps the company maintain one of the lowest expense structures in retail."

In the interview, Turner goes on to explain that the systems are generally the same, regardless of store location, which facilitates the smooth transfer of people from one store to another. And true to Sam's philosophy of sticking with what works and abandoning what doesn't, Wal-Mart developers continuously improve systems by going out and understanding the business. "That's one of our key things: We're merchants first, technologists second."[7]

Sam Walton hated spending money on technology but was smart enough to realize the investment in technology was a necessary evil. When presented with a technological solution by his team of IT professionals, his first question was always "How much is that going to cost?" I remember watching Sam cringe at a Saturday morning meeting as the then CIO, Bobby Martin, told him the bottom-line cost of a new technology in response to his question.

Every single item in a Wal-Mart store has a unique universal product code (UPC). Many competitors will assign a bar code to a class of merchandise but not to every individual unit. Bill Fields, the former chief merchandising officer of Wal-Mart, told me as an example each and every Christmas ornament had a unique UPC code. By attaining this level of detailed inventory Wal-Mart can track sales velocity of individual items and make decisions for future ordering to maximize sales dollars per square foot.

These bar codes eliminate the expense of the manual labor that would be necessary to individually hand-label the prices on each item. Products are simply scanned at the register. Shelf labels provide the necessary price information for the consumer. Inventory is tracked at the point of sale electronically, by UPC scanners at the registers. The store-inventory-management system allows for automated product replenishment by vendor partners, lowering costs, which in turn allows for lower prices. However, as Wal-Mart has grown, bar-code-label technology, with its historically impressive set of benefits, has become old technology as new supply-chain technology emerges.

The retail-technology standards are changing as you are reading this page. New technologies like radio frequency identification (RFID) and electronic product codes (EPC) are not just on the horizon—they have been tested and are about to be implemented. Technology will once again change everything for competitors and suppliers alike. These new technologies will improve the accuracy of shipping and inventory management and ultimately reduce shrinkage. Fast-adapting companies like Wal-Mart, partnering with world-class suppliers, will lead the way. In the process, the big discounter will once again lower its cost of doing business. As costs go down lower prices won't be far behind.

According to an article by Gene Koprowski, a writer for *TechNews World*, "Most professionals in the manufacturing industry have widely perceived RFID technologies as a threat to bar codes, so bar-code technology purveyors have begun to embrace the new RFID technology. RFID tag technology supports an array of warehouse and manufacturing activities, including pallet and case tracking, automated receiving, put-away verification, picking verification, cycle counting and kit building. At any stage in the manufacturing or shipping process, the RFID devices can transmit electronic product codes wirelessly. The tags can be used to track retail buying habits and can even help patients keep track of their prescription bottles. The technology easily could be deployed by amusement parks to track lost children."[8] Companies like Wal-Mart that ship products in full cases can more easily take advantage of this new technology. Companies that are forced to break cases down and "pick" items in less than case quantities for shipping from their distribution centers aren't going to be able to justify the cost of RFID. That could all change as this technology continues to evolve and costs come down.

I interviewed a K-Mart district manager for a job at Wal-Mart several years ago. He told me about the overwhelming technological challenges he'd faced when Wal-Mart started opening stores in Denver, Colorado. At that time, Wal-Mart was bound and determined to gain a toehold in the Denver market and its strategy of course was to have the lowest prices. He told me the Wal-Mart management teams were relentless in shopping K-Mart's stores and doing shopping-cart comparisons. They'd go back to their stores and with their computer technology instantaneously reprice all of the items they found that had prices higher than those at K-Mart. It became a real price war. K-Mart managers would go out to price-shop Wal-Mart stores but the problem was K-Mart at that time lacked the technology to reprice products electronically. K-Mart's people were forced to change the price labels by hand, and it became a real fiasco. Not only was Wal-Mart's technology a competitive advantage, but K-Mart's lack of technology drove up its labor costs.

The spoke-and-hub distribution strategy, along with the sophisticated store IT systems, cross-docking and vendor partnerships, enable just-in-time replenishment of product inventory. The company-owned fleet delivers merchandise in 24 to 48 hours to meet the demands of the stores. "Wal-Mart management sees itself as a distribution company rather than a retailer and it is this distribution expertise that distinguishes the company from every other retailer. The company defines distribution starting with acquiring a product from suppliers to ultimately getting it into a customer's car trunk. They strive to complete this transaction as efficiently and promptly as possible to minimize operating costs."[9]

Companies like GE, Proctor and Gamble, Home Depot, Toys "R" Us, FedEx and Disney all share ideas with one another to improve store operations, distribution, customer service, and the treatment of people: This is an approach known as "sharing best practices." I participated in these mutually beneficial best-practice benchmarking sessions with top executives from Home Depot and Toys "R" Us. A benchmark is a high- level standard, identified by studying other businesses, used by company leaders as a self-assessment gauge for the purpose of comparing, critiquing and setting performance goals. Every department in Wal-Mart uses benchmarking to create competitive advantage in their area of the operation. I was always struck by the interest shown by outsiders in understanding how and why Wal-Mart did things in a certain way. They were as interested, and possibly more interested, in learning from us than we were in learning from them.

Competitive advantage is what professional trade associations attempt to provide for their members. They bring together groups of competitors in formal meetings to discuss best-practice solutions to common problems. Trade associations like the National Association of Convenience Stores, the National Grocers Association, the National Retail Federation and the National Community Pharmacists Association are examples of organizations that provide valuable competitive tools and insights for their members. That's also one of the goals of a local chamber of commerce. You can take the initiative to create your own team of local companies to share best practices to help one another compete. Learn from the example of some of the biggest and best-run companies in the world: They know that they haven't cornered the market on good ideas and they aren't afraid to reach out to learn from others.

Like Wal-Mart, you too should steal shamelessly from the best ideas of your direct competitors as well as from other companies with whom you don't compete. Ideas are free for the taking, and other companies have already tested them at great expense. All you have to do is visit other stores and see what they are doing. Don't feel obligated to strain your brain coming up with new ideas. In all likelihood, the solutions to your problems have already been thought through and solved by one of your competitors or another retailer, and if you'll simply take the time to shop their stores, talk to their people and learn from their successes, you'll improve. Retail is neither brain surgery nor rocket science. Don't overly complicate things. The key to retail is and always has been to keep things simple.

One company with whom Wal-Mart does not openly share best practices is K-Mart. There was a time when K-Mart was a force to be reckoned with. Years ago it was known as the Genghis Khan of the discount business. For Wal-Mart to share information with a company like K-Mart would be tantamount to the Pittsburgh Steelers sharing their playbook with the Dallas Cowboys. K-Mart has learned the "Wal-Mart way" by hiring key executives out of Wal-Mart who could bring an insider's perspective to its operations. The problem for competitors is that many of Wal-Mart's strategies are easy to understand but painfully difficult to duplicate and execute. This is because Wal-Mart's culturally engrained standards enable the big retailer to execute strategies top-to-bottom quickly and efficiently with little fanfare.

Wal-Mart tries things that challenge conventional wisdom without spending a whole lot of time internally selling, marketing, or convincing its own managers that the new initiative is worthwhile. If the top executives direct the stores to implement an innovative new strategy, the stores implement it with no questions asked. Everyone is willing to take risks knowing that if something doesn't work the company will make the necessary adjustments, learn from its mistakes and move on. Wal-Mart's military-like execution at store level is captured in that saying, "Theirs is not to reason why." It is that discipline that is so pivotal to its operational excellence.

But don't think that Wal-Mart's benchmarking is reserved strictly to retailers. Company vendors are often tapped for ideas and solutions to problems Wal-Mart is experiencing. FedEx, for example, is one of the companies Wal-Mart highly respects for its logistics acumen and management practices. FedEx is a major supplier of shipping services to Wal-Mart. We used it as a primary vendor to expedite drug-screening results across the country on job applicants we were considering for hire. I led a Wal-Mart team that visited the FedEx hub in Memphis, Tennessee, to learn from its experiences. We took a tour of its facilities from 10:00 at night until 4:00 in the morning. That's when it all happens in Memphis, as the FedEx flights pour in from all over the country and the world with packages that are sorted and put back on the same planes. Everything has to happen by 4:00 A.M. to ensure on-time delivery.

On this particular benchmarking mission I picked up some new ideas from FedEx about staffing college students, the use of part-timers and second-income earners, and the use of supervisory stand-up communication meetings. We learned that each of the managers, at the Federal Express hub in Memphis, Tennessee, holds a five- to ten-minute information update meeting with the hourly employees in their workgroup before each and every shift. These meetings are liter-ally held standing up, like a football huddle and company news is shared with everyone attending. We also talked to FedEx managers about how to enable our Memphis-based drug-testing vendor to pick up our test samples at the airport as soon as they were on the ground in Memphis. This would enable our drug-screening vendor's third- and first-shift employees to send drug-test results to Wal-Mart via e-mail first thing in the morning. We could then hire new employees across the country more quickly, giving Wal-Mart a competitive advan-tage in staffing stores with a drug-free workforce. FedEx worked with us to help us do this.

At the time, many competitors, including K-Mart, weren't drug-screening their job applicants. In small towns across the country drug users quickly found out Wal-Mart required pre-employment drug tests and so they sought work at competitors that didn't perform drug test-ing, forcing retail competitors to hastily implement their own drug-screening programs at great cost or risk the deterioration of the quality of their own workforce. Ultimately K-Mart was forced to implement drug screening as the quality of its job applicants began to deteriorate.

Benchmarking best practices against the best companies is a way to distance your company from the competition. It's akin to the concept of a breakaway in the Tour de France. A small team of five to seven bicy-cle riders work together to try to create competitive advantage against the rest of the pack of 100-plus riders. In a breakaway this small team of riders works together to create distance between themselves and the rest of the pack. By constantly rotating the lead position, the team con-serves the energy of each individual, enabling all to go faster than they possibly could individually. They take advantage of the synergy of the breakaway team to defeat their competitors. Benchmarking best prac-tices and implementing key learned strategies can significantly improve your company's ability to outperform the competition.

Let's talk about the importance of synergy to improving your operation. Synergy can be defined as a phenomenon whereby the whole of the collective efforts is greater than the sum of the individual parts and that's exactly what happens with teams at Wal-Mart. I believe Wal-Mart's ability to make use of the synergy created by its teams is one of the towering strengths of its culture. Do you believe you have a great team of people working with and for you? I think most business leaders would answer this question "Yes," but let's drill a little deeper into what a team is and why teamwork is important.

In a business context, the concept of *team* is sometimes misunderstood. You can't just call a group of individuals a team and assume you can extract the benefits of teamwork from them. When a true team exists in a workgroup or a company it is apparent. It is just as apparent to the experienced leader when teamwork isn't there. Just about every company says it values teams and teamwork, but not every company has learned to create teams or make use of teamwork. Why is a team important? The answer is synergy. A team of individuals working together has the ability to achieve greater accomplishments than the same number of individuals working separately.

Synergy is a powerful concept. Studies have proven that a group working together on a complex problem will almost always come up with better decisions or solutions than one individual working alone. Group problem-solving is synergistic thinking. This is why companies depend upon focus groups, task-force teams and benchmarking to develop solutions to business problems.

The specific path to synergistic results at Wal-Mart has defined steps. The foundation, or first step, upon which synergy flourishes is "servant leadership." Servant leadership is serving or taking care of the people who report to you first, thereby gaining their respect and trust. Only then does the servant leader earn the right to lead the team. In practice, the supervisor never asks direct subordinates to do anything the supervisor hasn't already proven that he or she is ready willing and able to do personally. Group or team synergy is thus initiated by the team leader and synergy is built on a solid foundation of servant leadership.

At step two on the path to synergy, company managers demonstrate that they care about one another and the employees (associates). Indications of this regard are helping one another out, maintaining an open-door policy, knowing the employees by name, walking around to see and hear how things are going, and showing appropriate empathy and caring toward employees. Accomplishments of individuals and groups are recognized.

At step three if there is trust between managers and employees, people will feel that they can count on one another. They operate with integrity; if they say they are going to do something, it gets done, without the need for reminders. Once servant leadership has yielded caring and trusting relationships, step four is now the opportunity for the leader to develop a true team of motivated people working together to achieve the common mission or goal of the company.

This combination of servant leadership, caring, trust, and teamwork is the prerequisite for synergy. This is why directing, managing, or simply supervising people won't necessarily lead to workgroup prosperity; it takes leadership. Inspired, caring servant leadership of truly empowered people who trust and care about one another builds strong teams, which provides leaders the opportunity to achieve synergistic results. Servant leadership is the foundation and the secret of Wal-Mart's team synergy.

I believe Wal-Mart's servant-leadership philosophies are pivotal to its ability to get its entire team to line up behind company initiatives. Its ability to take a group of average people and shape them into a high-performing team is one of its great operational secrets. Sam Walton said it best: "There's absolutely no limit to what ordinary, working people can accomplish if they're given the opportunity, encouragement and the incentive to do their best."[10]

There is clearly a valued distinction between management and leadership at the world's largest retailer. Company managers are actually referred to as "coaches," downplaying the hierarchical structure of the organization in manager and associate relations which further encourages teamwork. This approach to human interaction has created incredible camaraderie within workgroups which makes the mundane work activities in the stores and distribution centers easier to bear for everyone involved.

Three questions you can ask to determine if synergy exists in your organization are: Do your managers take the time to get to know each member of the team? Do members operate with integrity and honesty? Do people in different departments work together to get work done or is there often a struggle? At Wal-Mart, managers who are egotistical recognition-seeking prima donnas are destined to fail. Team values and success are more highly valued than individual success. An individual who needs constant ego reinforcement isn't going to do well at Wal-Mart. Giving credit to others and recognizing their accomplishments is a way of life.

A good illustration of this point is the story of how Tom Seay, the former executive VP of real estate at Wal-Mart, designed the physical layout of his entire department in order to facilitate communication. His design was unique even by Wal-Mart standards. Instead of an office, Seay placed his desk in the middle of a large cavernous warehouse-like room without walls and surrounded himself with the 200-plus real-estate department associates who reported to him. I have to say I always found the experience of meeting with him under these conditions a bit disconcerting. One of the pioneers in open-office concepts, Seay told me the open design clearly improved communication. His open office showed the associates he was one of them. The fact that he cared about the people in his department created trust, which ultimately lead to improved team synergy. This was Tom Seay's way of increasing the speed of decision-making by facilitating communication, thus turning the real estate department into another fast-adapting competitive advantage at Wal-Mart.

Having been an insider at Wal-Mart, I had a unique opportunity to see the value of servant leadership firsthand. Sam talked about it all the time. When he would get up in front of the Saturday morning meeting he would often preach about the contributions of the store associates. In his own leadership, he modeled the behaviors he expected everyone else to adopt in their personal leadership. Servant leadership is even embedded within one of Wal-Mart's most famous cultural slogans, "Our people make the difference."

To know and understand what you are up against as a competitor you have to understand the concept of servant leadership. This is another of the powerful yet simple concepts used by Wal-Mart that is easy for competitors to understand yet extremely difficult for them to duplicate. Servant leadership is a top-down cultural concept. It has to be embraced and brought to life at the highest levels. Until and unless a company is willing to flip the traditional organizational pyramid, making the people who really do the work the most important in the organization, servant-leadership philosophies can't be implemented.

Another effort to improve operations is Wal-Mart's total-quality effort, established well over a decade ago. Total quality was embraced and promoted by Sam Walton because of his personal commitment to continuous improvement. By culturally focusing on a total-quality program, company leaders were able to integrate Sam's continuous improvement beliefs into the daily routine of the associates and managers. Wal-Mart has visions of becoming the first retailer to win the prestigious Malcolm Baldrige Quality Award. The Malcolm Baldrige Award Program was established by Congress and is run by the National Institute of Standards and Technology, an agency of the Commerce Department, and was designed to encourage American companies and workers to continuously improve themselves. Manufacturers, not retailers, have historically won this award. Sam was committed to constantly improving Wal-Mart in every operational area and he viewed total quality as a vehicle to help achieve that goal.

In his travels, Sam Walton learned about a management concept called "kaizen" which the Japanese business leaders used to focus their workers on continuously improving operations. *Kaizen* is a Japanese total-quality concept that when roughly translated into English means "continuous improvement." The truest Japanese definition of Kaizen is "to take something apart and put it back together again in a better way." That is what Wal-Mart does in every area of its operations. In fact, one of the pillars of quality at Wal-Mart is continuous improvement. The idea behind *kaizen* is the tireless pursuit of small improvements in processes everyday that yield big improvements over time. Wal-Mart encourages all of its million-plus associates to think and act like entrepreneurs (or *"intrapreneurs"*), to come up with small cost-saving ideas that can make a big difference if implemented across the chain of stores. As an example, if an employee at one store proposes an idea that saves ten dollars at that store, it can then be implemented across the entire chain of over four thousand stores to save the company forty thousand dollars. In this way small ideas can have a big impact.

Competitors need to take note that Wal-Mart sets lofty continuous-improvement standards for its business. It has even established the pillars of its total quality efforts, which are communicated through the Walton Institute: empowering people, productivity, diversity, expense control, continuous improvement, technology and customer service. The principle of continuous improvement is taught to all company managers when they attend cultural training at the Walton Institute at the University of Arkansas.

Whether or not Wal-Mart ever wins a Malcolm Baldrige Award is irrelevant; the fact that it is striving to achieve such high standards is what counts. The information-sharing and training partnerships it has established with key vendors provide them with current best-practice know-how in every area of the business. The goal of constantly achieving operational excellence sets Wal-Mart apart from the vast majority of the competition. Striving to continuously improve in everything it does provides Wal-Mart with a significant competitive advantage in the marketplace.

Wal-Mart competitors need to tap into their own supplier networks and demand greater support to improve their competitive ability. Proctor and Gamble is a Malcolm Baldrige Award–winning company. In its vendor partnership with Wal-Mart it has shared its technology, manufacturing and distribution best practices. By strategically aligning with experienced and market-savvy vendors, small and large companies can gain back some of their lost competitive advantage in the areas of technology, distribution, pricing, advertising, promotion and service. Strategic partnerships are in the best interest of retailers and vendors alike.

Competitors also need to tap into the creativity of their own people. Hourly associates at Wal-Mart are trained to make flow charts of business processes. These were typically people without college educations who were asked to get involved in what some would say is work that was over their heads. I, for one, wasn't convinced that the hourly associates had the intellectual capacity to grasp the complexities of mapping a business process; but I was wrong. Associates were encouraged to hold meetings to discuss how to continuously improve processes for which they were responsible. Great ideas were generated by groups of average people all the time. Wal-Mart believes in the potential of its people—in a lot of cases, more than the individuals believe in themselves. Sam Walton had a way of taking people to a place they had never been before with respect to their own job performance. In this context, he accomplished his own water-into-wine miracle by turning even below-average workers into solid to above-average performers. I saw this happening with my own eyes every day all around the company.

An example of hourly employee flow-charting that I personally experienced involved analyzing ways to improve staffing velocity. A group of hourly employees at the headquarters was challenged to try to figure out how to increase the speed with which open job positions were filled. The recruiting department's internal customers were dissatisfied with the time it took to fill vacant positions. The problem was amplified by the fact that unemployment in northwest Arkansas was extremely low. This group of hourly associates decided to make a flow chart of Wal-Mart's Home Office hiring process and determine what they could do to increase hiring velocity. They immediately determined that it was about two weeks from the time an applicant filled out an application until the first interview was scheduled. Recruits were being lost to more nimble competitors in the area. Competitors like Tysons and JB Hunt, whose corporate offices were nearby, gobbled up available talent as quickly as people applied for work. A simple solution for Wal-Mart was discovered through total-quality flow charts.

The interviewing process was changed so that walk-in applicants were screened immediately, as soon as they had completed filling out their application forms. (Wow, what a revolutionary thought, screening applicants while they are still here as soon as they complete their application forms.) Traditionally, most companies take applications, send recruits away and then call them back for interviews. We took the position that lack of speed in recruiting kills and we were letting talented people slip through our fingers. Obviously in a tight employment market great people have lots of options and the solution we decided on was to increase our staffing velocity.

I later visited Disney's "Central Casting" office in Orlando and observed its hiring process firsthand. As it turns out, Disney uses an "interview them while they are here" practice as well. The "casting" department recruiters screened all applicants immediately and made decisions on second interviews on the spot. Interestingly enough, the recruiters performed the initial screening over the telephone to reduce the likelihood of discrimination or bias on the part of the interviewers. Private telephone cubicles were set up just off the main lobby and all the applicant had to do was pick up the phone and a recruiter would be on the other end.

I have always believed that companies that let applicants walk out without screening them are missing a huge recruiting opportunity. On one hand, companies say people are their most important asset, and on the other hand companies make it too darn difficult to get a job working for them. As far as Wal-Mart is concerned, finding talented recruits is like panning for gold. The people who are hired are treasured like golden nuggets for their ability to serve the customers. That's why recruiting the best talent available is so critical to the company.

At Wal-Mart we placed a mobile recruiting placard out on the busy highway in front of the Home Office building that read, "Apply Today and Interview Today." Offices were set up just off the lobby for company recruiters who would interview walk-in applicants from 8 to 5, Monday through Friday. Qualified applicants were instantly referred for second interviews by hiring managers. The interviewing process was reduced from two weeks to one day. As word of mouth spread across northwest Arkansas about Wal-Mart's new streamlined hiring process, the number of applicants increased immediately and the number of open positions fell. The recruiting staff's internal customers were thrilled.

In keeping with Sam's philosophy of taking a good idea from one area and implementing it across the company, a modified version of the Home Office staffing practice was implemented in the stores. A clipboard was kept up at the customer-service desk, and when applicants came in to apply (if managers couldn't interview them immediately) they would immediately be scheduled to be interviewed within the next week. The applicant simply picked a convenient time to be interviewed on the designated interviewing day (or days) by placing his or her name on the interviewing schedule kept on that clipboard. Store assistant managers and department managers were assigned rotating responsibility for the interviewing schedule. This method of scheduling reduced the burden of calling people back to set up interviews, thus increasing the speed with which open positions could be filled. Applicants often expressed surprise when they were offered the opportunity for an immediate interview. This is a great example of how Wal-Mart used the good ideas of its people to improve the operation of the whole company.

This example can easily be implemented as a staffing tactic at almost any organization. It challenges the tried-and-true, conventional methods of filling open positions. In the world of overscheduled executives and managers this simple idea is really hard to accomplish. I highly recommend that companies having trouble filling open positions try to implement this powerful idea. What you will find, in all likelihood, is although this idea is easy to understand, the discipline and flexibility required will make it next to impossible to execute. Excuses will abound, insurmountable barriers will be thrown up, and anarchy will reign supreme, as company managers refuse to change the way they have always done things. Change is a way of life at Wal-Mart. Its managers and associates welcome new ideas and aren't afraid to try new ways of doing things. As the competitive landscape changes, whether they like it or not, companies, their managers and employees need to demonstrate flexibility and change with it.

Empowered associates at Wal-Mart solved operational problems like the one in this example in every area of the company. The people who are closest to the work almost always have the best ideas for improving operations. The same holds true for your employees. Take the time to tap into the brains of all of your employees and you will be amazed at some of the ideas they come up with that will make a world of difference in your business. Unless you ask, your employees won't necessarily come forward to help solve problems. In some cases they've been conditioned by years of neglect not to volunteer information. In other cases, supervisors have sent the message to employees that they feel threatened when employees recommend a better way of doing things. Ask employees and you will be shocked and awed by some of the great ideas that are hiding in your own organization just waiting to be discovered.

As you evaluate your own company from an operational perspective, sweat the operational details because that is what Wal-Mart does. A story illustrates the point: Sam Walton showed up at a Saturday morning meeting in late October dragging a sixty-pound mail bag behind him. When he got to the middle of the stage, he dumped the mail on the floor at his feet, explaining to everyone in attendance that the mail on the floor was that week's internal mail from the Home Office being sent to the stores. He reminded us that we were entering the busiest time of the year in the stores and asked if any of us had time to open and process sixty pounds of mail that particular week. From that moment through the end of holidays he forbade us all to send any more mail to the stores. To sum up, Sam said, "If you have something to communicate to the stores, go out and tell the store associates personally by going out to visit them."

The reality is that no one could process sixty pounds of mail in one week and still do the job of serving customers. In his sensitivity to the mission of focusing store managers on holiday sales and merchandising, Sam knew he had to minimize distractions. And that was the end of unnecessary written communication going out to the stores.

Some of the simplest things make all the difference in customer perceptions of your business. A customer can shop in your store in a leisurely manner for an hour, but when it is time to check out the customer wants to move through the registers quickly. I've seen customers walk up to the checkout lanes in some of Wal-Mart's competitors, look around at the three out of twelve lanes that are open, each with a line six or more people deep, abandon their carts and leave the store in disgust. Time-sensitive consumers frustrated by slow checkout lines may never return. Take a good hard look at dollar volumes versus work schedules to ensure you are maximizing service at key sales peaks, and learn to be flexible. Keep a close eye on wait times required in checkout lines.

Teaching employees the importance of restocking shelves throughout the day is another way of avoiding missed sales opportunities. Being out of stock is being out of business. This is particularly frustrating if you have the inventory in the store but it hasn't been put on the shelves. Vendor partnerships, state-of-the-art technology and great distribution systems are effectively neutralized if your in-store personnel don't constantly restock the shelves.

It is also important from a customer's point of view to maintain clean and neat facilities. I remember a story I heard about passenger perceptions of the major airlines on which they fly. Customers who walk into the cabin of a dirty, unkempt aircraft equate poor housekeeping and poor engine maintenance. Who among us relishes taking off in a jet aircraft whose engines he or she already perceives haven't been properly maintained? What is the likelihood those customers will fly on that airline again? Not that your floors, lighting, windows and bathrooms are life-threatening, but your customers may still vote with their feet by shopping at competitors who have their acts together.

Operational success comes down to one thing—execute, execute, execute. This sounds pretty easy to understand but operational disciplines have a tendency to break down for all kinds of reasons. Sometimes it's as simple as other pressing issues taking priority. More often than not training is the culprit. With high turnover of managers and employees the development of operational discipline is a matter of constantly educating and re-educating. You can have the best store location with the best product but if you fail to execute your product and promotional strategies at the store level you may as well be out of business. Clear goals to continuously improve your business, along with repetitious and redundant training and communication strategies are the keys to becoming operationally excellent. If you clearly communicate and integrate your standards your current employees can culturally reinforce those standards as new employees are hired.

The operational success formula begins with creating a convenient shopping experience that includes a good store location, good store hours, and enough staff. Always being in stock is critically important. To do this you must have the courage to buy deep enough to restock promoted items and backfill empty shelves throughout the sales day. *Visual merchandising* (VM) includes signage, graphics, product pricing, neatly merchandised shelves, and attractive current window promotional displays. Operational details are important to customers which include things like dust-free shelves and products, clean floors, windows, and bathrooms. Register lines have to be minimized and new registers opened as customer traffic demands. The key to everything in store operations is consistent execution. The rallying cry at Wal-Mart for store operations is "Execution, execution, execution!"

The lesson to be learned is to run your business like you're in it for the long haul. Sweat the operational details. Take a good hard look at your operations from the point of view of your customer. Does your operational preparation project to your customers what it says on the sign in your window, "Welcome, We're Open for Business?" Or does your lack of commitment to store operations send the subliminal message to your customers that you're "Sorry We're Open for Business?" You've only got one chance to make a first impression on your customers...make it a good one!

Operational Checklist

Review this checklist of operational success strategies and tactics designed to help you compete with big-box retailers like Wal-Mart and not only survive, but thrive.

Accessibility
✓ Make certain your store is easily accessible
✓ Evaluate the hours your store is open to ensure customer convenience
✓ Design your floor plan with ease of customer navigation in mind
✓ Schedule your store hours to meet or exceed those of your competitors
✓ Protect the customer parking closest to your store for your customers only
✓ Ask customers for feedback about your store's accessibility

Operations
✓ Keep floors clean and shiny. Rugs vacuumed each day
✓ Keep bathrooms clean and assign someone to regularly maintain them
✓ Maintain good displays, lighting, and cleanliness of shelving/ fixtures
✓ Clean windows regularly
✓ Keep stock clean and rotated
✓ Keep the aisles clear and free of restock merchandise
✓ Focus everyone on shrinkage (retail theft) control

In Stock
✓ Train and focus every employee on the priority of constantly being in stock
✓ Require employees to police the aisles to fill in inventory holes
✓ Develop aggressive reorder strategies to avoid being out of stock
✓ Make a statement to customers with first-class promotional product merchandising
✓ Know your back-stocked inventory to ensure responsiveness to customer requests
✓ Organize inventory so products are easily accessible
✓ Remerchandise shelves throughout the sales day, during slack sales periods
✓ Teach cashiers to proactively communicate restocking needs
✓ Talk with suppliers about their role in timely product deliveries

✓ Create a flow of new merchandise to replace sold out or poor performing product

Visual Merchandising
✓ Design signage to appeal to customers and increase sales
✓ Ask your suppliers for attractive graphics and change them out
often
✓ Make certain signage reflects current promotional activity
✓ Reevaluate your graphics and signage to make certain they tell
your brand story
✓ Display signs prominently promoting on-sale merchandise
✓ Make sure signage helps to clearly guide customers around the
store
✓ Label shelves and products for customer convenience
✓ Check signage and graphics for quality and continuity of your
store's theme

Technology
✓ Leverage point of sale scanning technology to improve service
and lower costs
✓ Make serving customers a primary focus and managing inventory
secondary
✓ Convert to shelf labeling versus individual product price labeling
to cut costs
✓ Talk to your suppliers and ask for support in managing inventory
via technology

Retail Team Synergy
✓ Require employees to work together as a team toward a common
set of goals
✓ Teach employees basic sales, product knowledge, and customer
service techniques
✓ Leverage the skills and abilities of individuals to improve service
✓ Empower employees to serve the customers
✓ Solve problems by fact finding, not fault finding
✓ Embrace diversity in staffing and in thinking, starting at the top
✓ Require managers to be active in customer service; leading by
example
✓ Set a standard that managers must know each and every
employee by name
✓ Run your business productively but make it a fun place to work
for employees

- ✓ Establish continuous learning and continuous improvement standards
- ✓ Builds positive employee relations and make good morale a priority
- ✓ Set goals that are easily understood and which lead employees to produce results
- ✓ Give ongoing employee feedback in the form of praise and correction
- ✓ Demand that group members cooperate rather than compete
- ✓ Instill ownership so employees manage company resources like their own
- ✓ Develop open and active communication with all employees
- ✓ Resolve issues quickly when conflict does arise
- ✓ Deal with nonperformers and recognize achievers promptly

3

Cultural Strategies and Tactics

"Empowering people turns Wal-Mart's culture into
a competitive advantage and the synergy created
unleashes the organization's full potential."

I remember sitting in one of the Saturday morning meetings when Sam
Walton announced the demise of one of our large regional discount competitors to the collected throng of 500 top managers of the company.
Initially, everyone leapt up and a jubilant cheer resonated off the walls and
ceiling. High fives and backslapping were evident around the room. In that
brief moment the true smash-face competitive spirit of the Wal-Mart leadership team was exposed for all to see. In an article entitled "The Two Sides
of the Sam Walton Legacy," Hugh Sidney references a similar experience he
attributed to Wal-Mart employees who were gloating over the misfortune
of failed competitors with the chant, "Stack it deep, sell it cheap, stack it
high and watch it fly! Hear those downtown merchants cry!"[1] Sam reacted
to this type of unsportsmanlike conduct quickly and directly.

He was embarrassed by this type of emotional display at the expense
of a failed competitor. As he regained control of the meeting, he assumed a
preacher-like persona, firmly scolding those in attendance for their out-
burst, reminding them that breadwinners had lost their jobs and families
had been hurt. This was no time to gloat. Sam reminded everyone that we
needed to stay focused on the things that had made Wal-Mart successful,
keep the competitive pressure on and not to rest on our laurels. He directed
the Operations VPs to do what they could to encourage the local Wal-Mart
stores to hire as many of the competitor's employees as possible to lessen
the impact on those families.

Sam Walton seemed to enjoy the competition more than the ultimate victory. He had won the marketplace battle against this particular competitor but in the process his empathy or humanity remained vigilant over the Wal-Mart culture. I can't imagine another Fortune 500 company CEO responding to the demise of a direct competitor in the way that Sam responded in this example. It was obvious to me, that in that moment of reprimand, that Sam intended to personally model the appropriate behavior and to train his leadership team in the correct way to deal with someone else's hardship.

This is an example of the charismatic leadership of Sam Walton. A great deal of the spirit of the man remains alive in the company to this day. His myth, folklore, and legacy still engender loyalty from his leadership disciples and associates. His guiding principles still provide a touchstone for company leaders more than a decade after his death. So strong were his disciples' beliefs in Sam's teachings that I'd even heard that someone made up bracelets like those that say WWJD (What Would Jesus Do?) that instead say WWSD (What Would Sam Do?). I know that in my own career I never met anyone in top leadership who was as charismatic and visionary a leader as Sam Walton.

Having worked in Wal-Mart's Home Office in Bentonville, Arkansas, as a writer I had a unique opportunity to see Sam Walton and the executive leadership team in action. In the process, I got to see how they compete in every area of the business. The work ethic I experienced was second to none that I had seen before or have seen since, and the company's leaders were driven by an unusual singularity of business focus.

I would arrive at work at seven in the morning and most nights didn't leave until seven in the evening. Add to that working from 7 to 3 on Saturday—and sometimes I had to go in to work on Sunday. I honestly couldn't find time to cut the grass around my house. I was working close to seventy hours each and every week! But that's nothing. There were other Home Office executives and managers who would arrive at five in the morning and they'd leave after I had left, every day. Because I arrived later, I'd see their cars when I walked in from the back of the lot in the morning and I'd see their cars still there when I left at night. These fanatically dedicated people were working 80 to 90 hours per week and more—it was crazy! Sam was one of the worst of all often arriving as early as four in the morning!

I'd been told by a long-tenured headquarters employee that divorces in Bentonville of workaholic associates weren't uncommon. This always seemed strange to me in a company that professed to be a family-friendly company. Helen Walton, Sam's wife, openly expressed her dismay with the time associates had to spend away from their families. If Sam was listening to her, it went in one ear and out the other, because the work ethic expectations didn't change.

I was never a big believer in the concept of burnout until I worked at the Wal-Mart Home Office. I've got to tell you that I was physically and mentally exhausted the entire time I worked there. I always had more to do in a given day than I could possibly get done. I think a lot of the other associates were feeling the same way I did. The high standards, workload, small staff, and long hours clearly take their toll. I don't know how the long-term associates are able to physically and mentally handle the pace year after year after year.

In addition to Wal-Mart's management work ethic, competitors are competing with an army of over a million associates in the stores, distribution centers, and fleet, all focused on doing battle in the retail arena. Wal-Mart's associates demonstrate unusual loyalty, which can be traced directly to the treatment they received from Sam Walton. He knew that individuals don't win in business but teams do. He treated managers and employees with respect and he wasn't afraid to challenge everyone to achieve the highest of standards. The term "associate" was used instead of the term "employee," customers were "guests or neighbors" and managers were referred to as "coach" in order to focus everyone on the importance of these roles in building positive employee and customer relations.

Associates are considered business partners and are empowered by the company to do whatever it takes to serve the customer. Empowerment is one of the pillars of Wal-Mart culture. These empowered associates are the ones who have implemented the strategies that have allowed the company to achieve so much against the competition so quickly.

When I went to work there I was given one of those management parable books about the thunder of empowerment. By passing out that book to all employees, the company leaders were reinforcing the powerful principles of employee empowerment. Clearly there was an expectation on the part of company leadership to leverage the horsepower contained within the hearts and minds of everyone in the company. Empowerment of its humongous workforce is an example of how Wal-Mart leverages the economies of scale and the synergies created by its team of motivated people. Empowering people is also a good business strategy as it often yields great ideas or better ways of doing things that end up saving the company considerable sums of money.

In its own recruiting materials, Wal-Mart stresses to the new management recruit how important it is for each individual's personal beliefs about people to coincide with Wal-Mart's own people philosophy. Established by Sam Walton in 1962, Wal-Mart's three cultural beliefs form the foundation of this philosophy: Respect for the individual, serve the customer, and strive for excellence. Wal-Mart does a better job than most companies of communicating its cultural beliefs to its people.

Using old-school Management by Objectives (MBO) performance-review processes coupled with New Age 360-degree internal customer-service feedback, grassroots employee-opinion surveys, and an open-door policy, Wal-Mart managers are held accountable. In the performance-review process, Wal-Mart uses the acronym SMART: Specific, Measurable, Action-oriented, Realistic, and Time-bound. The managers are measured in terms of typical hard-retail metrics like sales, payroll, and shrinkage, but they are also responsible for maintaining a soft touch with employees and customers. Getting a bad score on a grassroots survey is a sure way to get demoted or fired. Associates are encouraged to bring their concerns up the chain of command if their local manager hasn't satisfactorily resolved an issue. Treatment of people in the stores, fleet, and distribution centers was monitored via the open door policy and any issues identified were taken very seriously. Company leaders made every effort to resolve problems to the satisfaction of associates, whenever warranted.

One of the former Wal-Mart managers, Stan Fortune, provided insight into the open-door policy:

> I can remember my district manager saying, "I am going to reverse two or three out of ten decisions involving people that you've made and it's not because you're doing anything wrong but because your people need to understand they can talk to leaders higher up in the company and get some type of reaction through the open door." In the early years my district manager would call up and say you didn't do anything wrong but we're going to bring this associate back [that you fired]. The theory behind that is that they are going to come back and be so thankful that you brought them back that you'll never have another problem with them. If they were a problem it wouldn't be too long before they messed up again. It was something you did to give people a second chance.

This balance of people versus profit presents a difficult dilemma for the store-management team. As a manager, if you hit your financial goals for your store at the expense of the morale of your team, you may get demoted or fired. You can have the best morale, but if you don't hit the numbers, again, you may get demoted or fired. Show me a long-term store manager at Wal-Mart and I'll show you a manager who more than likely has solved the people-versus-profit equation in his or her store. By means of performance data and grassroots employee-opinion surveys, each store manager is evaluated from above by management and from below by employees. For the store managers it's like living and working in a glass box because there is truly no place for a poor performer to hide!

Adding to the performance pressures placed on the stores is the demand that everything be accomplished in a 24/7/365 business environment and that average people have to achieve above-average results. Imagine the responsibility placed on the shoulders of the store managers simply trying to hire, schedule, orient, and train 500 to 600 associates in this fast paced ever-changing environment. Additionally, Supercenters carry over 100,000 different products that must be stocked and restocked in 100,000 to 260,000 square feet of space. It is not uncommon for one Supercenter to have sales of over 100 million dollars in a year.

It is obvious that Wal-Mart's associates are the key to execution at store level. With so many new stores opening, the challenge becomes duplicating the operational and service culture across this country and around the world. Wal-Mart's cultural values and beliefs are reinforced through management training provided at the company's Walton Institute of Retailing. Cultural integration and buy-in by its managers are so important that all new managers are required to attend a weeklong cultural orientation and indoctrination session held at the University of Arkansas at Fayetteville.

Imagine the costs associated with sending all new managers for a week of cultural training. (Remember, Wal-Mart is one of the world's most tight-fisted companies.) That's how important culture is to the success of Wal-Mart. It's not just something that is nice to have; it is necessary to have. Cultural training is considered a positive investment in the business and is looked at as a necessary expense of doing business.

Topics and philosophies taught in the cultural training program include: company history, customer service, diversity, productivity standards for sales, treatment of people, expense control, total quality, continuous improvement, union-free philosophy, performance management and performance coaching. Emphasis is placed on skills like Management by Walking Around (MBWA), behavior-centered leadership, communication, and listening skills. The actual modules taught in the Walton Institute include: Goal Setting, Communication Skills, Behavior-Centered Leadership, Applied Behavior Analysis, Group Problem Solving, Situational Leadership, Time Management, Performance Appraisal, The Customer is "The Boss," Developing Associates, Positive Discipline, Task-Force Preparation, Team Building, Task-Force Presentation, and Behavior Contracts.

The core modules are taught by Home Office executives as well as professors from the University of Arkansas. Once they have received a thorough cultural indoctrination, management "Wal-Martians" leave the orientation with a clear understanding of their role in creating a focus on "one company, one culture." Said another way, they attempt to clone the culture across the world (some say in a cultish way) to make the customer-centered shopping experience consistent, whether you shop in Frankfort, Indiana or Frankfurt, Germany. Even the Wal-Mart cheer is the same, although as you travel stores around the world you may hear it in one of nine different languages.

On the final day of the training week, all those attending the Walton Institute attend the World Famous Saturday morning meeting. Held at the company Home Office headquarters in Bentonville, Arkansas, the meeting starts bright and early at 7:00 A.M. As many as 500 of the top company managers are in attendance. It is the place where the Wal-Mart executives discuss the company's current performance, and more importantly, focus the leadership team on the goals for the week(s) to come.

Attendees get a unique look into the strategies of the organization as leaders openly discuss and plot competitive tactics in an open forum. Everyone in attendance is free to express an idea, concern, or potential solution. The agenda is freewheeling and flexible. Bring a problem forward and you're likely to get any number of supportive ideas to solve it from your fellow teammates. The atmosphere is collegial, in that Wal-Mart leaders treat one another as equal business partners who are serious about their work but relaxed about the way they go about getting it done.

The meetings start promptly and often include surprise visitors like the GE or Disney executive leadership teams, singers like Garth Brooks and Donnie Osmond, or the now-deceased wrestling great Andre the Giant. You never know who will be there. That's part of the excitement and the company leaders always have time for fun and laughter. The humor is more often than not quite elementary but always clean, somewhat like that of Bob Hope. The meetings are one part theater, one part business, and one part pep rally, and none of it is rehearsed or choreographed. Walton Institute participants gain insights into their own company that they'll never forget. What they learn about the culture they will take back and use immediately in their own stores or distribution centers.

It wasn't unusual to see Sam's bird dogs running loose around the headquarters on a Saturday morning. He'd bring them into the lobby and set them loose to run the halls. The security guards would follow them around with brooms, dustpans, mops, and buckets to clean up behind the dogs when they had an accident. It was all part of the fun of never knowing on Saturday morning what Sam would do next to create excitement and fun to take the edge off the ever-present stress associated with executing Wal-Mart's aggressive strategies.

I have always felt the Saturday morning meeting is the place where Wal-Mart culture is personified. It's almost like the "twelfth man" concept in football, where the home team has the advantage of its hometown fans. If you haven't been to one of these meetings you haven't really experienced the strength of the corporate character of the organization. Every one of the leaders in attendance hears the same messages presented the same way. It is one of the competitive advantages of the company. It is also the place where strategies are plotted and communicated to everyone against competitors. I was always careful to bring money to the meeting because I had to pay for my own coffee and donuts at the honor bar!

On Saturday morning, while 99 percent of the other corporate offices in America are closed down for the weekend, Wal-Mart's competitive strategies are discussed and implemented at its Saturday morning meeting. At the earliest, competitors might respond to Wal-Mart's strategies by midweek if they are lucky and astute enough to realize that new tactics have been put in place against them. But most are too slow to respond and besides, come next Saturday, Wal-Mart leaders will simply change or modify the strategy again. This lopsided competition is going on fifty-two weeks a year.

Wal-Mart is known for its lockstep execution and these meetings are critical to getting all the company leaders on the same page; they also provide retail training opportunities for everyone in attendance. Wal-Mart does a nice job of teaching all company leaders to be retailers and to think like merchants. It doesn't matter whether you are an accounting manager, IT professional or lawyer, everyone is taught to think like a retailer first. In fact, corporate Home Office employees are clearly second-class citizens when you consider the importance placed on the associates in the stores. Wal-Mart is one of the only companies I know of that has flipped its organizational pyramid, placing the associates who service the customer at the top and everyone else below them.

I believe competitors who are losing the competitive battle against Wal-Mart (or who have already lost) probably don't even understand the significance of the Saturday morning meetings to Wal-Mart's competitive advantage. It's as if the company leadership has a management retreat every Saturday of the year. Competitors may pull their leadership teams together once a quarter, every six months, or once a year for a pump 'em up, rah-rah conference, but that's not the same. Unless competitors are willing to go to a six-day workweek and hold meetings with all of their top executives each week to plot counter strategies, I don't know how they can even think about competing directly.

In addition, every week Wal-Mart's leaders are in the field visiting company stores as well as walking through the stores of competitors. At the end of the week, the Store Operations Leadership meets all day on Friday in Bentonville, discussing what competitors are up to. It then begins plotting strategies to counteract the competition's efforts. Wal-Mart's leaders seem to know more about the execution of their competitors' strategies and tactics than top executives of those companies do themselves. By having their top store-operations executives tour markets across the country and visit competitors' stores each and every week, Wal-Mart's leaders are able to orchestrate counter-competitive strategies with the flexibility to focus on specific markets and even on an individual store.

In concept, these Saturday morning meetings are easy to understand, yet they would be hard for another company to duplicate. Even if a competitor wanted to hold similar meetings each Saturday, its leadership teams wouldn't support it. The mere mention of the idea might lead to management protests or even riots in the halls of their corporate offices. You'd think the concept of executives working and meeting on Saturday is downright un-American. The quality of their executives' personal lives would suffer, marriages would end, and morale would go down. And forget about getting your team to perform your company cheer at seven on Saturday morning!

I'll be the first to admit that the work ethic of Wal-Mart's executives and managers "ain't quite right!" Working from 7 to 7 Monday through Friday and then coming in to work from 7 to 3 on Saturday is taking your business a little too seriously. But because of this, hard work and long hours are the price that competitors have to pay to compete successfully. An analogous lesson from the world of boxing captures it best. Trainers say, "The more you sweat the less you bleed."

Ninety percent of Wal-Mart's strategy is tactical execution and the Saturday morning meetings provide the perfect forum for disseminating the game plan. They also provide monitoring and direction to ensure operational discipline in every process. But even at Wal-Mart the executives realize that ideas or strategies are the easy part—it's the implementation or tactical execution that is tough. I remember one time when David Glass, CEO, challenged the store operations VPs to execute a television set promotion for which the company had bought a ton of TVs. He asked each VP to bring a Polaroid picture of the massive TV set promotional display set up in each store, under his or her direction, to the next Saturday morning meeting. That next Saturday David rolled a wheelbarrow out onto the stage and dumped out Polaroid photos showing every store in the chain with that TV promotion set up on time. His message, albeit theatrical, was that as well as Wal-Mart executes, the company must keep the focus on promotional activity and maintain 100

percent operational discipline across all stores. He said this was probably the first merchandise promotion Wal-Mart could prove it had executed across the entire chain. As good as it is, even Wal-Mart struggles
with execution.

There are lots of ways to communicate the need to improve promotional execution. The story I just shared with you is an example of company folklore. Wal-Mart often uses theatrical methods to illustrate a point.
By doing so, company leaders are able to get people to focus on a single
important issue in what seems like a forest of important issues all around
them. The stories they used would grab people at an emotional level, creating a Significant Emotional Event (SEE). An SEE is like a slap in the face
or being doused with cold water. These stories would wake people up and
remind them of what was really important. The beauty in using stories to
illustrate a point is that downstream in the organization stories are told
and retold weaving their way into the fiber of the company culture. Sam
Walton was a master storyteller who used illustrative stories to reinforce
his cultural standards. Company executives, mentored by Sam, continue
to reinforce the culture with a plethora of spellbinding stories many of
which were first told by Sam himself decades ago.

Clear communication is difficult in every organization. Wal-Mart has
crafted several communication vehicles to streamline and simplify the
process of getting the message out with one voice. Saturday morning
meetings, satellite broadcasts, the retailing institute, training programs,
policy and procedure manuals, employee handbooks, orientation videos,
the company web site, and the intranet provide integrated channels of
cultural communication with a common theme and content.

If I were to boil down a recommendation for creating cultural competitive advantage it would be communicate, communicate, communicate! It's hard to over-communicate in any organization. Just as they teach
in Marketing/Advertising 101, repeating the same messages over and
over again is the key to getting through to people. Communication using
one voice is another one of the great secrets of Wal-Mart's culture.

John Morrison, the state director of the Missouri Grocers Association,
said, "It is a lot easier to put a directive out from Bentonville to 100 stores
and have it done overnight then it is for us to work together with 100 different owners and get the same thought and idea out and across. We are
certainly at a disadvantage in terms of communication and interaction."

At Wal-Mart, store managers meet with associates every day. They
also do a Wal-Mart cheer three times a day, one at each shift change, in
the twenty-four hour stores. That's over a thousand Wal-Mart cheers each

year in one store. These standup meetings are held at the front of the store for all the customers to see. Associates are provided with updates on issues of current concern within the company and associates are provided with the opportunity to ask questions or discuss any concerns they might have. Managers also use this public forum to give individual associates or the entire team recognition for a job well done. It is through these daily meetings that new and seasoned associates gain a clear cultural indoctrination into the company's operational standards, values, and beliefs. By meeting daily, associates and managers form bonds that link them all together as members of the same team. By reaching out to communicate with associates each day, the managers form relationships with the associates, which humanizes the environment in an otherwise depersonalized brick-and-mortar atmosphere. It all goes back to treating employees (associates) like business partners.

Wal-Mart's leaders figured out a long time ago that a paycheck alone doesn't sufficiently motivate employees. In this day and age a major segment of the working population brings a different set of values and expectations to the job than those of their parents and grandparents and there is a widening gap between traditional supervisory techniques and employee expectations of treatment. Wal-Mart recognizes achievements and motivates employees, using positive reinforcement techniques, to close this gap.

Recognition is acknowledgement that encourages the repeat of desirable behavior. Recognition can be monetary and it can be non-monetary. Using employees' names, saying thank you, and asking about the kids are a few simple examples of recognition. The use of positive-reinforcement techniques breeds camaraderie in the workforce and, when used properly, will lead to higher productivity. Sam Walton expected company leaders to take the time to get to know the associates. He realized that if company leaders took the time to show the associates they cared, the associates would in turn care about the company's goals.

If the only time employees hear from the supervisor is when they screw up, poor morale will result. You reap what you sow and in this case you will reap disgruntled and negative employees. Good supervisors show their appreciation to their team in many different ways each and every day. The employee perception of positive treatment by supervisors has a tremendous impact on retention and productivity. Treating people right, through the use of positive-recognition techniques, is also the right thing to do. A good rule of thumb is to follow the lead of great leaders like J.C. Penney and Sam Walton and treat people the way you would want to be treated.

People are starved for information, attention, and recognition. The associates at Wal-Mart and employees of companies everywhere are no different in this regard. As hokey as it sounds, the fact that Wal-Mart managers take the time to meet with their associates and give them information and sincere recognition for their accomplishments, and even perform a company cheer, engenders associate loyalty and gives the associates a nice warm feeling about the company. The understanding of company goals also drives average people to above-average levels of performance. High fives and telling people they did a good job, or simply thanking them for going the extra yard, are powerful forms of non-monetary recognition. Fully engaged and motivated people also provide better customer service, which drives sales.

Wal-Mart leaders embrace a philosophy called "servant-leadership," which simply means that if you are a leader you need to put the needs of your people first. Said another way, company leaders need to serve their employees (associates). When you boil it all down, the secret to Sam Walton's leadership philosophies is servant-leadership. His belief was that to truly be an inspirational leader, you must serve those whom you lead. In this regard, Sam was as much an amateur psychologist as he was a merchant.

When Sam visited stores, the company associates would walk right up to him and strike up a conversation with no fear. He was so down to earth that people were attracted to him like steel to a magnet. People could tell he was genuinely interested in what they had to say. Sam was a people person and there was nothing he liked better than rubbing elbows with the troops. Upon arriving at a store he'd often pull the associates together in the front of the store and talk with them about the company. Before he would leave he'd always lead a Wal-Mart cheer.

Sam modeled those servant-leadership behaviors to the very end of his life. I can still remember in his final days, seeing Sam Walton in his office laying flat on his back in a hospital type bed taking chemotherapy treatments while he continued to work. I can assure you he didn't do it to make people feel sorry for him; he did it because he intended to keep working until the very end of his life. This is another true story that has become part of the folklore of the company.

When I think of Sam Walton and the influence he still has on the Wal-Mart culture, I think of this quote by Teddy Roosevelt that personifies Sam's spirit of servant-leadership and his beliefs about the contributions of his store managers and buyers:

> It is not the critic who counts; not the man who points out how the strong man stumbles, or where the doer of deeds could have done them better. The credit belongs to the man who is actually in the arena, whose face is marred by dust and sweat and blood; who strives valiantly; who

errs and comes up short again and again, because there is no effort without error and shortcoming; but who does actually strive to do the deeds, who knows the great enthusiasms, the great devotions; who spends himself in a worthy cause; who at the best knows in the end the triumph of high achievement, and who at the worst, if he fails, at least fails while daring greatly, so that his place shall never be with those cold and timid souls who know neither victory nor defeat.[2]

This quote captures nicely the competitive spirit of Sam Walton and Wal-Mart's leaders as well as their beliefs about servant-leadership. If you really want to communicate to your own people what it takes to win at retail, share this quote with them. Within this quote are threaded the cultural beliefs embraced by the company leaders, which I saw in action. Enjoy your work, do whatever it takes to win, and if you can't win go down trying! You can rest assured that Wal-Mart executives and managers work their tails off to win at retail. They are tenacious competitors who "leave it all on the field" each and every day.

Sam Walton ultimately died of bone cancer, but in those final weeks he continued to work in a weakened state, lying down in that hospital bed, while he wrote notes with an antigravity pen on his clipboard! Imagine the influence of his behavior on all of the Wal-Mart associates. There is no way an associate would even think about calling off sick with a cold or a case of the sniffles when the company chairman was fighting cancer and continuing to provide leadership to the organization. The sight of him lying there in his office in the final days of his life, continuing to work from a hospital bed, is an inspirational image burned forever into my memory.

Every company has a treasure trove of rich stories from the past that historically define what it is today. It is through these stories that company culture and store brands come alive. Leveraging the past through storytelling is an excellent way to train new employees and get them up to speed quickly on company standards. Remember, when employees are trained they will quickly forget the boring facts you present but they will remember cultural stories forever.

Sam attributed some of the most innovative ideas the company had implemented directly to the associates. As an example, all Wal-Mart stores have greeters to greet and assist customers as they enter the store. Michael Eisner liked the idea so much that he put greeters in his stores, to make Disney's customers feel welcome and to answer their questions.[3] The greeter job serves two purposes: greeting customers and store security. The idea for greeters at Wal-Mart was originated in a Wal-Mart store in Crowley, Louisiana. Once Sam saw the greeters for the first time, he was committed to implementing them across the chain, which he did immediately. As in this example, entrepreneurial thinking by the people closest to the action was not only encouraged, it was expected.

The people greeter example has been told and retold by managers and staff at Wal-Mart. The result is the creation of corporate folklore. One of the challenges in a company the size of Wal-Mart is the proliferation of the culture itself. As the company expands into new markets or when new associates are hired, how do you teach people the company's shared cultural values and beliefs? As in the greeter illustration above, the answer is through myths, folklore, and storytelling.

In my experience, executives of organizations are hesitant to tell stories. Maybe they think it wastes time or that it is simply unimportant to achieving business goals. One of my mentors, Bill Gove, the first president of the National Speakers Association, taught me a lesson about story-telling that I'll share with you. At that time, Bill had delivered over five thousand paid speeches to audiences all over the world. He said, "Audiences will forget the facts you provide to them in a speech very quickly. If you reinforce the facts with stories, although they'll still forget the facts, they will always remember your stories." He went on to say, "Make a point and tell a story or tell a story and make a point but on one side of your point or the other tell an illustrative story." Sam Walton was a storyteller and so are many of the other top executives of the company. To this day, they bring the vision for the company alive using rich stories representing the folklore of the company.

There was one such story told over and over again about a Wal-Mart store opening back in the 1960s. The company was small enough that Sam was personally directing the store managers. He was also buying product, merchandising shelves, delivering products to the stores, and doing whatever it took to run the stores more efficiently. Back in those days, as the story goes, he had already implemented his low-price dis-counting strategy and he was selling merchandise stacked on tables, out of bins, or off of pallets. One of the current Wal-Mart executives, who was working for a competitor back in those days, told the story of attending this new store opening. He said it was awful! That particular summer day it was stiflingly hot; well over 100 degrees with high humidity and no wind. Sam had set up a corral in front of the store and offered free donkey rides to attract families with children to the store. He'd also bought hundreds of watermelons, which he had merchandised directly on the ground in the parking lot. The asphalt was so hot you could fry eggs on it! As the heat of the day rose the watermelons began to pop and the juice of those watermelons covered the ground. The donkeys did what donkeys do and that too was mixed with the watermelon juice and the customers tracked that godawful concoction throughout the store on the bottoms of their shoes. The store was a mess and it smelled terrible. It was the worst store opening this executive had ever seen. This story has become part of the folklore of the company, representing its humble roots. It has been told countless times and like a child's bedtime story never loses its appeal.

One of the former Wal-Mart managers told me this cultural story. "I met Sam Walton many times. I still have two handwritten letters that he wrote to me. Keep in mind, this is the richest man in America. He could have dictated a letter to his secretary and she could have rubber-stamped it. Once he met you he always remembered you. He walked up to me and shook my hand and said it was good to talk to me when we didn't have a crisis. He could remember stuff about people. It was just unreal—he'd come in the store and see people he'd talk to once a year or every year and a half, when the company was still small enough that he could do that. He said to this female associate, "The last time I was here your husband was in the hospital—is he okay?" How did he remember all these people? He was very personable and able to communicate with every single hourly associate no matter what their status was, no matter what their position was, how much money they made, it really didn't matter. When the company lost Sam Walton they lost someone really special." He was one of those rare people you meet in life who never met a stranger.

"Our people make the difference" is what I call the branding of the Wal-Mart culture. This phrase is prominently displayed on the company trucks, on the walls of the distribution centers, and in the stores. To Sam Walton this wasn't just a catchphrase, it was a hardwired cultural belief. Sam always referred to the store, distribution, and fleet associates using the most glowing terms like *wonderful* and *terrific*. In satellite broadcasts to the stores, in his charismatic way, he constantly communicated to the associates how much he appreciated their efforts and results. Sam may have been the leader of the band but he realized it wasn't a one-man show. Even though competitors try to copy Wal-Mart's easily observable merchandising and operational concepts in their stores, the one thing they can't duplicate is the company's army of associates. Wal-Mart has a whole variety of rich cultural beliefs that bring its culture alive and make it hard for competitors to duplicate.

I heard Sam Walton, at the Saturday morning meeting, tell the company leaders on several occasions to refer to and use the golden rule in their treatment of people. His belief was that if you take care of your people profits will follow. He always emphasized leading by example; his culturally engrained servant-leadership philosophy required that managers never ask anyone to do anything that they wouldn't do themselves.

He believed in treating customers like neighbors or guests and the employees, his associates, like family.

I learned that Sam's golden rule and servant-leadership philosophies were driven by his belief that everyone is equal; that we all put our pants on one leg at a time. I also learned that employees, Wal-Mart's and yours, want the same thing that their managers and executives want. Employees want to be treated with respect and they want to be recognized for a job well done. Just like you and me they want to be members of a winning team. Employees want the responsibility and authority to complete the task at hand and they want a supervisor who listens and uses their ideas. Of course, everybody wants to know what's going on in the organization. By receiving fair pay and benefits for their work, employees want to be able to provide for their families, pay the rent, and send their kids to college. Whether they will admit it or not, the vast majority of employees want training and development so they can do their current jobs well and so they are prepared for potential promotional opportunities. Finally, all of us want to be part of something special—no one relishes being a member of a last-place team.

If you look at Sam's beliefs about the treatment of people purely from a behavioral-psychology standpoint, you'd think Sam was trained by Dr. Frederick Hertzberg himself. Hertzberg's list of the five most important motivators of people at work include: achievement, recognition, the work itself, responsibility, and advancement. Intentionally or by accident, Wal-Mart's culture emphasizes these five top motivators of people. Sam provided average people with above-average job opportunities that were beyond their wildest expectations, and then, through company profit-sharing, he rewarded them accordingly. The same opportunities exist today for the associates of Wal-Mart to achieve their dreams.

In reading the book *Mainstreet Merchant* (the story of J.C. Penney) by Norman Beasley, I began to understand that many of Sam Walton's leadership philosophies were learned or developed during his association, early in his career, with J.C. Penney. Penney had the nickname "Golden Rule Penney" and Sam, being a continuous learner, quickly picked up these philosophies on how to treat employees and customers.

I heard Sam say many times, "If you take care of your people, your people will take care of the customer and the business will take care of itself." I don't know that he originated this statement but I can tell you he believed in it. He truly believed that if you take care of your people first profits will follow. The golden rule also applies to customers; if your customers are not treated as they expect to be treated you can bet they'll become customers of someone else who treats them right. The entire focus of the Wal-Mart culture as designed by Sam Walton is to lower prices and improve the quality of service to the retail customer, but never at the expense of the associates.

One of the former Wal-Mart store managers reminisced about Sam's cultural influence, saying, "He was an excellent businessman, there is no doubt about that. He had a lot of his success because of the way he was able to treat the people around him and that he was able to make every single associate in that store that he met with feel like he was their friend as well as their boss. He didn't just do it with lip service, he did a lot of things for the associates; he tried to make things better. In fact I think back in the late eighties and early nineties, when they were in the smaller towns, in the middle part of the country that was the job to have. You had benefits back then that were comparable with anyone else. You had a steady job, you knew Wal-Mart was going to be there. You were working for a man that you knew appreciated you."

To understand the Wal-Mart culture you have to gain an understanding of the character and personality of its founder, Sam Walton. From the moment I met him I knew I had met someone special. Whenever I was around him I watched him interact with people and I was struck by his down-to-earth, folksy, and friendly manner. He had a unique ability to instantaneously establish rapport with people from all walks of life. His approachability was downright disarming but behind that backwoods country charm was a man who was no country bumpkin, he was dumb as a fox.

Deep in his DNA he was hardwired to be honest, competitive, courageous, caring, hardworking, frugal, driven, disciplined, curious, humble, stubborn, decisive, and ambitious. He was also street smart, team-oriented, a people developer, a tight-fisted negotiator, a great communicator, a teacher, and an aggressive competitor. As the organization's powerful charismatic leader he wore a variety of hats including those of servant-leader, trailblazer, risk-taker, change agent, chief merchant, storytelling pontificator, team-builder, entrepreneur, visionary leader, theatrical performer, motivational expert, comedian, psychologist, and preacher.

He was a "tinkerer" with the status quo. Whoever said "if ain't broke don't fix it" never met Sam Walton. He believed in looking at every area of the operation, all the time, with an eye on improvement. Small improvements in a company the size of Wal-Mart, multiplied across the chain of stores, potentially represented huge improvements. Everyone was taught and empowered by Sam to look for those improvement opportunities and implement those changes to improve the business.

Sam was one of the best motivational speakers I ever had the pleasure of listening to. He was a master of communication. He used his voice inflection, pace, volume, and pauses as effectively as any television preacher I've ever seen. As I watched and listened to him speak I think I discovered the secret to his communication; it was storytelling. By painting pictures with words he was able to hold an audience in the palms of his hands. He talked about what had been, what was, and what might be. Often he'd reminisce about great successes or great failures from the past. Sometimes he'd tell the story of a Wal-Mart hero who had accomplished some great feat, using the story of that accomplishment as a way to culturally engrain that performance as a company standard or benchmark. At the Saturday morning meetings, on occasion, he talked in abstract terms about his dreams for the future, firing up the creativity of those in attendance. When Sam told a story everyone focused on his message and those stories would later be told to others, becoming part of the folklore of the company culture.

One of the great folklore stories about Sam himself involved his induction into the Sales and Marketing Hall of Fame. He was inducted that year along with Bob Hope and Liz Claiborne. It was a black-tie affair held at the Waldorf-Astoria; Sam Walton was forced to wear his tuxedo, which he referred to as a monkey suit. Tom Peters presented the prestigious award and when Sam was given the opportunity to make an acceptance speech he noted that the stage lights were too bright, so he pulled a baseball cap out of the pocket of his tuxedo and put it on his head. In typical showman fashion, he made his acceptance speech memorable by wearing that Wal-Mart baseball cap with his tux in the middle of the Waldorf-Astoria ballroom.

Just as when he played football in school or tennis as an adult he was driven to win. Sam wasn't an imposing physical presence, in actuality he was a lanky and lean fellow who made up for his lack of size with lots of heart. Lombardi-like in his will to win, Sam hated to lose so he devoted himself to outthinking and outworking his competitor. His competitive nature in athletics evolved into his beliefs about business competition. Doing a good job was never good enough; there was always room to improve. With his clipboard in hand, he constantly took notes, preparing lists to challenge the status quo in an effort to make the company better.

More than anything he enjoyed competing with and learning from others. He required the buyers to get out into the stores to talk to the customers about their product preferences. The saying I remember hearing was, "you can't merchandise America from Bentonville, Arkansas." His passion for visiting his own stores and the stores of competitors bordered on an obsession. He was somewhat opinionated and he was very demanding but he always led by example. Oh, by the way, if the personality I've described in the list above reminds you of the attributes of a Boy

Scout—trustworthy, loyal, helpful, friendly, courteous, kind, obedient, cheerful, thrifty, brave, clean, reverent—I have to point out that when Sam was a teenager he achieved the distinction of becoming an Eagle Scout.

His integrity standards were extremely high and I heard him say more than once, "if you say you're going to do something then do it" and a "promise we make is a promise we keep." Culturally, executives, managers, and associates know they must follow through on their commitments or they will suffer being labeled as lacking in integrity. At Wal-Mart, that label is at least career-limiting and in severe cases is likely to be career-ending. Breaches of integrity or honesty would lead to termination faster than lapses in job performance. Remember what I said earlier: Sam would walk a million miles with someone with a performance problem but he wouldn't take the first step with someone who lacked integrity.

He was the kind of person who would never ask anyone else to do anything he personally wasn't willing to do. At Wal-Mart they called it walking the talk. He preached his servant-leadership concept, which he believed was the most important attribute of great leaders. To be a true servant-leader requires that you be a servant first, by serving the people who report to you, and a leader second with the respect that you gained by serving first. Servant-leadership comes from the heart and requires that the leader sincerely care about people. In the process of serving others respect and trust are generated as a by-product. The concept of servant-leadership is unique to Wal-Mart and really sets its company leaders apart from everyone else.

As you can tell, I have a great deal of respect and admiration for Sam Walton. Having worked for lots of bosses in my career, I had never met anyone who inspired me like he did. I feel blessed to have had the chance to work with a world-class charismatic leader like Mr. Sam. To this day I use his leadership standards as a yardstick for comparison when I'm faced with a tough business problem.

When I remember Sam, a quote attributed to William Shakespeare comes to mind: "Some men never seem to grow old. Always active in thought, always ready to adapt new ideas. Satisfied, yet ever dissatisfied, settled yet ever unsettled, they always enjoy the best of what is, and are the first to find the best of what will be." Wal-Mart lost a truly one-of-a-kind, visionary leader the day that Sam Walton died.

Fortunately for Wal-Mart and unfortunately for competitors, Sam Walton's values and core leadership beliefs were forever integrated into the culture of the company for posterity. The adjectives I listed above to describe Sam rubbed off on the leaders around him. His influence on the company is not only still felt today, but he has been made a cultural icon promoted and immortalized in company literature, his quotes even appearing on domestic and international web sites. Posthumously, Sam has become a brand character or icon not unlike Colonel Sanders at Kentucky Fried Chicken. His memory provides a cultural rudder for company leaders to help them steer true to the course originally set by Sam himself. As you read about the company on its web sites you'd almost think Sam is still alive and providing personal direction! That's how important his visionary leadership was and is to the success of the company both then and now.

Each company has certain core company competencies that have been pivotal to that particular company's success. Each organization also has key leadership competencies. In some companies, these competencies are simply known to everyone, and have never been formally collected and committed to paper for all to see. The same is true for the company vision or mission. Clearly communicating vision, mission, and company competencies is pivotal to any organization's past, present, and future success. Your organization is no different. Wal-Mart has a specific vision and competencies that they have identified, which have been critical to their success in the past and will still be pivotal to their success in the future.

Let me illustrate the importance of having a clear delineation of your company's vision/mission and core competencies by using Wal-Mart as an example. Wal-Mart's vision, as established by Sam Walton, was to be the best retailer in the industry. Simple and straightforward, this mission was easy to explain and left little to the imagination. The vision or mission was to be the best in retailing. Everyone understood this goal and company leaders constantly reinforced this message. Sam often said, "Our goal was never to be the biggest retailer in the world; our goal is to be the best retailer in the world."

Coupled with that vision/mission, Wal-Mart has certain core company competencies for which it is known and that have led to its phenomenal success. Wal-Mart's list of competencies includes: innovation, merchandising, store operations, customer service, technology, distribution, cost control, and culture. These eight core company competencies are the reason the company has been so successful. By doing these things the best it can it has become the biggest and best retailer in the world.

Wal-Mart translates these company competencies into action by focusing the leadership team on a set of its own key leadership competencies in order to achieve company performance goals. Sam and his executive team were directly involved in the forced ranking exercise used to identify Wal-Mart's key leadership competencies in two areas: people skills and work processes. These key leadership competencies have been communicated to leaders throughout the organization. They provide a solid foundation of skills from which managers execute company strategies. The key leadership competencies are broken down into two specific areas, people skills and work processes:

People Skills	Work Processes
Communication	Continuous improvement
Developing others	Sense of urgency
Motivating others	Team development
Customer focus	Organization/Planning
Listening	Expectations/Accountability
	Resolving problems

Here is a description of each of Wal-Mart's key leadership competencies in cultural terms:

Communication—The role of managers is to give associates the help, information, and motivation needed to run the business. It is important for associates to know what problems the company is experiencing as well as the opportunities it faces. Daily standup meetings conducted by store managers keep the team constantly updated on what is going on around it. Sam knew that if he wanted to get employees behind his vision he had to clearly communicate that vision to them.

Developing others—The ability to develop the talents and potential of each and every Wal-Mart associate is one of the company's greatest advantages. Wal-Mart managers are expected to teach and train associates for their jobs today, but, just as importantly, they are expected to prepare associates for future opportunities. Wal-Mart believes in the importance of cross-training people throughout the organization from all functional areas. To accomplish cross-training, headquarters employees are routinely moved into jobs in other departments to gain additional knowledge, skills, and experience. In the stores, assistant store managers are rotated through assignments in merchandising, operations, and human resources. This ensures that a pool of internally promotable, well-rounded company leaders will be available as promotional opportunities become available.

Motivating others—A manager's true success is measured by his or her ability and desire to help others be more successful. Wal-Mart cheers are conducted each day by all managers and associates to break the boredom and create esprit de corps. Associates are recognized by their managers for their personal achievements and are awarded lapel pins for their accomplishments for all to see. In the process, caring managers transform average people into above-average performers. The company philosophy on motivating people is that if you put the interests of people first, profits will follow.

Customer focus—Associates are empowered at every level to respond to the needs of customers. The "ten-foot rule" directs all associates to drop everything to help customers with whom they come in contact. The company embraces a very high external and internal customer-service standard.

Listening—Company leaders are expected to get out from behind their desks and spend time with the associates. MBWA—Management by Walking or Wandering Around—is practiced by all of the company's leaders. Associates who have concerns are encouraged to take advantage of the company's open-door policy. The open-door policy provides a progression of proactive steps that employees can follow to bring issues up the management chain of command to progressively higher levels of authority in order to seek resolution to their concerns.

Continuous improvement—Entrepreneurial thinking is not only encouraged at Wal-Mart, it is expected. It is called "intrapreneurship," and the company can attribute some of its best ideas and greatest improvements to the associates. Nothing is sacred. Any process, policy, or practice can potentially be improved and everyone is expected to take a critical look at ways to improve the business.

Sense of urgency—Don't put off until tomorrow what you can today is the company's "Sundown Rule." Erring on the side of action and getting things done is part of the work ethic for which Wal-Mart is known. "Do it now" accurately describes the company's bias towards action.

Team development—A manager's primary responsibility is to serve the associates he or she leads. Leading by example and using the golden rule are what Wal-Mart refers to as servant-leadership. Wal-Mart believes in the spirit of teamwork and the synergy it creates. Associates are business partners and need to be treated with respect.

Organization/Planning—"Plan your work and work your plan" is a phrase that characterizes the importance at Wal-Mart of seizing control of the work environment rather than being at the mercy of it. Even with the best of plans unanticipated problems that throw the best intending managers off course come up all the time. Staying focused and managing time effectively are critical to thriving in the often chaotic environment of retailing.

Expectations/Accountability—Wal-Mart's associates are hard-working overachievers, who individually and collectively have achieved great things. High expectations are the key to everything and operational excellence is the standard company leaders constantly strive to achieve. Managers and associates are held accountable for achieving established goals.

Resolving problems—When problems occur, as they often do, everyone is expected to get involved. Managers pull together with associates at Wal-Mart to determine how a situation can best be resolved. The people closest to the work almost always have the best solutions to day-to-day problems. In many companies the employees are an untapped reservoir of creative ideas and solutions, but not at Wal-Mart.

These 11 key competencies formed the basis of management-performance feedback resulting from the company's 360-degree internal customer-service performance appraisal process. Understandably, by focusing on this narrow set of competencies the company realized that it might be excluding other important competencies. Sam Walton and his executive leadership team agreed that the use of one set of leadership competencies would serve as a touchstone with which to clearly focus company expectations.

In business, what you measure is what you get. By defining key leadership competencies and training all the managers on their usage, Sam was able to put his head on his pillow at night confident in the knowledge that his entire leadership team was focused on the same things. Everyone was expected to not only embrace these competencies but to internalize them and then demonstrate their use in personal work habits and values.

The challenge faced by any company, but especially a company the size of Wal-Mart, is replicating the culture as it moves into new markets and opens new stores. The notion behind the identification of key competencies for leaders is to ensure that everyone is singing from the same sheet of music. Retail is detail. There are probably 100 different leadership competencies to choose from. The fact that Wal-Mart chose these 11 competencies to the exclusion of others is not to say the other 89 aren't important skills for leaders to have also. It simply says that Wal-Mart believes these are the 11 most important skills for its leaders to have for the company to be successful. I was directly involved in surveying Sam Walton and the other executives to develop the forced ranking that led to the final list of 11 core competencies. The executive team clearly understood the importance of selecting the right skills and marrying ourselves to them with the knowledge that other skills would be excluded in the process.

Once selected, the key leadership competencies were then integrated into all of the standard human resources practices for purposes of focus and efficiency. They become a living, breathing part of the company culture. This means that current and future company leaders are recruited, interviewed, and hired against them, oriented and trained against them, and their performance reviewed against them. As selections are made for promotion individuals are evaluated and promoted against the list of core competencies. Just as at Wal-Mart, selecting the right competencies is critical to ensuring everyone in your organization is marching in the same direction.

Wal-Mart's list of leadership competencies is a good place for you to start as you attempt to define and develop your organization's key competencies. As you are identifying the appropriate competencies for your success today and into the future, ask yourself these questions: Who are we and who do we want to become? Often companies rely on competencies that represent the founding entrepreneurs' skill sets but that do not necessarily represent the current or future reality of the company. I learned that the founder of a company isn't always the person most suited to turning a company around, building the company's infrastructure, or taking the company to the next level. I've seen organizations and entrepreneurs stubbornly stick to the way they have always done things even when today's competitive environment dictates change is necessary. Companies change, markets change, and competition changes requiring organizational flexibility at different points in a company's growth and development. I have worked successfully with many organizations to identify or develop lists of core company competencies and key leadership competencies through a quick survey process of their leaders.

I can't overemphasize the importance of culture to the expansion of Wal-Mart into new markets. Culture is who you are and what you stand for. Internationally, Wal-Mart has found it necessary to adapt its American culture to fit the attitudes, values, and beliefs of people in countries around the world. What works here doesn't necessarily work in Germany, China, Argentina, or Japan. Although cloning store culture is important for multinational organizations intent on creating a uniform customer-service experience, adaptations have to be made to international cultural differences. Culture is important to the single-site operator as well.

Burke and Litwin define culture "as the way we do things around here."[4] Culture is a product of the collective attitudes, values, beliefs, and behaviors of the people who work within an organization. What makes a company culture unique is folklore and stories, inside jokes, values and beliefs, slogans, and a common language. Culture is reinforced in the selection, orientation, training and development, performance appraisal, and the rewards and recognition of employees. It is important to have a culture that is aligned with your organizational vision or mission.

Establishing a clear cultural mission begins with creating an organizational strategy and then communicating and integrating your vision into the DNA of your company. Ownership is the personal acceptance or buy-in into company values and is evidenced in employee behaviors. Empowerment is delegation to employees of the responsibility along with the authority to do the job without the need for management intervention. Standards are the cultural expectations or norms providing a measurement of the achievement of company goals.

In that cultural saying, "our people make the difference," lies another one of the secrets to the success of Wal-Mart. It's as true today as it was when Sam was alive. Armies of associates going the extra yard to provide outstanding service to customers, restock the shelves, and get customers quickly through the registers. Every retail store would come to a grinding halt without the efforts of the people working in them. Show me a well-merchandised, clean store where service to the customer is a priority, and I'll show you a store that is ready to compete because of its people. Learn a lesson from Wal-Mart by never, ever losing sight of the importance of your culture and your employees to the success of your company.

Cultural Checklist

Review this cultural checklist of success strategies and tactics designed to help you compete with big-box retailers like Wal-Mart and not only survive, but thrive.

Culture
- ✓ Communicate your "brand story" to your employees and customers
- ✓ Use stories and folklore of both successes and failures to communicate culture
- ✓ Develop and communicate your vision and mission to all employees
- ✓ Fill key openings by promoting from within to maintain continuity of culture
- ✓ Measure the performance of each employee every day
- ✓ Establish standards of performance as an example for sales: "dollars per hour" or "units per transaction"
- ✓ Create a reward system tied to productivity goals
- ✓ Use stories from your company history to reinforce your cultural values
- ✓ Catch employees doing things right

✓ Send a message about performance by dealing with nonperforming employees

✓ Teach managers to personally model your customer service standards each day

✓ Establish the same standards for customer experience at every location

Key Questions about Your Current Managers

✓ Are managers holding employees to high standards?

✓ Are the highest-caliber people available hired?

✓ What has been each manager's success rate in selecting people?

✓ Are managers building bench strength to allow promotion from within?

✓ Are managers training and developing employees?

✓ If they wanted to, do managers have the ability to attract and recruit great talent?

✓ Is turnover at an acceptable and manageable level?

✓ How would you characterize the morale of employees?

✓ Are managers dealing with nonperformers and recognizing the stars?

✓ Can managers drive sales and control costs?

4

Key Item/Product Strategies and Tactics

"Sam Walton instilled ownership of the products in the stores into the collective consciousness of every associate regardless of what job that associate did for the company."

Everybody is expected to think like a merchant at Wal-Mart. In every department, from information technology to accounting to human resources, every associate at the headquarters must be a retailer first. Only when they've assumed retailers' hats can they secondarily assume functional identities like systems developer, accountant, or trainer. They are expected to visit the company's stores as well as those of competitors, know the issues, and have a point of view on business problems. In this way, functional agendas are eliminated and everyone in every department focuses on the retail agenda, which is improving the stores, products, and customer service. Think about the powerful team synergies created when many people are focused on a common goal. If you ask people from the Wal-Mart Home Office what they do for the company don't be surprised if they tell you that they are retailers. And trust me when I tell you they mean it!

Every week, following the Saturday morning meeting, selected buyers are asked to present, to the cross-functional corporate managers who are in attendance, potential future products they are hoping to sell in the stores. I'll never forget Sam Walton holding an item, like a new-fangled toaster, as he talked to the buyer who had found it in front of the entire leadership team. He'd ask questions about the price point, margin, and number of anticipated units per store as well as when it was intended to be in the stores. He'd then ask the management team, which is a cross-section of leaders from every functional area, to judge each individual item by giving the buyer a thumbs-up or a thumbs-down on it. Sam would personally walk across the front of the stage displaying the item in one hand, over his head, and ask the throng of managers, "What do you think, what do you think?" For some items you'd hear cheers and others items you'd hear jeers. Those receiving a thumbs-up would be purchased as part of the store's merchandise assortment. If a product received a thumbs-down from the audience, the buyer was told by Sam himself, for all to hear, to go find a different product.

This was Sam at his best—being a merchant and a showman. He was in all his glory when he had the chance to pick products for the stores. I watched his face light up while he handled and sized up merchandise. He looked like an auctioneer trying to find just the right words to describe an item, right before he took bids on it to insure he'd get the most money for it.

What was the point of this exercise? This product-selection event each week was intended by Sam as a way to get all company leaders thinking like retail merchants. Culturally, he was instilling ownership of the product in the stores into the collective consciousness of each and every associate regardless of what job that associate did for the company. Each buyer at Wal-Mart is responsible for dozens and dozens of products and they were only asked to bring one of them out as an example to show at this meeting. Sam was trying to get the whole team excited about product selection, to feel the same excitement he had felt when picking products as a young entrepreneur and merchant. He was training everyone in attendance to think like a merchant so that by understanding the stores and its products they could all better serve the customer.

Years earlier I had traveled with a long-tenured sales VP at Frito-Lay who had that same enthusiasm for product. I'll never forget the way he dressed up the snack-food shelves in one of the Wal-Mart stores we visited. I watched him as he carefully picked up each bag with two hands, one hand holding the top seam and the other hand holding the bottom seam. When he pulled his hands quickly apart the bag straightened up without damaging the product inside, making the display look neat and uniform. I remember he was painstakingly careful to avoid crushing a single chip, handling those bags as if they were hen's eggs. He romanced the product as if it were 24-karat gold. When he was done we both stood back and admired the perfectly merchandised shelves. It is hard to explain but he had that same look in his eye that I saw in Sam's when he was handling product. By the reverence they showed for product it was clear that both realized that "product equals paycheck." It is just this type of fanatical attention to detail for which great merchants have always been known. Great merchants like Sam Walton have a passion for product and he expected everyone else at Wal-Mart to share that same passion.

Having worked in several Fortune 500 companies, I know from my own experience how unusual it is for the functional managers at head-quarters to understand the inner workings of the business. There is a ten-dency for functional experts to create a functional agenda or operate in silos, as opposed to aligning themselves with the overall business agenda. Accounting managers provide thorough accounting, human resources managers worry about people issues, and IT professionals keep the systems running—each almost in a business vacuum with little knowl-edge of the real issues affecting service to the customer. It's not the same at Wal-Mart. Functional managers are expected to travel to the field, work in the stores, and develop an understanding of the real issues related to customers. Everything else they do is secondary to developing strategies that improve the level of service in the stores.

They even ask their vendors to get into the customer-service act. Examples of customer-service vendor partnerships were cited in a Forbes.com article: "Looking to sell food to hunters who already fre-quented its sporting goods departments, [Wal-Mart] asked Hormel Foods to come up with a snack that it could place alongside the rifles and fish-ing rods. Within weeks, "Spamouflage"—Spam in camouflage cans—was blowing out the doors of 760 rural Wal-Marts."[1]

I think Wal-Mart's has a fanatical focus on having all of its employ-ees and their vendors think like merchants because it knows that having the right products, merchandising them well, and providing outstanding service are pivotal to creating an exciting shopping experience and build-ing customer loyalty. Knowing the variety of shopping choices available to customers today, Wal-Mart's buyers and store managers do all they can to make their stores the destination of choice for value-driven shoppers. The price points are sharp and the merchandise is tailored to meet the needs of middle America. This customer-centered focus makes customers wonder, "Why shop elsewhere?" By "flowing" new merchandise into the stores each and every week and having the widest selection of low-priced seasonal merchandise, Wal-Mart ensures that customers return again and again almost afraid they'll miss a great bargain. As large and diverse as Wal-Mart has become with its Supercenters, Sam's Clubs, Convenience Stores, and Neighborhood Markets, even it can't be, in retail terms, all things to all consumers though it continues to try. Herein lies a potential opportunity for competitors to create a niche to compete and survive.

Retail stores have a choice of areas in which to compete, including: service, price, assortment, quality, location, fashion, and product selection. By identifying and targeting a specific market or pocket, retailers all over the world have found ways to compete and thrive. Once you figure out your own brand story, you need to earn your "retail PhD" in all of the problems and opportunities associated with that market. A retailer who focuses on a specific market can provide a unique product selection and develop expertise to better serve its customers.

By now I hope you are convinced that it is suicidal to attempt to compete directly with Wal-Mart on the same product with comparable pricing. Part of the reason is that the vast majority of Wal-Mart's products are made at low-cost manufacturing facilities overseas. By contracting directly with the manufacturers and buying unbelievable quantities, Wal-Mart pays a unit cost far lower than the price at which any of your suppliers can purchase those same items. In fact, unless you intend to buy hot merchandise, there is no way you can buy from your own suppliers at prices that come close to allowing you to go toe to toe with Wal-Mart. Your expense structure may also be a deterrent.

John Morrison, director of the Missouri Grocers Association, said:

> We [grocers] are still very engrained in selling USA-produced products; unfortunately, Wal-Mart has moved well beyond that into a global marketplace. They have been forced to do that because of economies of scale to maintain their product price position. They have to find companies that will make the same product at a cheaper price and in many cases they have to go outside the United States to do that. If you want to buy something cheap, someone's got to make something cheap, and if someone makes something cheap somebody's got to work cheap . . . you can't break that cycle. There is a difference between buying something cheap and paying fair market price for it. That fair value goes back to the people who made it, giving them adequate wages to incent them to come up with more products and better products. "A great opportunity could now exist and that is to promote in an arena Wal-Mart can no longer control and become the primary retailer of our neighbor's products by strongly promoting and selling USA and regional products. Such an effort could send a valid reason of where consumers should shop and why."

Unless you are a discount store don't try to act like a discounter. Wal-Mart is a jack of all trades but I can't really say that it is a master of none. With its store-within-a-store strategy, Wal-Mart has specialty divisions including tire and lube express, optical, pharmacy, health and beauty aids, electronics, jewelry, garden centers, photo lab, and so on. In my opinion, its sheer size and number of departments still limits its ability to focus on any particular product line at store level to the extent that you can. That's good news for competitors; you can capitalize on your strengths by providing products and services that are more narrow and deep. Find your niche and buy products to create a merchandise mix and services that clearly differentiate your business and clearly makes you an expert at what you do.

Your differentiation strategy could be as simple as focusing on providing American-made products to your customers and advertising that fact. By adopting a differentiation strategy, you can carve out a competitive niche, thereby catering to local customers with more discerning tastes. By doing so you can actually sell higher-priced merchandise. Wal-Mart can't cater to local tastes to the extent that you can.

There is no doubt that Wal-Mart's entry into new markets has decimated many small and large retailers. Some simply failed to offer a distinct selection of products. Others just got caught in the wrong place at the wrong time when Wal-Mart came to town. Some local stores have simply surrendered to the feeling that they will fail anyway by closing their doors without a fight. Wes Ball, president of the Tennessee Grocers Association, said this about competing with Wal-Mart: "They come in like gangbusters and if you can stay on your corner eighteen months you're likely to stay there for twenty years." So, before you throw in the towel, it's important to realize you can compete and not only survive but thrive in the Wal-Mart economy. By sticking to what you do best and by stepping back and strategically identifying markets, products, and services ignored by big-box retailers you can carve out a successful niche to serve in your community.

In the study *Small-Town Merchants Are Not Using the Recommended Strategies to Compete Against National Discount Chains: A Prescriptive v. Descriptive Study,* author Christopher Achua stated,

> A retailer's product strategy is revealed in the variety and assortment of products it chooses to carry out. A discount store chain and a local independent retailer may offer similar merchandise, but the discount store will tend to offer more variety but limited assortment of merchandise. These elements of product variety and assortment form an integral part of the retail market structure, since it is the retail offering that ultimately distinguishes between discounters, department and specialty stores. The question to respondents was how competition from major chains had affected their product offerings. When asked to describe what responsive actions they had instituted to stay competitive, respondents' answers varied as follows:
>
> - No change—52 percent
> - Expand product line—34 percent

- Decreased product line—10 percent
- Complete new line—3 percent
- Changed retail format—2 percent

Of the 62 merchants who responded to this question, about a third of them (34%) indicated that they expanded their product line offerings rather than contracting or eliminating some lines. Only 10% (six) indicated that they took this line of action. Half (52%) did nothing to adjust their product offerings. Very few (3%) offered a completely new product line or changed store format as a competitive response (2%).[2]

It is interesting to note that 52 percent of the stores chose to do nothing to adjust their product assortments even though they knew they were directly in the competitive path of a big-box discounter.

I asked Kerley LeBoeuf, president and CEO of the National Association of Convenience Stores (NACS), what kinds of problems Wal-Mart and Sam's Clubs are causing the convenience-store industry and he said, "What they are doing is fundamentally using gasoline as a leader, I'm not going to say a loss leader but a leader to attract traffic. If you've got a parking lot out there you can put some gasoline pumps in it, perhaps a little outpost-type operation, and all you are trying to do is get more people to come into your store and buy your products that have higher margins. So that's what's happening around the country and that tends to press the margins in a particular area."

Dick Wood, chairman of the 546-store Wawa convenience store chain, stated, "As it turns out, there are a multitude of competitors, not just Wal-Mart, trying to take market share away from every other retailer out there. It's fast paced, dog-eat-dog competition, and flexibility and perseverance are critical to success." Historically, convenience stores haven't viewed Wal-Mart as a direct competitor. Now that Wal-Mart has introduced gasoline pumps onto its parking lots, everything has changed and its fuel sales are directly and negatively affecting convenience stores.

The rules of competition are continually changing and retailers have to adapt to those changes or face severe consequences. Those convenience stores that rely on gasoline to drive company profits are destined to fail. Reliance on one product as a source of income is a risky proposition for any business. Businesses that have chosen to offer a unique assortment of products to drive sales and profits have a much better chance of surviving.

Unfortunately, there are businesses that have toyed at differentiating themselves from Wal-Mart, as if they were rearranging the deck chairs on the *Titanic*. The outcome of this ill-advised tactic is both predictable and fatal. However, the good news is that lots of businesses throughout the country successfully reinvented themselves when Wal-Mart came to town. Learn from the retailers that are currently thriving in proximity to Wal-Mart and try to copy their example.

Sam spoke about the importance of being merchandise-driven:

> If you are going to show the kind of double-digit comparable sales increases that we show every year and grow a company the way that we've grown ours, you have to be merchandise-driven. Otherwise you become like everybody else. In retail you are either operations-driven—where your main thrust is toward reducing expenses and improving efficiency—or you are merchandise-driven. The ones that are truly merchandise-driven can always work on operations. But the ones that are operations-driven tend to level off and begin to deteriorate.[3]

The point is that you can't save your way to prosperity and even if you have the best-run operation around you still have to be merchandise-driven. The trick is that you have to simultaneously increase the top line by increasing sales while you manage the bottom line by controlling expenses. The retail formula is quite simple: Find a great location, buy the right products, merchandise them properly, promote the heck out of them to create store traffic, hire great people to serve the customers, and do whatever you can to run an efficient operation while staying in stock and controlling costs. In reality, many factors are pivotal to your success in retail, not the least of which is having the right products and a little luck to go along with them!

But how do you identify your niche when Wal-Mart owns so much of so many markets? As an example, according to an article in *Fortune* magazine entitled *One Nation Under Wal-Mart*: "Wal-Mart now has captured market shares of: 36 percent of the dog food market, 32 percent of disposable diapers, 30 percent of photographic film, 26 percent of toothpaste, and 21 percent of pain remedies."[4] The list of gigantic market shares goes on and on. The good news is that there is still a 64 percent market-share opportunity within which you can carve out your niche if you want to sell dog food.

Here is an illustration of a market that is wide open. The top five sporting goods retailers in the United States are: The Sports Authority/Gart Sports, Dick's Sporting Goods, Galyan's, Big 5, and Hibbett. These companies represent billions of dollars of sporting-goods sales across America, yet collectively their sales only represent 11 percent of the total sporting-goods market.[5] That means that 89 percent of the sales in this market are made by other retailers, many of which—like Wal-Mart,

Target, K-Mart—don't specialize in sporting goods. This statistic provides a great insight into the sales opportunity available to the sporting-goods specialty store that can figure out ways to garner a larger share of the market. The sporting-goods market is just one example of the potential sales that are out there in every market for the retailer that can differentiate its brand and become a destination for shoppers. Grappling for market share is what business is all about; the sales are out there for the taking, you just have to figure out how to get your fair share.

Focusing on the customer is and always has been the most important element of retailing success. Wal-Mart strategy has always been pretty simple: Offer customers what they want at the best possible prices. Its buyers go to great lengths to understand the customers' wants and needs and then they buy to those needs, supplying products that provide quality and value to the consumer. They also shop competitors' stores in search of great new product ideas. This is the same product-selection path you should take to make your business successful. Talk to your customers, find out what they want, and buy to those needs. Brand marketers call this process an "outside in" approach to customer and product strategy.

Remember, change and adaptation must become a way of life for your business. If you stand still you'll get run over by the competition. But it works both ways. As you take ideas from your competitors they are doing exactly the same thing to you. Competition creates a never-ending tug-of-war between competitors. As you attempt to provide a unique selection of products and services to create your niche, your competitors are also adapting to steal your best ideas and grab an increased share of the market.

Business and brand competition are kind of like the story of the crab in a bucket. A lot of us have gone to the seashore and caught crabs by the dock using a piece of chicken at the end of a string for bait. Once you pull a crab up and you've netted it, you put it into a bucket. If you have only one crab in the bucket you have to put a lid on that bucket because that crab will do everything within its power to crawl out of that bucket or it will die trying. But you know, if you have two or more crabs in a bucket, you don't have to put a lid on that bucket. Every time a crab tries to crawl out of the bucket those other crabs will reach up and pull it back down. That's the same thing that happens in business. Every time you come up with a unique idea or niche and you are the only one offering that product or service to the customer you competitively blow the lid off as you, alone, capture market share. You in essence own that market. You are, so to speak, the only crab in that competitive bucket, but not for long. As your competitors race to replicate your unique strategy, others climb into your competitive bucket in an effort to grab market share and take away your competitive advantage. In the process, they level the playing field. As that happens, you no longer own the market as your competitors have pulled you back into the pack. What was once a unique product or service quickly becomes readily available everywhere. This is why you must constantly consider adapting and changing your product mix as the market conditions change, cycling out of previously successful products as you ramp up new ones.

I've heard merchandise managers say that buying too little merchandise is just as bad as buying too much. Some who purchase products seem to subscribe to the philosophy that shorting a promotion by underbuying product is a safe way to avoid getting hung with too much merchandise. It's also a way to avoid risk. Inherent in the very nature of buying is the risk associated with one human being trying to predict the future buying habits of a consumer who is not always predictable. Picking products can be risky business, and those making buying decisions won't always be right. But I've always heard that if you want the chance to hit a home run you've got to step up to the plate and swing the bat. You'll never be truly successful until you courageously select a product, buy it deep, promote it, merchandise it, sign it properly, and keep it in stock. As a result of conscious or unconscious fears, many retailers never realize their true sales potential because of their aversion to risk-taking in buying and promoting products. Operationally, buying short represents empty shelves and empty shelves represent lost revenue.

Let's talk about some strategies you can adopt to better position yourself to increase your chances to survive but also to thrive. One of the things you can start to do immediately is learn from the success of Wal-Mart and other respected competitors. Most of the world-class retail companies have perfected the art of displaying products and creating sales velocity through the use of promotional activity and signing. The standards they have set for window design, fixtures, and signage are what consumers have come to expect from every retailer. Compare how your business stacks up as you shop their stores. Once you've determined the standards you need to achieve ask your vendors to help you merchandise your store to world-class levels.

Good merchandising is one of the skills that are pivotal to the success of any retail merchant, but it is important to remember that no amount of great merchandising and selling can generate sales of a product nobody wants. On the other hand, items that consumers perceive as hot may fly off the shelves with little merchandising gymnastics required. Properly signed and priced merchandise, if it is in demand by consumers, should sell if merchandised properly and if your store generates sufficient customer traffic.

Educate your customers so they understand the depth and breadth of your product offerings. Once they cross your threshold educating them is easy. Train your employees to discuss the features and benefits of your product selection. You can even give customers promotional handouts or bag stuffers. For those that don't walk in the door a targeted direct-mail campaign or newspaper inserts directed to the homes of your ideal customer base will help get your promotional message out.

It's no surprise that inefficient merchandising or poor product selection leads to sluggish sales, driving up inventory costs and increasing the necessity for mark-downs. When you have too much inventory and the product isn't turning over, that's when good merchants cut their losses early. They quickly replace slow movers on valuable shelf space with products offering better sales potential. Wal-Mart employs this same strategy; if a product moves too slowly through their system they'll promptly drop that line in a heartbeat. As sales slacken, as they often do, be prepared with new products in the pipeline for a fresh mix of products on the shelves.

"Flowing" in new merchandise monthly or seasonally keeps the shopping experience fresh and exciting. A good product strategy I saw used at American Eagle (AE) to keep the stores interesting and fresh was the use of core items, key items, and fashion items. American Eagle flowed new AE-branded merchandise into their stores using this approach. An example of a core item is AE blue jeans and tee shirts bought in large quantities. Customers knew core items would always be in stock. A key item is bought in large quantities also and AE cargo shorts in the summertime are a good example; a fashion item is a current "hot" AE fashion item bought in small quantities to satisfy the fashion-forward customer.

If you are a merchandise-driven company, as most retailers are, you have a responsibility to constantly evaluate and adjust your mix of product offerings. Buyers have a tendency to lose objectivity when products they have selected underperform. There is no reason to be sentimental about poorly performing product. Learn from your mistakes, cut your losses and move on.

A mistake merchants often make is riding a successful product into the ground rather than cycling out of it and ramping up a new product to replace it. Sameness is boring and makes for a dull shopping experience for the customer. Sam's Club does a great job of keeping its ever-changing product mix full of surprises. You never know what you will find when you shop there. My wife, Sheryl, and I find it hard to shop at Sam's Club without impulsively spending 200 dollars every time on things we just have to have. We feel pressure to purchase items on the spot because we've found that if we don't buy the item that moment, it will be gone by the time we return to shop again. You too can keep your store exciting with in-store specials and new products to keep your customers coming back again and again.

Sam Walton truly expected his buyers and store managers to take risks and make mistakes. Michael Eisner, CEO of Disney, made this point and captured what I feel are also Sam Walton's beliefs when he said, "We set our goals, aim for perfection, inevitably fall short, try to learn from our mistakes, and hope that our successes will continue to outnumber our failures."[6] Making an honest mistake at Wal-Mart is rarely career ending. Errors and mistakes are inevitable with the workload, sales volume, and expansion of the company. However, a buyer who knowingly fails to move quickly to correct a known mistake in order to cut losses early is making a second more heinous error by acting dishonestly or without integrity.

Errors normally occur by commission but they can also occur by intended or unintended omission. Retailers also lose sales when they pick a winning product but fail to buy it deep enough to insure a sufficient back stock of inventory to match sales. Buying in sufficient amounts is particularly critical for products being promoted. Being out of stock is unacceptable from a consumer's perspective and from a retailer's point of view no stock equals lost sales. You have to have the product the customer wants when the customer wants it. A sufficient back stock is one of the costs of doing business. Excellent vendor partnerships with wholesalers and distributors may save the day when customer demand for a product exceeds your projected sales and inventory projections.

Wal-Mart seems to value merchant skills more than most companies. That's probably because Sam Walton was always a merchant at heart, having grown up in retail from the bottom up. The key competencies of successful merchants have historically included the ability to pick the right product, promote it, merchandise it properly, and sell it off. These skills have also provided the greatest satisfaction for retail entrepreneurs. Wal-Mart hasn't lost sight of this fact and has maintained a degree of merchandising autonomy in the hands of local store managers. With computerized space-management software and store planograms much of the creativity has been taken away from the on-site managers of many retail chains as product placement decisions for stores are made by buyers at the headquarters. Wal-Mart is no different. Knowing this, Sam took steps to ensure that store managers always retained a degree of autonomy.

One of the contests Wal-Mart created to focus the entire team on entrepreneurial discount merchandising was the Volume Producing Item or VPI Program. Managers pick an item and promote that item in-store using extremely large merchandising displays or end caps. VPI brings Sam's discounting principles alive by demonstrating to everyone involved that when you buy a lot of product, charge as little as you can for it, and display it as if you are serious about it, big-time profits will follow. The VPI program significantly increases the sales volume and velocity of the promoted item but it is more a way to teach merchant skills and create fun competition between in-store department managers. By stacking product high and watching it blow out, managers throughout the chain of stores learn the relationship between good merchandising of a product and its sales velocity. Wal-Mart has always liked the idea of healthy competition. Contests are also a great means of exceeding customers' expectations by doing unusual things to set Wal-Mart apart from the competition. Leading by example, the Home Office executives are active participants in stoking the competitive fires by directly participating in these product contests.

Those that manage smaller retail companies must by default still rely on old-fashioned merchant skills in their stores because they continue to wear all the retail hats. If you are one of them, this is an advantage for you with respect to your ability to compete with larger, nationally controlled retail chains. A local retailer has a great deal more flexibility in selecting product and merchandising it to best fit the needs of the customers in his or her own community. This local buying advantage must be leveraged to the hilt. Local consumers need to know you offer specialized products and services that can only be found in your store. This could include items manufactured locally that only appeal to your geographic area. Big-box retailers can't specialize to the extent you can in providing products that meet the needs of your local customers.

Stores that currently carry a line of merchandise that is also carried by Wal-Mart need to work with their vendors to differentiate their product offerings. They might do this by stocking higher-end products rather than cheap ones. A good source for developing a product-mix strategy is to gather ideas from your own customers. Teach your employees to engage customers in conversations about products to help you determine what the customer is looking for. Keep a list of product requests you receive from customers, over the phone and in person, that aren't in your current inventory. As you make future buying decisions take those product ideas into consideration. Talk to your vendors and ask them for ideas concerning fast-moving product they might already be supplying to other retailers. You might also ask your vendors for examples of stores comparable to your own that are successfully competing with Wal-Mart in other towns nearby. By visiting them you can pick up plenty of good ideas you can use in your store.

Success in retail does not require a whole lot of original thinking. Remember, imitation is the sincerest form of flattery. Sam Walton did just that in the early days, shopping K-Mart stores and anybody else with a good idea, and then emulating their best strategies. You, too, can use this idea to your advantage. Just as Sam Walton and his Wal-Mart disciples embrace continuous improvement and continuous learning, you too should learn from the success of others. Shop other stores and don't limit yourself to your direct competitors or your own industry. Look for subtle ideas concerning product mix, placement, pricing, signage, graphics, and employee sales activity, and also check out point-of-sale merchandising for impulse-sales ideas.

Marketing your business through local advertising can be one good way to increase customer traffic and build your brand. As you well know, advertising can be very expensive. As a merchant you must look at advertising as an investment that over time pays dividends to you in the form of increased customer traffic and sales. I'm not talking about a one-time shotgun approach here. Effective advertising requires focus and the courage of your conviction along with enough cash to maintain an ongoing ad campaign to promote your business. Work with your wholesalers and distributors to develop a well-planned marketing strategy to focus your advertising around product promotion. Check into the possibility of receiving manufacturer advertising coop subsidies when you promote their products in your advertising. Promoting aggressively through advertising and in-store promotion are proactive ways to take charge of increasing your business. Even Wal-Mart, with its unbelievable customer traffic, uses promotional newspaper and television advertising to build even more brand identity and traffic.

I've noticed that in the last couple of years Wal-Mart has been making a big push into branded fashion apparel and simultaneously concentrating on building its private-label product business. That's no surprise when you consider the benefits of manufacturing its own brands have in terms of margin improvement alone. Wal-Mart carries some respected national brands like Levi's, Bugle Boy, Jordache, No Nonsense, Fruit of the Loom, Wrangler, and Hanes. Side by side with these it also offers its own private-label merchandise. Wal-Mart has become a destination store for back-to-school apparel for kids of all ages. The price points are sharp and their apparel represents knockoffs of current basic fashions you'd find in the mall. It isn't what I call fashion-forward or edgy and for the targeted customer it doesn't need to be.

Historically, Wal-Mart has not been known for fashion apparel but it's obvious the chain is making a concentrated effort to capture market share from companies like Old Navy, American Eagle Outfitters, the Gap, and Eddie Bauer. These private-label, mall-based retailers sell tons of blue jeans and T-shirts. As you walk around a Wal-Mart store or any retail mall, observe what the customers are wearing. A lot of customers are decked out in blue jeans and T-shirts. It's a huge core business for mall-based retailers with entire stores built around those two items. Walk into the Wal-Mart apparel section and you'll see a serious commitment to these two businesses in the children's, men's, and women's areas.

Generally speaking, you won't find the fashion snobs who typically shop at high-priced stores like Abercrombie and Fitch shopping for clothes at Wal-Mart but that has little impact on sales volume. Fashion seekers represent the minority of consumers. Wal-Mart clothing is targeted toward the masses and its prices are the cheapest around. You could probably buy two or three pairs of comparable-quality jeans at Wal-Mart for the price of one pair at one of the mall-based, private-label stores. For families on a budget, that represents real value. Specialty-apparel retailers like Old Navy and American Eagle Outfitters are perfectly happy targeting the same mass-market consumer who shops for clothing at Wal-Mart.

Apparel is just one example of Wal-Mart's push into private-label product; you can find its private-label product all over their store. Most specialty retailers discovered the power of creating their own private-label brands years ago. Fortunes have been made by Donald Fisher, who created the Gap brand, Jay Schottenstein, the visionary behind American Eagle Outfitters, and Les Wexner, founder of the Limited, who turned those stores into destination shopping experiences for teenagers. This fact has not gone unnoticed in Bentonville, Arkansas. Wal-Mart is developing more and more private-label products knocking off more expensive, branded mall merchandise. The margins are significantly higher on private-label product and the cost per unit is much lower when you are able to build your own line.

A *Fortune* magazine article provides insight into the shift of consumer perceptions: "Store brands aren't for losers anymore. In fact, they're downright sizzling. And that scares the soap out of the folks who bring us Tide and Minute Maid and Alpo. An almost imperceptible tectonic shift has been reshaping the world of brands. Retailers—once the lowly peddlers of brands that were made and marketed by big, important manufacturers—are now behaving like full-fledged marketers. And here's the earthquake part: It is their brands—not those of traditional powerhouses like Kraft or Coke—that are winning over the customers in the greatest numbers."[7]

Sam's Choice® is a Wal-Mart brand and registered trademark established by Sam Walton. Each package in the Sam's Choice line carries the brand story: "Sam Walton, founder of Wal-Mart, listened to his customers, understood their needs and found ways to offer quality products to them at every day low prices. The Sam's Choice brand continues his legacy by offering innovative products that have been made to our own higher standards with the finest ingredients from around the world. We believe these products, available only at Wal-Mart and Wal-Mart Supercenters, offer exceptional quality and better value then the leading national brands at our always low Wal-Mart prices. We think you'll agree, or we'll refund your money, no questions asked! Better products at the always low Wal-Mart prices...always...we guarantee it. Sam Walton [signature]" Sam's personal signature appears on every package as a reinforcement of his product guarantee. Sam's Club also has its own private-label program called Members Mark, which was developed in response to Costco's private-label program called Kirkland Signature. One of the perceived values of these brands is that the consumer receives more value at the same or better quality than the national brands.

Once happy to serve as passive landlords of shelf space on behalf of established national brands, "Retailers are now becoming brand managers," says Dan Stanek, executive vice president at consulting company Retail Forward. "Retailers love this trend. Because overhead is low and marketing costs are nil, private-label products bring 10% higher margins, on average, than branded goods do. But more than that, a trusted store brand can differentiate a chain from its competitors. Shoppers will drive the extra mile to Costco to buy Kirkland cashews, filling their carts with other goods while they're at it. All told, one in five items sold in US stores is now store branded, which sounds like a lot—until you learn that in Europe that percentage has reached 40 percent. Consumers here keep warming to them. A 2001 Gallup poll found 45 percent of shoppers more likely to switch to a store brand, while only 31 percent said so in 1996."

The lesson to be learned here is that consumers are willing to purchase cheaper, private-label store brands if those products are of equal quality to national brands. Many vendors offer private-label programs for their retail clients. This is an excellent way to differentiate your product mix while at the same time improving your profitability. No one can buy your brand anywhere but at your store. This creates a unique shopping experience for your customers. The possibilities are endless for creating your own brand identity.

Product-differentiation strategies, like private-label programs, require executives to step back and analyze the market. That's not always easy for tactically-oriented business leaders. I've found in the years I've worked in retail that executives and managers of stores are execution-oriented to a fault. They seem to subscribe to the philosophy "When in doubt about what to do, err on the side of action." Generally speaking, ready, shoot, aim is retail leadership personified. The nature of the beast in retail is to roll up your sleeves and do something now. The retail reality is that 90 percent of strategy is execution; ideas truly are often quite easy to come up with, it's the implementation that's always tough. A flurry of the same or unfocused activity is not the correct strategy for competing with Wal-Mart or anyone else. Develop a well thought-out plan and execute it.

My recommendation to those who always err on the side of action is to stop what you're doing and re-educate yourself about the market within which you are competing. Embrace the fact that change is inevitable. Develop a well thought-out, ongoing strategy based on your firsthand competitive analysis of the market. Talk to vendors, competitors, the chamber of commerce, trade groups, your employees, and your customers. Challenge the way you currently do things in every area of the business. This shouldn't be a one-time activity; it needs to be done constantly. Get your finger on the pulse of your market and keep it there. A competitive self-assessment and a strategy-and-tactics questionnaire are included in the appendix of this book to help you develop your own competitive game plan.

Remember, the definition of business insanity is doing things the way you have always done them while expecting a different result. Take as much control of your own destiny as you possibly can by becoming current in your knowledge of the competitive landscape. Heed the warning implied in the Chinese proverb that says, "If we don't change the direction we are going, we're likely to end up where we are headed."

Find and observe other retail companies that do what you want to do, in your vicinity or in another town nearby. Learn from their proven track record of successfully competing with Wal-Mart. Shop their stores and talk to their managers. Look at their merchandise and then shop the local Wal-Mart and compare. Observe and copy its strategies and tactics. Look at its visual merchandising, product assortment/mix, customer service, convenience, promotional activity, prices, location, and people. Do what they do, in other words. There are businesses successfully competing with Wal-Mart in your niche; find out what they are doing and try it in your business. If one can do it successfully all can do it!

Most successful entrepreneurs are happy to help others succeed. As you attend local chamber of commerce or rotary meetings, develop your own network of successful entrepreneurs with whom you can share ideas. By joining your national trade association you can stay current on competitive developments in your particular area of expertise. These associations exist to help companies in your industry compete successfully. Share what you learn with other business people in your community to strengthen everyone's ability to compete and survive.

A strong and viable shopping market with healthy stores is in the best interest of all the businesses in the local area. Retail merchants are by nature very competitive with one another. In a Wal-Mart retailing world, smaller competitors need to get over any petty jealousies they feel towards one another and work together to keep downtown areas, shopping malls, and suburban strip centers viable. I've heard it said that the rising tide lifts all boats but that's not always true when a big-box retailer like Wal-Mart plants one of its 200,000-square-foot megastores just down the street and begins taking market share. Some businesses do experience some improvement from the increased consumer traffic and money flooding into the area but the majority of businesses see a significant decline in sales. One of the ways to survive the big-box onslaught is for local retailers to cooperate with one another instead of just fighting among themselves over the leftover scraps.

Don't wait for someone else to initiate; get proactive. Ask your suppliers to go out for lunch and discuss current developments in your market. Ask them what other companies are doing to successfully compete with the big-box retailers. Finally, ask for some suggestions and constructive feedback about your business and how your suppliers would recommend improving your operations.

Just as in any other competition it is important for you to understand what you are up against by studying your competition. Become obsessed with understanding Wal-Mart's product, pricing, placement, and promotion, the "four Ps of marketing." Watch carefully and emulate how they execute the "four Cs of retail," which are customer service, customer service, customer service, and customer service! You get the idea. Talk to its customers and your own to find out what their needs are so that you can best meet them. Understand its mix of products in your category and its prices. Do whatever you can to meet or exceed your customers' expectations. In other words, become a student of retailing and a continuous learner.

I remember the first time I met with the Chief Merchandising Officer of Wal-Mart. At that time it was Bill Fields. I had to ask him how his buyers could possibly buy to the kind of volume for which they were responsible. With the number and the size of the stores it seemed a Herculean task just to get the proper mix of products onto the shelves. Bill explained to me the Wal-Mart store-within-a-store philosophy of one store at a time, one department at a time, one customer at a time.

This meant that each Wal-Mart Buyer needed to think in terms of the smallest common denominator or the buying task would truly become an insurmountable challenge. In other words, they realized the "buying pie" couldn't be consumed all in one big bite, but once reduced to smaller slices it was then edible and digestible. The key is what Wal-Mart refers to as the KISS. (keep it simple, stupid) principle to break big, onerous tasks down into smaller, easier-to-manage, bite-size pieces.

There is an old saying in traditional business—"think big, start small, scale up." Wal-Mart contradicts that way of thinking with their own version which I summarize as "think small, start small, scale up." They do everything they can to simplify everything they do by making the seemingly impossible look easy and the easy look downright invisible. Big companies aren't supposed to be so focused, quick on their feet, and fast-adapting—but this behemoth has all the right moves at all the right times!

Bill explained the buying strategy to me in the simplest terms possible. He said Wal-Mart has different sizes of stores: A, B, C, D and E. Within each size store classification is identified a specific planogram for product placement. Each classification requires a different quantity and mix of products. (With the technology available, Wal-Mart could also differentiate within store classification high-, medium-, and lower-volume stores. Restocking strategies would take into account purchase velocity and then replenishment would occur in partnership with the vendors.) By categorizing the stores by size, Wal-Mart makes the buying job, which at first glance seems impossible, more manageable. Using technology it has even developed individual product strategies to avoid sending snow shovels to Miami.

It would appear that UPC codes may become a thing of the past. Wal-Mart's technological leadership is moving into new directions including Radio Frequency Identification (RFID) and Electronic Product Codes (EPCs) and it is requiring its vendors to get up to speed quickly on these established technologies. Alex Daniels reported on a conference called "Emerging Trends in Retailing," held at the University of Arkansas on October 9, 2003.

> At the event, sponsored by the Sam M. Walton College of Business Center for Retailing Excellence, Wal-Mart officials emphasized the importance of suppliers understanding the benefits of Radio Frequency Identification, or RFID. The technology, used for years to track large items such as trucks and livestock, consists of tiny computer chips that allow goods to be followed throughout the manufacturing and distribution process. The promise of RFID, according to Wal-Mart officials and other retail experts, is that costs can be taken out of the distribution process, because the chips can accurately measure when and where goods are shipped, stored and displayed on the retail floor.[8]

A 2003 article in *InformationWeek* magazine entitled, "Wal-Mart To Brief Top Suppliers On RFID Plans," states,

> Wal-Mart wants all of its suppliers to be ready for RFID in 2006, and will itself have RFID readers in all its distribution centers as well as in its more than 2,900 stores by the 2005 deadline . . . Procter & Gamble Co. says it will begin using RFID with Wal-Mart in major markets by next spring, and Unilever says it, too, will meet the deadline.[9]

Key suppliers like Procter & Gamble, Unilever, and GE have had strategic alliances with Wal-Mart for years, which include electronic-data interchange to expedite product replenishment. It is estimated that between 500 and 600 of Wal-Mart's supplying companies have even set up shop in Bentonville (which has been nicknamed "Vendorville") and have dedicated teams to support the sale of their products to Wal-Mart's buyers.

Katherine Bowers of *Women's Wear Daily* writes:

> Vendorville is a Fortune 500 microcosm, with everyone from Procter & Gamble to Exxon and Mobile [sic] running offices dedicated to serving Wal-Mart. Kraft redefines "branch office" with 200-plus employees ensconced in a 50,000-square-foot building . . . The thought of working in Bentonville might initially send chills down the spines of many vendor executives. But many big-city expats become enamored with the region's mild seasons, low cost of living, and wide, green spaces and decide to stay. Many switch to another vendor, rather than take a promotion back to corporate headquarters. Locals call it "vendor hopping." . . . The job-hopping goes both ways. Sources say vendors, in hopes of getting insight and an inside track, are luring away Wal-Mart buyers and other junior staffers with higher salaries . . . Given that Wal-Mart has 27,000 vendors, it's logical that Vendorville is in its fetal stages in terms of clout and scope. A persistent rumor traveling local circles is that Wal-Mart has mandated that all vendors of a certain size will have to open branch offices in the next 18 months if they want to do business with the retail behemoth.[10]

Vendor partnerships have proven to be critically important to Wal-Mart's ability to lower costs and remain in stock. Many manufacturers, but not all, would love to be a supplier to the world's largest retailer. Most companies don't have the manufacturing capacity nor do they have the logistics capability to supply their products across the chain. If they did they would be placed in an undesirable business position of supplying 50 percent or more of their production capacity to one customer, Wal-Mart. That is not a sound business strategy and could lead to a disastrous outcome should that overcommitted supplier be dropped by the Bentonville Colossus.

"[Wal-Mart's] goal is to have a 30 percent share of every major business they are in and they are pretty serious about it," says Linda Kristiansen, a retail analyst for UBS Warburg Equity Research. With the volume of business Wal-Mart generates, and its lofty market-share goals, it makes sense for vendors to have branch offices in northwest Arkansas. Wal-Mart has pioneered vendor relationships built on honesty and integrity and open sharing of information. Some of the most respected suppliers are even leveraged for their knowledge of best practices in other key business areas.

When I was at Frito-Lay we were a supplier to both Wal-Mart and Sam's Club. I used to travel with account sales representatives from time to time as they sold temporary modular displays (TMDs) to grocery store managers. You would have thought Frito-Lay owned the place the way its TMDs were scattered throughout the stores. Whenever it was time to reset the snack-food aisle Frito-Lay took on the responsibility. Because of Frito-Lay's state-of-the-art, 10,000-truck, store-door delivery system, grocery store managers were only too happy to let Frito-Lay do the work for them. In the process Frito-Lay almost always picked up more square feet of selling space.

I remember that when Frito-Lay first started making palletized deliveries to the Sam's Clubs, we had no idea how large our sales volume would be. At first, we didn't even have the tactical ability to deliver palletized and shrinkwrapped shipments to the wholesale club market. It was a brand-new concept and when it took off the Frito-Lay route sales drivers doubled their annual salaries. Volumes were so great and the velocity of merchandise turnover so rapid that the poor route sales rep job turned into a pure delivery job requiring multiple trips between the clubs and the distribution center each day.

Wholesale clubs became an entirely new distribution channel for Frito-Lay in addition to the four other existing distribution channels: vend sales (vending machines), route sales (convenience stores), account sales (grocery stores), and institutional (military, hospitals, and restaurants), each with a different sales organization.

One of the competitive advantages Frito-Lay always has enjoyed is its ability to provide fact-based data to retailers concerning sales of each and every product in each and every store. Using Fugitsu handheld computers all of the 10,000 store-door delivery salespeople have instantaneous access to sales volumes and trends for their individual stores and routes. Frito-Lay's account sales representatives have a command of compelling sell-through data on each and every product currently on the shelves. Snack foods are one of the fastest-turning items in a grocery store and Frito-Lay's market share was in the neighborhood of 50 percent or more. Grocery-store managers are well aware of that fact, and of Frito-Lay's contribution to overall store sales. Sales reps typically gain approval for placement of TMDs from local store managers interested in pumping up their sales volumes through in-store promotion of Frito-Lay's proven products.

Brand marketing has created a perception in the minds of consumers that Frito-Lay's premium-priced products represent a solid value, leading the company to garner a 50-percent share of stomach nationwide in the highly competitive snack-food industry. It's no wonder Frito-Lay's products are so well represented in supercenters, grocery and convenience stores across America. Frito-Lay was one of the pioneering companies in forming a true vendor partnership—including electronic data interchange—with Wal-Mart. It remains to this day one of Wal-Mart's largest suppliers.

The relationship between you and your wholesalers and distributors has changed. You are both successful only if you satisfy the retail customer. To that end, you have a right to expect better prices, product selection, promotional support, and on-time delivery. If you find your current vendors are unresponsive, start shopping other suppliers. Be demanding in your relationships with your vendors because you owe that to your customers. Building solid relationships with vendors and forming partnerships is an important strategy, which in the long run is in the best interests of retailers, suppliers, and customers alike.

Stephen L. Giroux, R. Ph., a board member of the National Community Pharmacists Association (NCPA) and owner of five independent pharmacies, recommends to other retailers, "Work very closely with a regional or national wholesaler that can help you develop goals and objectives, pricing models, merchandising tools and techniques. They can make you tremendously successful. National wholesalers will partner with retailers to develop their competitive ability." These days vendor partnerships aren't just nice to have, they are absolutely mandatory for retailers to survive.

The rule of thumb for suppliers of Wal-Mart merchandise is that they generally do not supply more than 30 percent of their production to Wal-Mart. This strategy makes a great deal of sense if you think about it. Manufacturers who allow too much of their production to go directly to Wal-Mart lose control of their own destinies. There are several large companies that do an inordinate amount of their total sales volume through Wal-Mart, including Tandy Brands (39 percent), Clorox (23 percent) Revlon (20 percent), RJR Tobacco (20 percent), and Procter & Gamble (17 percent).

Companies in this position are flirting with disaster should Wal-Mart decide to switch vendors or develop its own exclusive private label line.[11]

Imagine the negotiating advantage Wal-Mart has with vendors who count on the retail giant for such a large proportion of their annual sales volumes. I've even heard horror stories of vendors who manufacture product for Wal-Mart and end up trading dollars. In other words, they break even on the proposition or even lose money. It is hard to believe but some suppliers don't make any money selling unbelievably huge quantities of product because of Wal-Mart's negotiating prowess and low prices. Then why do they do it? They keep their manufacturing facilities running and they get excellent brand advertising by being a vendor of choice at Wal-Mart.

The manufacturer/retailer relationship has forever changed as a result of Wal-Mart's size and power. When it says jump, manufacturers ask how high. Unfortunately, their elimination of wholesalers has un-leveled the playing field for every other retailer. In an article entitled "Can $250 Billion Wal-Mart Think Small," Emily Kaiser talks about the global impact of Wal-Mart:

> From its nondescript headquarters in a remote corner of Arkansas, Wal-Mart Stores Inc. decides whether to buy T-shirts made in Guatemala or Guangdong Province, and if stylish clothes from its British stores will sell in Brazil. Love or loathe it, Wal-Mart is the world's biggest company by revenues, and the decisions made in Bentonville affect economies on five continents and dictate prices (and products) at other discounters, department stores and grocery chains. Wal-Mart accounts for roughly 9 cents out of every retail dollar spent in the United States, excluding autos. The U.S. Federal Reserve phones Wal-Mart executives to check up on sales as a gauge of the nation's economic health.[12]

Unfortunately, if your company is small you may not be in a position to form a truly strategic alliance with suppliers like Procter & Gamble or GE. You can, however, form vendor partnerships with your own network of suppliers, or you can join a buying coop that provides some of the same strategic and tactical advantages on a lesser scale. Change the way you look at your buying relationship with your vendors. Increase your expectations of their role in that partnership. Partners share both the risks and the successes of doing business together. Historically, many suppliers have acted somewhat cavalier and parasitic in their relationships as if they were not worried whether or not the products or services they supply are mutually financially beneficial. For your vendor relationships to work in this day and age your relationships have to be symbiotic. When you are successful your vendor is successful and vice versa. Get your suppliers and distributors to start carrying their share of that responsibility for the failure of their products in the marketplace or identify new suppliers who will. The buying standards have changed and it's up to you to take the lead in being an advocate on behalf of your business. No one else will do it for you.

Key-item promotion is an important aspect of generating store traffic and creating incremental sales volume. By constantly putting in promotional product you keep the shopping experience fresh and interesting for customers, generating repeat visits. The key to accomplishing a sound promotional strategy is twofold. First you must understand customer wants and needs using an outside-in approach, by asking customers for input; secondly, you must partner with vendors strategically to meet those wants and needs. A change is required in the relationship with, and on the part of, suppliers. Both retailer and supplier have to work in tandem to serve the ultimate customer, the purchaser of products at retail. As in most aspects of retail, execution of your key item-promotion strategy is critical to driving sales. Remember the six *P*s of retail,—*profits* result from having the right *product* at the right *price* in the right *place* with the right *promotion*, and well trained *people*, to provide great service.

As you compete, remember these ten two-letter words I learned at a Rotary Club meeting I attended: "If it is to be, it is up to me!" You control your own destiny; your success or failure depends on you. You have to be proactive. Anticipate the worst-case scenario and plan your strategy as best you can. By anticipating the drop in sales when Wal-Mart or a Neighborhood Market comes to town, or a remodel of a discount store creates a Supercenter, you can proactively develop a product-differentiation and promotional strategy to reinvent your business. As in any competition, size up your opponent and develop a strategy to leverage your strengths and minimize your weaknesses. Believe in your business and convey enthusiasm as you compete each day. If you really focus on the customer and you've created a unique retail pocket, the rest is in the hands of your customers and the retail gods!

Key Item/Product Checklist

Review this key item/product checklist of success strategies and tactics designed to help you compete with big-box retailers like Wal-Mart and not only survive, but thrive.

Vendor partnerships
- ✓ Question your suppliers about competitors' product successes and failures
- ✓ Discuss with suppliers how they can help you build your business
- ✓ Talk to your suppliers about partnering with you to help you compete
- ✓ Communicate a sense of urgency to your suppliers
- ✓ Require vendors to work with you to develop promotional strategies
- ✓ Ask suppliers for successful strategies other retailers are currently executing
- ✓ Demand in-store product-training support for your employees
- ✓ Ask suppliers how to differentiate your product assortment
- ✓ Request discounted or special sale merchandise for your customers
- ✓ Verify that your current product mix provides differentiation from competitors
- ✓ Ask suppliers to help you develop a promotional-calendar strategy

Merchandising
- ✓ Remember that out of stock is out of business
- ✓ Talk to your suppliers and ask for creative promotional-product offerings
- ✓ Make your shelves look full . . . send the message you're serious about the business
- ✓ Fill in holes in inventory with back-stock merchandise
- ✓ Make use of the temporary modular displays offered by suppliers
- ✓ Cross-market products if it makes sense (as an example, tortilla chips and salsa)
- ✓ Create impulse sales through effective point-of-sale merchandising
- ✓ Become a student of merchandising by shopping other stores

Assortment
- ✓ Develop a product mix that appeals to local tastes and interests
- ✓ Offer higher-quality and higher-priced merchandise than Wal-Mart

✓ Develop a unique selection of product in your niche
✓ Offer a changing variety of promotional products to create store traffic
✓ Ask customers how you can improve your product assortment

Private label
✓ Ask suppliers about their private-label product programs
✓ Find out if your vendors are offering private-label products to your competitors
✓ Shop other stores to find out which suppliers are offering private-label programs
✓ See if other stores like yours have successful private-label programs
✓ Ask your customers if they'd purchase generic or private-label products

Promotion
✓ Promote like you mean it...buy deep and...make a statement
✓ Drive promotional merchandising by the calendar as planned
✓ Teach employees to be merchants...let them help pick products and display them
✓ Create merchandise contests to keep the store exciting for your employees
✓ Teach employees to suggest promoted items at the register to all customers
✓ Require employees to demonstrate an understanding of current promotions
✓ Critique your own store...is the signage clear and properly placed?
✓ Make certain promotions are merchandised on time, every time
✓ Purchase enough promotional merchandise to satisfy the needs of all customers
✓ Honor rain checks in the event you run out of promoted items

5

Expense Control Strategies and Tactics

"Wal-Mart has changed the traditional standards of expense control, evolving or morphing them to a previously unheard-of level, disproving the notion that you can't save your way to prosperity."

At one of the Saturday morning meetings, Sam Walton showed up late because that morning he had dropped by one of the Bentonville distribution centers to have a cup of coffee with the truck drivers. He would often spend time with the drivers in the wee hours of the morning in an effort to keep current on what was really going on out in the stores from their perspective. Company drivers seem to know everything that goes on in a company and their networking amongst themselves is phenomenal. Because Sam was so down to earth and unthreatening the drivers felt free to tell him what was going on. As a continuous learner, Sam used these opportunities to pick up fresh and unbiased intelligence about his own company.

So just like anyone else who arrives late for the Saturday morning meeting, even Sam Walton was forced to park in the back of the Home Office parking lot. There were no exceptions. On this particular day, for whatever reason, he took note of the kinds of cars parked in the lot as he made his way to the offices. When he finally arrived at the cavernous auditorium, which was packed to the rafters with company leaders, he was mad as a hornet. You could tell by his body language when he walked out on the stage that for some soon-to-be-apparent reason he was not a happy camper!

I remember he apologized for being late for the meeting but he explained the reason so all those in attendance would understand. He then described his walk through the parking lot that morning. In a way that only Sam Walton could, he scolded everyone there that day, saying, "I must be paying you Home Office managers and associates too much money. There are an awful lot of high-priced BMWs and Mercedes out in that parking lot." His concern was that company leaders were getting too big for their britches and too full of themselves and he was fearful everyone would forget that frugality had made the company successful. You could hear a pin drop as he completed his diatribe. It felt as if he had knocked the wind out of everyone present in one fell swoop.

To fully appreciate this story you have to understand that Sam drove a 1979 red-and-white Ford pickup truck with bird-dog cages in the back to and from work. I was one of the fortunate ones that day who also drove a pick-up truck to work. I've always made a practice of driving a "beater" to and from work. At my house it was my wife that drove a Mercedes! Many of the Wal-Mart managers were faced with an immediate conundrum. Sam didn't directly threaten anyone but the clearly implied message was that people needed to take a good hard look at their personal values and beliefs and how they aligned with the company's. A funny thing happened the next week. I noticed a change in the parking lot. Those who owned expensive cars either parked them in their garages or traded them in at a car dealership. At that next Saturday morning meeting there were more old beat up junkers and clunkers in the parking lot than you could shake a stick at. It seems everybody read between the lines and decided it was better to err on the side of public frugality than to display wealth ostentatiously for all (or just Sam) to see.

We'll never know but Sam's mood that morning could have been spurred by his conversation with those truck drivers who may have challenged him or clued him in about the luxury cars in the Home Office parking lot. One of the pillars of success of Wal-Mart is and always has been its ability to maintain the lowest possible cost structure. By doing so, it drops billions and billions of dollars to the bottom line in direct savings. "A penny saved is a penny earned" aptly describes Sam's belief about managing expenses. In asking company leaders to tone down public displays of wealth he wasn't asking them to do anything he wasn't already doing.

To understand this story you have to understand Sam Walton's personal lifestyle. Even though he was a billionaire many times over, you wouldn't know it if you met him on the street. He drove that old white pick-up truck, and he lived in a humble house in Bentonville that almost anyone with a job could have afforded. His home phone number was even published in the local phonebook. He was a common self-made man who stubbornly refused to change his simple lifestyle throughout his life.

He was self-admittedly cheap as the day is long and those beliefs permeated the Wal-Mart culture. His personal lifestyle choices about wealth and frugality affected his beliefs about controlling costs within the company. Wal-Mart's bottom-line success can be attributed equally to Sam's fanatical focus on expense control and everyday-low-price philosophies. Wal-Mart's leaders are proud of the tightfisted perception they have created around the world: Cheap is chic at Wal-Mart!

Sam Walton never wanted to be known as the richest man on the planet so he skillfully divided his fortune among his heirs. Had he kept his fortune together, his family's amassed wealth would be actually double that of Bill Gates! The top ten richest people in the world (in billions of dollars), as estimated by *Forbes* Magazine in 2002, included five members of the Walton Clan:

1. Gates, William H. III, United States, $52.8, Microsoft
2. Buffett, Warren E., United States, $35.0, Berkshire Hathaway
3. Albrecht, Karl and Theo, Germany, $26.8, Retail
4. Allen, Paul G., United States, $25.2, Microsoft
5. Ellison, Lawrence J., United States, $23.5, Oracle
6. **Walton, Jim C., United States, $20.8, Wal-Mart**
7. **Walton, John T., United States, $20.7, Wal-Mart**
8. **Walton, Alice L., United States, $20.5, Wal-Mart**
9. **Walton, S. Robson, United States, $20.5, Wal-Mart**
10. **Walton, Helen R., United States, $20.4, Wal-Mart**

The Walton family's collective fortunes total more than 100 billion dollars! Most people can't even begin to imagine how much money that is. I know I have trouble comprehending that kind of wealth. Think of it this way, one billion dollars is equal to a stack of 1000 million dollar bills. Now to understand the total fortune you have to realize a hundred billion dollars is equal to a pallet load of 100,000 million dollar bills! Who among us wouldn't change their lifestyle given wealth beyond our wildest dreams? If you think about it that way it becomes easy to understand why Wal-Mart's hardworking executives and managers, who had become wealthy as a result of the phenomenal growth in value of their stock options, had a right to display their success publicly. Sam Walton felt otherwise.

To help you understand the incredible impact of expense control on the success of Wal-Mart you have to understand the history of its stock. On October 11, 1970, Wal-Mart offered 300,000 shares of its common stock to the public at a price of $16.50 per share. On that day, the musical duo the Carpenters had a hit on the U.S. singles chart with the tune, "We've

Only Just Begun," a strange coincidence that may have been a portent of things to come for Wal-Mart. Since that time, Wal-Mart has had eleven two-for-one stock splits. On a purchase of 100 shares at $16.50 per share of the first offering, the number of shares has grown as shown in Table 5.1.

Allow me to share some more staggering statistics with you. If you had purchased 100 shares of Wal-Mart's stock on October 1, 1970 at the IPO price of $16.50, your total investment would have been $1,650.00. If you had been smart enough to hold on to that stock until today, after eleven two-for-one stock splits those original 100 shares would now be worth (at $58.00) a total of $11,878,400. If you had purchased only one share of stock it would now be worth (at $58.00) $118,768. That's why so many of the associates at Wal-Mart are able to afford luxury cars and that's why the members of the Walton family are so filthy rich!

To put the value of Wal-Mart's stock in perspective, a stock story in Michael Eisner's book *Work in Progress* helps capture by comparison the incredible success Wal-Mart has achieved. Eisner describes how Warren Buffet purchased $4 million worth of Disney stock in 1965 and how he then sold that stock a couple of years later, earning about two million dollars. Had Buffet kept that stock it would have been worth $869 million dollars 28 years later. However, if Disney had purchased $4 million worth of Buffet's Berkshire Hathaway stock in 1965 it would have been worth $6 billion 28 years later.[1] If Michael Eisner or Warren Buffet had purchased $4 million worth of Wal-Mart stock at the IPO price of $16.50 in 1970, 28 years later (at $46 a share) that stock would be worth over $22 billion! This fact, by the way, hasn't gone unnoticed by Warren Buffet.

Table 5-1   Wal-Mart Stock Split History

2 for 1 Stock Splits	Number of Shares	Cost Per Share ($)	Market Price on Split Date ($)
October 1970	100	16.50	—
May 1971	200	8.25	47.00
March 1972	400	4.125	47.50
August 1975	800	2.0625	23.00
November 1980	1,600	1.03125	50.00
June 1982	3,200	0.0515625	49.875
June 1983	6,400	0.0257813	81.625
September 1985	12,800	0.1275	49.75
June 1987	25,600	0.064453	66.625
June 1990	51,200	0.032227	62.50
February 1993	102,400	0.016113	63.625
March 1999	204,800	0.008057	89.75

Source: www.walmart.com.

According to *Motley Fool* (7/30/98), Buffet, known as "the Sam Walton of Investing," has actually owned a large block of Wal-Mart stock (reportedly over a million shares) for many years.

So depending on when associates joined the company and began accumulating stock, you can see how financially well off many of them have become. It's amazing what the success of the company has done for the finances of the average long-term associate at Wal-Mart. One of the managers who reported to me, who was not eligible for stock options, made regular payroll deductions to purchase company stock and participated in the company profit-sharing program during her 17 years of employment and was able to retire a millionaire. By the way, the associates who do participate in stock options are under an unheard of nine-year vesting program. Talk about golden handcuffs!

I met a buyer at the Home Office who told me a story that brought tears to his eyes. He said he had borrowed money from the bank in the late seventies in order to purchase some of Wal-Mart's company stock. He fibbed to the bank, saying the money was for a motorcycle. Along the way, he had a change of heart and decided he really did want to buy a motorcycle, so he switched directions, took the money and bought the bike. He said if he had bought Wal-Mart company stock at that time, as he had originally intended, that stock would now be worth a fortune. That million-dollar motorcycle, he said, is still sitting out in his storage shed and serves as a constant and painful reminder of the dumbest decision he ever made!

Sam's brother Bud cashed in some of his stock to build a dream home in Bentonville. Because he paid cash for that house, it ended up costing him millions in lost stock appreciation. Sam, however, lived in the same house that he and his wife, Helen, had brought the kids up in. He was one of the most frugal people around, subscribing to the old Will Roger's adage, "the quickest way to double your money is to fold it up and put it back in your pocket."

Not all of Wal-Mart's executives shared Sam's beliefs about frugality, an error in judgment one executive in particular would later regret. He actually built a mansion outside Bentonville with the riches he had earned from his Wal-Mart stock options while he was still employed by the company. He was dumb enough to invite Sam and his wife Helen to dinner at his opulent estate. As the story was told to me (by a Wal-Mart headquarters employee) that executive was terminated by Sam the following day. Obviously, Sam didn't like ostentatious displays of wealth by his leadership team.

Out of necessity, Wal-Mart owned a fleet of airplanes. Ever fearful of projecting an air of "lifestyles of the Rich and Famous," Sam shunned jet aircraft in favor of 17 propeller-driven planes that were hangared at the Rogers, Arkansas, airport. Sam had been trained by the military as an aviator and was known for flying his own plane when he visited stores. As Wal-Mart expanded its operations across the country it became increasingly difficult for executives, including Sam himself, to physically get out to the stores to visit. It is one thing to fly to Dallas or Kansas City from Bentonville in a prop plane but it is still another to go to Seattle or Boston in one. In earlier times Sam had prided himself on visiting every store in the chain every year. That had become logistically impossible. Even though there was a clear business need for them, Sam refused to purchase jet aircraft because he believed they would publicly create a negative perception of Wal-Mart's leaders living a high-roller lifestyle. He worried so much about company leaders creating a negative perception that when he flew on a commercial flight he made sure he was seated in coach!

To save money, when Wal-Mart Home Office associates needed to fly to distant locations they used the fleet of small turbo-prop planes to carry them to Kansas City, Memphis, Tulsa, St. Louis, or Dallas where Wal-Mart's corporate travel department would arrange a commercial flight to the final destination. That commercial flight, by the way, often involved multiple connecting flights in order to allow the purchase of the cheapest ticket possible. Adding insult to injury, any frequent-flyer miles earned by individual travelers had to be turned in to the company!

Each week, like clockwork, the store operation regional VPs, who all lived in northwest Arkansas, would fly out on those 17 planes to the four corners of the country. Sam was a big believer in management by walking or wandering around. He liked company leaders to get out from behind their desks to visit stores and talk to customers and associates. The planes departed on Monday mornings to visit stores across the country, returning on Thursday evenings. On Fridays company leaders would disgorge their competitive findings at all-day store operations meetings. Rob Walton, Sam's son (who replaced Sam as chairman when he died), finally said enough's enough and while Sam was still alive he purchased a jet aircraft for his own business travel. Sam would have nothing to do with corporate jets because he believed corporate jets sent a negative message to Wal-Mart's investors, employees, and customers. A regional airport has since been built just outside of Bentonville, accommodating daily direct commercial jet flights to places like New York City.

When you know the family financials, the stock-split history, and the expense folklore of the company the story of BMWs and Mercedes in the parking lot seems all the more incredible. Retail merchants are by nature entrepreneurs and they personify capitalism. One of the spoils of war in business, in this entrepreneurial world, is the displaying of the trappings of your success. You have to realize that the Home Office executives, managers, and even the hourly employees all own company stock.

With those eleven stock splits over the past 30-plus years, those associates who dedicated their careers to the company are in many cases multimillionaires themselves. That includes many of the truck drivers, distribution-center and store hourly employees who participated in the profit-sharing and employee stock-purchase plans.

Sam Walton believed that a happy employee meant happy customers and that a happy customer of course meant more sales. He and his wife, Helen, believed that by giving employees a part of the company through profit-sharing they made individual success dependent on the company's success and that because of this the associates would do whatever they could to drive sales and control expenses. Sam's commitment to sharing profits engendered loyalty among the associates who then willingly helped him build his retailing empire. He used to tell the associates, if anyone asks you who owns Wal-Mart tell them that YOU do!

Because of the company profit-sharing plan and the potential for increasing the value of the company stock, Wal-Mart's associates are highly motivated to do everything possible to hold down costs. I even remember the associates in the Home Office voluntarily bringing office supplies from home to help hold down costs for the company. They would bring in their personal paper clips, pencils, pens, notepads, and staplers in order to contribute to keeping costs as low as possible in the hopes that profits would rise, the stock would go up, and profit-sharing would be paid out. This was not a company-directed mandate by any means; it was a grassroots employee effort to help the company have the lowest costs in the industry so the savings could be passed along to the customer. The associates at Wal-Mart are absolutely fanatical about saving the company money. Cost control is so integrated into everyday life that the associates themselves police wasteful practices. Peer pressure is a powerful motivator of the desired expense-control behavior.

I know you find this hard to believe but it is true and I saw this happening with my own eyes. The associates at Wal-Mart spend company money as if they were writing the checks out of their personal checking accounts. They call that cultural value "ownership." Since the inception of Wal-Mart's profit-sharing plan in 1972 and the inception of its 401(k) plan in 1997, Wal-Mart has contributed nearly three billion dollars toward the retirement funds of its associates.[2] No wonder union organizers have so much difficulty getting Wal-Mart associates interested in joining a union.

I'll never forget a college recruiting trip I took while at Wal-Mart. I traveled to two schools in Pennsylvania with one of the regional HR managers who was responsible for stores in the Northeast. We were recruiting assistant store manager trainees at Slippery Rock and Penn State. We had interview schedules set up on Tuesday at Slippery Rock and on Wednesday, Thursday, and Friday at Penn State. This trip was made interesting by Wal-Mart's expense policy on business travel, which requires that you double up with someone (of the same gender) in a hotel room each night that you travel together. This was the first time I had shared a room with someone else on a business trip. We roomed together for five straight nights! We didn't return to Bentonville until Saturday.

By the way, we weren't allowed to stay at Hyatts, Mariotts or Hiltons. We stayed at less expensive LaQuintas and Quality Inns. We didn't even pay the rack rate, as our hotel rooms were negotiated by Wal-Mart at much less expensive corporate rates. I remember attending a business conference held at a downtown premium-priced hotel and I was required by the company to commute to the conference from a bargain priced hotel, outside the downtown area.

There was a story in *Vanity Fair*, about Wal-Mart's current CEO that didn't surprise me in the least it said, "Wal-Mart President and CEO H. Lee Scott, Jr. was so frugal that on business trips, he often booked a spartan Days Inn room—and shared it with the company's CFO." Can you imagine the executives of any other Fortune 1000 company sharing hotel rooms to save money? The executives at Wal-Mart were true servant leaders who led by example. Culturally, I often heard this referred to within the company as executives "walking the talk."

If you think these efforts to control costs are penny wise and pound foolish, think again. In a company as large as Wal-Mart, managers and employees have tremendous opportunities to drift into gluttonous and wasteful behaviors with all the accolades the company receives in the news over new sales accomplishments. But if Wal-Mart expects to convince its customers and suppliers that it is doing everything possible to keep prices as low as it can it won't be very convincing if it is publicly demonstrating wasteful behavior. Historical expense-control stories and folklore are powerful cultural touchstones with which Wal-Mart's leaders can illustrate company expectations about managing expenses. When you have over a million employees focusing on accomplishing everything they do as inexpensively as they can, expense management becomes a competitive advantage.

Wal-Mart's employees take the concept of cultural ownership of expense control to a new level. It is as if each and every one of them were responsible for paying the company's bills at the end of the month. Cost control at Wal-Mart is sort of like an extreme sport! Analogously, it's as if competitors are playing by the traditional rules of the game of basketball while Wal-Mart is playing "slamball" using trampolines and a completely different set of rules. The point is that most competitors are playing the expense-control game by an antiquated set of rules while Wal-Mart has reinvented the game. By challenging conventional expense-control wisdom Wal-Mart has changed the traditional standards of expense control, raising the bar to a previously unheard-of level.

The necessary changes—in the way expenses are managed by executives at some companies in order to effectively compete—are so severe that I think the majority of those leaders would be unwilling to make the personal sacrifices necessary to personally model the desired behaviors themselves. Walking the talk would require them to shed the visible perks of the executive world including company cars, designated parking, and club memberships. Wal-Mart's cultural integration of cost control is easy to understand in concept, but it is probably one of the more difficult and painful things for competitors to emulate and implement in their own companies.

There is so much more to the low-price strategy at Wal-Mart than simply buying from the manufacturer at the lowest possible price. The excellent job its buyers do to negotiate the lowest possible prices from manufacturers and the cost savings generated are plowed back into the lowest possible prices for consumers. Wal-Mart associates are trained in total-quality principles like flow-charting, idea generation, and continuous improvement. Everyone is encouraged to find cost-saving ideas and to find ways of doing things that save time, energy, and effort. I'm not talking about million-dollar cost-saving ideas; I'm talking about ways to save a dollar here and a dollar there.

Great cost-saving ideas are generated every day through a formalized process called "Yes We Can Sam." Associates are encouraged to come up with ways to save a dollar, five, ten, twenty, or even more. Every once in a while one of the associates will come up with an idea that will save $50, $100, $500, or $ 1,000 dollars at a store. All of the best cost-saving ideas are then communicated across the chain, creating the potential for a small idea to create a million dollars in savings. These savings are used to lower prices, allowing the company to leverage the economies of scale provided by a 260-billion-dollar, 4,000-plus-store chain with over a million employees. A ten-dollar idea multiplied across a 4,000-store chain quickly becomes a 40,000-dollar cost saving for the company. There really aren't any small cost-saving ideas at Wal-Mart because it can replicate any idea in stores around the world.

From an expense standpoint, Wal-Mart not only squeezes its vendors but also looks for cost savings in every other area of the business. Need supplies for your office at the Bentonville headquarters? I was told to go shop the sample room and outfit my office with vendor samples. Need a cup of coffee or a doughnut while you're working? No free coffee here; ante up at the honor bar. You want to wear blue jeans to work on Friday? Cost you a buck donation to the *Children's Miracle Network* to do it. As you can see, Wal-Mart doesn't leave a lot of money on the table: It pinches pennies to an extreme. Wal-Mart even panned for gold through federally and state-subsidized tax programs.

I had a department reporting directly to me called Government Programs. The manager of that department was responsible for generating tax credits if a newly hired employee met certain government-specified criteria. Working directly with a third-party vendor we actively worked to take advantage of the Targeted Jobs Tax Credit (TJTC) and Job Training Partnership Act (JTPA) programs. Some tax credits were available at both the state and federal levels. In one year we generated over fifteen million dollars of tax credits by simply understanding the law and being aggressive in applying for the tax benefits provided.

One of the more interesting cost-saving ideas I experienced involved a pretty simple idea with major bottom-line impact. Wal-Mart doesn't waste much of anything. The company has a practice that theoretically reduces paper costs by 50 percent. It uses the back side of every piece of paper! Write a memo to someone and once the recipient is done with it he or she will use the back side of the page. This is another simple example of creating a visual cultural message of cost control. Wal-Mart truly focused on the small stuff in order to create a culture of fanatical spendthrifts.

Even the janitor gets into the cost-control act. One morning I walked into my office and the night before the janitor had carefully placed a "Grim Reaper paper waster" card squarely in the middle of my desk to point out to me I was wasting company resources. As it turns out, I had thrown paper that hadn't been used on both sides into my trash can. Being a creature of habit, I had not been thoroughly indoctrinated into the culture of the company yet and this was my rude awakening. That was the last time I wasted a piece of paper. I became obsessed like everyone else about controlling paper costs. I even felt a bit paranoid that Big Brother was looking over my shoulder and watching my every wasteful move! This is a great example of how the cost-control culture is reinforced by everyone in the company. Try implementing this simple cost-saving program in your company and you'll likely have an employee uprising on your hands! Unfortunately, as I think about this simple expense control technique and your implementation of it, I'm reminded of the old saying—you can lead a horse to water but you can't make it drink!

Having worked at Wal-Mart's Bentonville Home Office and having visited the K-Mart headquarters in Troy, Michigan, I have seen two companies with diametrically opposed expense-control philosophies. At one extreme you have Wal-Mart, with its Home Office that was formerly a warehouse. Its cheap linoleum floors, painted concrete-block walls, fluorescent lights, basement-style drop ceilings, and mix-and-match furniture all scream cheap. Even the top executives' offices had cheap basement-style paneling on their walls and some, not all, did have windows. The lobby looks like a state unemployment office with its stark fixtures. But that was all part of Sam's grand plan to clearly send the cultural message to employees, vendors, customers, and Wall Street alike that being frugal is a good thing. The Home Office accoutrements reflect the expense-control expectations of the company for all to see. The quality of the decorating and construction of the Home Office is equal to the quality of the construction you see in Wal-Mart stores.

At the other extreme you have the K-Mart headquarters. The massive structure is like a palace in comparison with the unimpressive one in Bentonville. You'll likely see limousines pulling up on K-Mart's beautifully landscaped driveway to drop off important visitors who are greeted by a massive atrium-style lobby. The upscale headquarters building and the brand image it reflects seem incongruent with what you see in K-Mart's discount stores. Thinking about their own headquarters building and all those limousines, K-Mart's store managers and employees must experience cognitive dissonance every time they receive a corporate directive concerning expense control.

I remember one of Wal-Mart's executives poking fun at K-Mart at the Saturday morning meeting the week K-Mart rolled out its "Big K" logo. He joked that it had paid millions of dollars to an ad agency to design its new competitive look, the Big K. The Wal-Mart executive's response was to suggest a new Wal-Mart Logo, the "Big W," at no cost to the company! The launch of the K-Mart logo, and the dollars wasted to do it, have proven to be an exercise in competitive futility. The state of K-Mart today makes me wonder if the outcome for its business would have been better if it had had different leadership over the years.

In retail, payroll cost is one of the most important and controllable expense items upon which management can focus. As a member of the turnaround team at American Eagle Outfitters I focused heavily on the costs associated with payroll, including schedules, overtime, and starting salaries. We became so fanatical about controlling payroll costs that we even required newly hired employees to provide us with a copy of their last paycheck stubs from their previous employers to prove their prior pay levels. Through reference checking I estimated that up to half of those applying for jobs were falsifying their pay histories in order to negotiate a better pay package with us. Other executives of the company thought I was too conservative in my estimate and that up to 75 percent falsified pay history. Once exempt and non-exempt recruits knew we were requiring documentation of pay history, falsification problems were eliminated. Whether it's 50 percent or 75 percent falsifying pay history it is a big number and this simple technique helped us eliminate the problem and hold down our costs.

At Wal-Mart, top management also focuses constantly on managing payroll expenses. If for whatever reason a store manager is going to miss hitting the sales plan for the week you can bet he or she will do everything possible to make certain not to also miss his or her payroll budget. This constant focus on payroll as a percentage of sales is a dynamic process that has to be managed every day of the year. Great store managers make schedule management look easy but obviously it is not. With 400 to 600 associates working 24 hours a day, 365 days a year at a Supercenter, managing schedules and the associated cost of payroll is a science that requires computer software. Schedules must take into account the ebb and flow of sales volume throughout the week and the day. Wal-Mart is disciplined in managing payroll expenses and that discipline is driven from the top.

By coupling its disciplined schedule management with its low-wage-and-benefit cost structure, Wal-Mart creates an unlevel playing field for many of its competitors. Wal-Mart leaders manage the costs associated with pay, benefits, work schedules, and overtime better than almost anybody. Add to that the fact that Wal-Mart operates all of its stores in the United States non-union and store payroll becomes a competitive advantage for it in the predominately unionized grocery industry.

When Sam was running the company just before he died in 1992 the company had a total of 350,000 employees and a headquarters staff of only 2,300 to support them. The head count of the Home Office staff represented less than one percent of the total company headcount!

The first year I worked in the headquarters at Wal-Mart we added 100 stores, which in terms of people is more than 30,000 new store associates and lots of additional headaches to deal with. I remember trying to budget additional headcount to increase my staff to cover the increased workload. My request was flatly denied. In fact, every department had the same budget for overtime—unfortunately that budget had zero dollars in it. Wal-Mart's leaders have zero tolerance for working overtime. Herein lies another huge expense advantage versus competitors who routinely dish out overtime to employees who view it as an entitlement. Wal-Mart has complete disdain for wasting money, which is how the use of overtime is perceived. It's also a black mark on the record of any manager who can't manage the work without the expenditure of overtime.

If you think about it, the control of overtime makes sense. Wage costs go up 50 percent or more on holidays when employees are working overtime, which rapidly erodes profitability. So you may be asking yourself, how does Wal-Mart get the work done when the hourly employees go home after 40 hours of work? It's simple. The exempt managers, who don't get paid overtime, stay and do the work that isn't finished. With that requirement in mind, managers get really good and efficient at directing the activities of the hourly employees to maximize the productivity of the straight time hours when they are working. Managers who use overtime in their stores are likely to be demoted or terminated for wasting company resources. That's a pretty good incentive for company leaders to manage work schedules efficiently and eliminate the use of overtime.

Even the payroll week at Wal-Mart was strategically designed to help lower costs by cutting payroll expenses. It began on Saturday at 12:01 A.M. and ended on Friday at midnight. By setting the pay week up starting on Saturday managers can load the schedules up with associates to match the peak weekend selling days. If sales are off plan over the weekend, managers can adjust their cost-of-sales for payroll percentage by cutting scheduled payroll hours in line with the lower projected sales for the week. Managers knew that if they were going to miss their sales target for the week they sure as heck better not miss their payroll-budget percentage as well. To say the least, under these conditions, scheduling is an extremely dynamic process requiring tremendous patience and flexibility on the part of the associates.

According to the book *How Wal-Mart Is Destroying America and the World and What You Can Do About It* by Bill Quinn, "The bulk of Wal-Mart's employee base work at Wal-Mart stores. They are part time workers who are paid the local minimum wage. Most employees are not entitled to any benefits, as it takes a part-time employee over five years to become eligible for benefits, profit-sharing, or other such compensation. There is a high turnover rate among these employees, which means most do not reach the required level of seniority."[7]

It is for this reason that Wal-Mart enjoys significantly lower wage and benefit costs than competitors with lower turnover. Turnover leads to the majority of associates being at lower pay levels with no benefits. It's hard to believe, but turnover drops millions of dollars to the bottom line in cost savings for the company. When an experienced associate leaves the company he or she is replaced by an entry-level associate at a lower wage. Turnover of associates, for this reason, actually appears, from an expense standpoint, to be a competitive advantage.

Having worked in specialty retailing for years I learned from the National Retail Federation that the common rule of thumb for store retail turnover was "30/60/120/240." Translated that means that on average, store managers turn over at the rate of 30 percent, assistant managers at the rate of 60 percent, full-time sales at the rate of 120 percent, and part-time or seasonal sales at the rate of 240 percent. There is quite literally a doubling effect of turnover at each level. The cost of turnover is quite high and unfortunately seems to be a cost of doing business in retail. I'm not suggesting that high turnover is a good thing but for Wal-Mart it does lead to lower wages and less benefits for replacement workers, which reduces the cost of payroll.

Wal-Mart's distribution and logistics functions provide still another expense advantage for the company. It uses an inventory-management technique called cross-docking of merchandise in their distribution centers which reduces the amount of time inventory sits idly on the floor in a warehouse. Retail cross-docking is a form of just-in-time distribution. Product in the pipeline has already been allocated for distribution to specific stores against automatic replenishment orders from Wal-Mart's vendor partners. Cross-docking is a means of creating efficiency in the supply chain from point of manufacturing origin to point of sale in the stores. By cross-docking, merchandise flows through the distribution facility to customers in the shortest time possible, reducing operating costs, which helps drive down prices and increase company profits.

Using its own fleet of tractors and trailers Wal-Mart replenishes its own stores 24 hours per day from its own distribution centers. Of course the overall goal of distribution and logistics at Wal-Mart is to insure the company shelves are always kept in stock. After its trucks make a delivery to a store, Wal-Mart's truck drivers backhaul merchandise from suppliers' warehouses whenever they can. Because of this, Wal-Mart reduces the costs associated with moving products through its supply chain. This practice also reduces the costs of and the reliance on third-party haulers, putting Wal-Mart in control of its own destiny. It is estimated that Wal-Mart is successful in arranging backhauls of merchandise 60 percent of the time, dramatically reducing the cost of shipping and improving efficiency.[8]

Advanced technology is pivotal and goes hand in hand with Wal-Mart's best-practice distribution strategies. Electronic data interchange (EDI) via satellite with vendors, distributors, and its own headquarters, point-of-sale (POS) registers, and individual product bar-coding form the basic foundation required to technologically manage hundreds of thousands of SKUs (stock-keeping units) via cross-docking. Sam Walton hated to talk about the costs associated with implementing new technology, but as much as the cost of it drove him crazy, he was smart enough to realize the cost-saving benefits of great IT systems. Wal-Mart has always invested in technology and from a cost standpoint it actually invests more than its competitors as a percentage of total sales in technology.[9]

To manage the millions and millions of products flowing through its stores and distribution network Wal-Mart uses a satellite-based inventory-control program called Very Small Aperture Terminal (VSAT) systems. The VSAT technology enables "real-time" inventory control. As customers make purchases, VSAT systems instantly adjust inventory and place orders through Wal-Mart's distribution and replenishment network.[10]

The cost-reduction benefits of cross-docking, backhauling, and satellite technology create significant competitive advantages for Wal-Mart. Controlling the movement and timing of product delivery to its stores is another way Wal-Mart leverages its economies of scale. Using its own fleet of trucks and cross-docking techniques enables it to reduce the steps in product handling, compared to warehousing of products, significantly lowers costs. The increased velocity of distribution allows products to turn over more quickly in the stores, reducing out-of-stock scenarios and increasing sales dollars per square foot. Less product handling automatically reduces the volume of damaged merchandise. The stores benefit by minimizing the amount of dedicated inventory storage required. With each distribution center supplying as many as 80 to 100 stores in a 300-mile radius, the cost savings in minimizing warehousing and inventory costs are phenomenal.

Wal-Mart has endless opportunities to leverage the economies of scale to reduce costs in the areas of distribution and logistics. Most competitors, except for the largest, can't begin to compete with sophisticated distribution strategies like cross-docking, electronic data interchange, backhauling, satellite inventory-management technology and RFID. Most receive drop shipments of product using third-party carriers and always will. So knowing the cost advantages Wal-Mart possesses because of its sophisticated technology and distribution, competitors should feel the pressure to initiate cost-saving strategies of their own wherever they possibly can in other areas of their business.

To give you a sense of how far Wal-Mart will go to reduce costs let me tell you about my personal relocation from Dallas, Texas, to Bentonville, Arkansas, as an example. On the day of my scheduled move a tractor-trailer pulled up in front of my house. Emblazoned across the side of the trailer was the "Wal-Mart Everyday Low Prices" logo. I should have known that as cheap as Wal-Mart is it would figure out a way to lower the cost of my relocation. As it turns out, because of the number of store-manager moves happening all the time, the company has its own moving trucks. Following the Wal-Mart moving truck were two carloads of associates from the local store. In addition to the truck driver, who was a professional mover, there were ten associates assigned to load my belongings!

On the other end, Wal-Mart hired ten employees from the Manpower temporary agency to unload our belongings into our new home. It was a nightmare! I left my three-year-old daughter, Heather, and my pregnant wife, Sheryl, at the hotel so they didn't have to experience the stress first-hand! Five days after we moved into our home my son, Paul, was born at a hospital in Rogers, Arkansas. (Upon his birth, Paul's immediate "claim to fame" was that he was born in the town where Sam Walton had opened the first Wal-Mart Store!) If you'll picture that Wal-Mart truck pulling up to my house you'll begin to understand how far Wal-Mart will go to save money.

Assistant managers and store managers were encouraged to either rent apartments or purchase trailer homes in order to expedite their moves and lower costs. Wal-Mart even has dedicated drivers and trucks for moving trailer homes. I heard stories of managers finding out on Friday they needed to be at a new store on Monday and that they were expected to pack and move over the weekend. It was not unusual for assistant managers to move multiple times prior to getting their first store-management position. Store managers also had to move to assume responsibility for larger-volume stores.

In order to compete, your goal must be to control expenses throughout the year. You don't have to be Albert Einstein to figure out the retail expense control formula. It's $E=MC^2$ or *Expenses = Management × Cost Control × Cultural Integration*. Translated, this means that your expenses are a product of your managers constantly taking the necessary steps to control, challenge, and cut costs, while at the same time culturally integrating standards and accountability for expense management throughout your organization.

Managing expenses as a percentage of sales by definition means that expenses will float up and down as sales rise and fall. That's why from a store-operations standpoint store managers have always been measured on sales, payroll, and shrinkage. If sales rise and expenses remain the same, dollars should drop to the bottom line. If sales drop, good retailers reduce expenses within the week, minimizing losses. Cost control is not static in retail, it is dynamic. In teaching managers the skills and discipline required to manage expenses, I simply ask them to approach cost control as if they owned the business and they were responsible for writing the checks personally.

Many of the cost-saving ideas at Wal-Mart are easy to understand, yet you'll find them difficult to duplicate and implement until you change your culture and the way you do business. Company leaders need to project a fanatical enthusiasm for controlling and cutting costs and eliminating wasteful practices. Only then will those habits become culturally engrained in the company.

Sam Walton used to say that overhead is one of the most crucial things any business has to fight in order to maintain profit margins. The Wal-Mart cultural-expense philosophy is that every time it spends a dollar foolishly it takes a dollar out of its customers' pockets. It sweats the details by getting everybody to try to save pennies, which ultimately leads to savings of lots of dollars. These savings are in turn plowed back into lower-priced products.

Expense Control Checklist

Review this expense-control checklist of success strategies and tactics designed to help you compete with big-box retailers like Wal-Mart and not only survive, but thrive.

Cost control/operational expenses

✓ Manage your schedules to avoid having your employees work overtime

✓ Place the appropriate emphasis with your staff on shrinkage control

✓ Recycle everything you possibly can

✓ Culturally communicate that waste reduces profitability

✓ Ask all your employees to think and act as if they owned the business

✓ Develop a "wastebuster" expense-reduction idea program and get employees involved

✓ Design work schedules that reflect the peaks and valleys of sales volume

✓ Run the pay week from Thursday to Wednesday so necessary labor cuts are made on the slowest retail days

✓ Make certain all managers are working at least a 48-hour work week

✓ Ask employees to contribute one good methods-improvement idea per week

✓ Reward and recognize expense-reduction ideas that actually reduce your costs

6

T alent Strategies and Tactics

"Wal-Mart hires average people but squeezes above-average performance and results out of them."

When I was first offered the opportunity to interview for a position at the Wal-Mart Home Office, I was more curious to go there than I was actually interested in taking the position. At the time I was living in Dallas, Texas, working for Frito-Lay and living in the North Dallas suburbs in an area that had sprung up out of the semi-arid ranch land—only minutes from the South Fork Ranch made famous by the "Dallas" TV show. We shared the neighborhood with a host of other yuppies who had relocated to Dallas, just as we had, for a career opportunity. I really liked living in Dallas and enjoyed my job at Frito-Lay's headquarters. You can imagine my reluctance to move my family out to live in the Ozark mountains, especially with my wife about to give birth to our son, Paul.

I interviewed that Saturday morning with the chief merchandising officer, the VP of people (HR) and the chief operating officer. At the end of my interview with the COO, I noticed he was looking over my shoulder toward the doorway behind me, and when I followed his gaze found an old man wearing overalls standing in the doorway. For just a moment, I thought it was the janitor walking in to pick up the trash. It then hit me that this was Sam Walton.

I'll never forget the introduction I received from the COO to Sam Walton. In his southern accent he said, "Mister Sam, this is Mike Bergdahl." Sam narrowed his eyes and tilted his head, looking at me kind of funny, and said, "Bird Dawg?" For just a moment, I didn't know whether being known as "Bird Dawg" was a good thing or a bad thing.

As it turns out, Sam was a prolific bird hunter and liked nothing better than to go out hunting with the pack of bird dogs he owned. In that moment I had a new nickname, and I had become instantaneously endeared to the most successful entrepreneur in the world.

My interview with Sam Walton was really quite a surprise. He had already read my résumé and through his questions demonstrated a good understanding of my background. He was very interested in my experience with Frito-Lay, a major supplier of snack food to Wal-Mart and Sam's Club. I still remember him saying, "Frito-Lay is a company I have the greatest respect for, what do you think is the key to their store-door delivery systems?" As a continuous learner he was taking advantage of this opportunity to gain a better understanding of one of his key suppliers.

As I drove out of Bentonville after my interviews and headed for the Fayetteville Airport, I remember hoping, for the first time, that I would get a job offer. The chance to work directly with Sam Walton was an opportunity far too attractive to pass up. The whole interviewing process at Wal-Mart was turned into a serendipitous event for me. I truly hadn't expected that it would be as exciting as it turned out to be. When the offer did come, although I was committed, I never expected I could convince my wife to move to the Ozark mountains, but she agreed, and I accepted it.

I was in awe of Sam Walton and he is the reason I decided to accept the job in Bentonville. After I had joined the company, I still remember seeing Sam walk into the Home Office bathroom—the same bathroom used by everybody else. To me he seemed superhuman and he was clearly a living legend. It sounds funny, and it truly is more than you need to know, but multibillionaire Sam Walton didn't have a private executive washroom. He used the same facilities that everybody else used. This was quite a contrast for me from the executives I had known at Frito-Lay, who enjoyed a private underground parking area, private bathrooms, and an executive dining room.

At the time I moved to Arkansas, a sign leading into Bentonville advertised a population of around 10,000 people, but in truth about 12,000 worked for Wal-Mart in the various facilities in Northwest Arkansas. I remember asking my real-estate agent about the homes in the neighborhood my wife and I were originally considering, wondering which were owned by other Wal-Mart associates. She said it would be easier to tell you which ones weren't. In fact, only a couple of the homes we passed were owned by individuals who weren't affiliated with the company—talk about a company town! We moved out onto a farm off a dirt road to insulate ourselves from Wal-Mart overload. We even made the decision as a family to attend church in Fayetteville, Arkansas, which is about 25 miles from Bentonville, to allow us a degree of privacy as we worshipped. If I took my family shopping in Bentonville in the evening or on Sunday I was always sure to run into lots of fellow Wal-Mart associates everywhere we'd go. It got old, real old!

There is a tradeoff of one set of problems for another when you decide to live way out in the country in the Ozark mountains. Southwestern Missouri, northeast Oklahoma, southeast Kansas, and northwest Arkansas have to be the hog-, pig-, chicken-, and turkey-producing epicenter of the world. The sights, sounds, and smells of animal husbandry are everywhere. Even when the weather was beautiful on spring days, you had to keep your windows and doors closed because if the wind blew just right the air was a veritable cornucopia of godawful smells.

You're probably wondering why in the world a company like Wal-Mart would locate its headquarters in the middle of nowhere. Think about it this way. If I asked you to stand in front of a wall map of the United States and stick a pin into the absolute geographic center of the country, I'm willing to bet that Bentonville, Arkansas, would be real close to the point you chose. In fact, if you drove to the farthest corners of the USA from Bentonville, Arkansas, it's 1,415 miles to Spokane, Washington, 1,316 miles to San Diego, California, 1,357 miles to Portland, Maine, and 1,232 Miles to Key West, Florida. That's not exactly dead center, but darn close. Lest you think there was some master planning involved in locating the world's largest retailer and Fortune's number-one company dead center in the United States, think again. Early on, Sam chose Bentonville for the location of his Ben Franklin 5-and-10 store and by locating there was able to bird-hunt in the four-corners area within an easy drive from his home where Oklahoma, Arkansas, Kansas, and Missouri converge. Getting four different hunting licenses effectively allowed him to load his bird dogs up in the back of his old pickup truck and drive a short distance to hunt birds all year round.

Once I had a chance to settle into my job at the Home Office I began to notice how rare it was for an outsider to actually get hired by Wal-Mart and be moved in from outside northwest Arkansas. The company prided itself on promoting people from within, especially from the stores, to fill open Home Office positions. I was brought in over a team of 30-plus associates who had all been home-grown. Only two or three of them had actually gone to college, and all were in highly responsible positions. My job was to focus the individuals, train them, and bring out their full potential as a team. I ran into other outsiders like myself around the Home Office who had been brought in under similar circumstances to develop a team of hardworking, well-intentioned, yet inexperienced professionals. I would soon find out that this staffing model of seeding externally hired seasoned professionals in the organization and promoting associates out of the stores was actually part of the talent strategy of the company and served as another powerful competitive advantage.

Sam had a unique ability to gather a team of great leaders and inspire them to achieve toward a common goal. One of the greatest challenges he faced was gathering top executives who were willing to suppress their individual egos in favor of the overall Wal-Mart team. I'm talking about high-powered executives that the board of directors of a great number of other companies would have loved to have at their helms. Some of his hand-picked executives did move on to become CEOs of other organizations, but the majority have stayed. A savvy headhunter who was able to infiltrate the executive ranks of Wal-Mart would find a treasure trove of high-potential "CEO stock." I'd guess almost all of these people feel that they are locked in due to the golden handcuffs their stock options provide.

At Wal-Mart, everybody is a retailer first. It doesn't matter what job you perform or what functional area you work in. All associates are trained to think like merchants and to be retailers. Executives, managers, and supervisors of every functional area visit and work in the stores periodically in order to understand the business. By doing so, the culture encourages them all to add value to the stores by sharing their individual thoughts and ideas. As a result, managers and executives at Wal-Mart act like business owners. Many of its Home Office employees were transplants from the stores who added value to decision-making by leveraging their firsthand experience working in the stores.

In comparison with other Fortune 500 companies, Wal-Mart generally hires what would appear on paper to be average and even below-average people. Many of its Home Office associates have no college degrees and were hired from off the farms or from small towns from as far away as Oklahoma, Kansas, and Missouri to work in highly responsible headquarters jobs. Wal-Mart hires for attitude and then teaches the necessary skills for the job. It's up to the management team of seasoned professionals to orient, train, and develop the associates into a cohesive team.

Folks who grew up on the farm are by nature hardworking and often humble individuals used to taking on any challenge. These home-grown people form a core team that can be described as nothing less than gung ho. Their enthusiasm is unlike any I've seen in other Fortune 500 companies for whom I've worked. It is as if the company leaders believe in the ability and potential of its people so much that their success becomes almost self-fulfilling. Using the power of positive thinking, company leaders instill in their people the belief and philosophy, "If you believe you can, you can, and if you believe you can't, you can't." Wal-Mart has a unique ability to take the energy of average people and channel that energy into a highly efficient execution-oriented retail army.

I saw lots of examples of individuals with no prerequisite experience for their jobs being placed in positions with great responsibility. To prove they were equal to the challenge they worked long hours and did what was necessary to learn their jobs in order to make an impact quickly. By relying on one another, the associates helped each other to succeed and in the process the company prospered. If there happened to be a weak link in the chain other associates would step in to shore it up. Team success is more highly valued at Wal-Mart than individual success.

Each individual associate's role is very narrow, minimizing the impact of any failure by an individual on the organization. If someone leaves the company, the team orientation allows others to quickly converge, pick up the pieces of the open job, and move on with little fanfare. It is for this reason that any single individual has little impact on the overall workings of the company. Though people are important, virtually everyone is replaceable, and there are plenty of willing and inexperienced yet trainable replacements available.

The staffing strategies and tactics I saw at Wal-Mart challenged everything I had been trained to believe about what was necessary for an organization to be effective. My personal staffing paradigms had been formed while I worked at PepsiCo's Frito-Lay division. We tried to hire 75th- to 90th-percentile people for every position we filled. If a candidate didn't have five to seven years of prerequisite experience and "sparks coming out their butt," we wouldn't even consider them for an interview. Because of their limited credentials on paper, the vast majority of the home-grown people I saw walking the halls at Wal-Mart wouldn't have gotten a courtesy screening interview at most Fortune 500 companies. The irony is that Wal-Mart's associates accomplish more real work in a given day than the employees at any other company!

Early in my own career I worked for a Fortune 500 company where form was more important then an individual having "substance." Said another way, looking good, appearing to be physically fit, and making a great presentation were valued more at times than actually being competent! Value was placed on wearing starched and monogrammed Ralph Lauren shirts, salmon, red, or yellow neckties, Hickey Freeman suits and Gucci shoes, having a great haircut, driving a BMW, and writing with a Mont Blanc pen. A great set of PowerPoint slides with a well-delivered presentation in front of the right audience could be your ticket to the top.

At Wal-Mart it is just the opposite; team performance is much more highly valued than individual performance. Substance or good perform-ance is everything and form or how you look doing it means very little. Doing a good job and working hard are the keys to success at Wal-Mart.

Driving a Beemer or a Benz in Bentonville didn't help your image in the eyes of the executives—in fact it hurt how you were perceived. Believe it or not, it actually helped your image if you were seen driving a pickup truck. When they interviewed me for the job at Wal-Mart one of the more unusual questions asked was what type of vehicle I drove. Being from Texas I had driven a truck for years, and when I said so I passed one of the more important hurdles to getting hired.

Wal-Mart's practice of hiring or promoting inexperienced people for professional opportunities was initially a shock to my system. The asso-ciates seemed to know how lucky they were to have the chance to per-form a job for which they knew no other Fortune 500 company in America would hire them. They worked hard to prove they were worthy of the responsibility entrusted in them. If associates brought 50 percent of what the job required, they would bust their humps to get up the learn-ing curve, close the gap on knowledge, and strive to begin to add value. If this required long hours to accomplish, so be it. Pressure and responsi-bility were placed on higher-level leaders to cultivate the people within their area of responsibility. One-on-one nurturing and training of inexpe-rienced people is an everyday reality for company leaders.

But it's also important to understand that Wal-Mart's selection strat-egy of hiring or promoting average people initially developed as a realis-tic response to its environment: The fast growth of the company and the demographics of the Ozark mountains made the decision to staff inexpe-rienced people a necessity by virtue of the fact that experienced appli-cants were few and far between. The company understood the limitations of the people it had hired and placed in these responsible positions. Still, Wal-Mart leaders seemed to like the fact that inexperienced people didn't bring professional baggage or preconceived notions about how a job needed to be done. They could be molded in any way the company wanted to mold them. This also was in keeping with cultural beliefs about simplifying everything. Associates who didn't know other ways of doing things couldn't needlessly complicate solutions to problems.

I was told that externally hired professionals had a tendency to develop complicated and cumbersome proposals to solve business prob-lems because that was how other companies they had worked for had trained them to do things. As outsiders enter the Wal-Mart Culture they are forced to relearn methods for getting things done. What worked in a pre-vious job wouldn't necessarily work at Wal-Mart. Anything that involved posturing, positioning or politics, which was typical in other companies, was perceived as time-wasting self-aggrandizement at Wal-Mart.

The "Wal-Mart Way" is to present your ideas in a simple, straightforward, and honest way. Because of the importance of continuous learning in the Wal-Mart culture, its leaders value the many good ideas outsiders bring to the company. Often those ideas just need to be "dumbed down" so they are easier to understand and implement. At Wal-Mart, the leaders believe in simplifying everything by embracing the KISS (Keep It Simple Stupid) principle. I learned that it is actually easier for people to create and recommend complicated solutions to problems than it is to design simple ones. Wal-Mart trains its people to make the difficult look easy and the easy look invisible.

In retailing, as we all know, ideas are easy; it's the implementation that's tough. But in retail, the simpler the idea the better the odds are it can be implemented effectively at store level. Sam Walton would become impatient with ideas that were overly complicated and that wasted people's time. I always felt he didn't want to hear about the labor pains, he wanted to be shown the baby. At PepsiCo, I had learned this same aggressive approach to competing and winning. Frito-Lay executives often talked about the distinction between effort and results. Working hard in itself wasn't valued if those efforts didn't yield bottom-line results. Sam Walton shared those same beliefs about business.

The difference in compensation between top-notch, experienced talent and inexperienced trainees provided another cost advantage for Wal-Mart. Based on my experiences before coming to Wal-Mart, I knew that the home-grown Home Office staff was paid about 30 to 40 percent less than comparable associates at one of Wal-Mart's competitors. Associates accepted lower salaries because they understood that their own inexperience and the low cost of living in the Ozarks warranted them. They accepted that the way to riches was via associate profit-sharing and associate stock ownership, rather than through salary, and for this reason were able in their own minds to justify delayed gratification. And they had abundant examples of their peers walking the halls who had become wealthy believing in that formula.

This pay philosophy created a two-tiered pay structure with professionals hired from outside Northwest Arkansas getting paid the appropriate market rates needed to attract, retain, and motivate them. The vast majority of jobs were filled through internal job posting, giving internal people an opportunity for enhanced roles in the company.

Failures are inevitable when you hire and promote inexperienced people into responsibilities for which they aren't prepared. Sam Walton called it "pickin 'em green." I came to find out that almost everybody at

Wal-Mart is on some kind of learning curve because the company is blazing trails in every department, outstripping the existing skills and knowledge of its people. The talent of the company is stretched to beyond capacity and sometimes to the breaking point. Promotions sometimes fail and have led to many associate demotions. Demotions are referred to as "stepping down." No stigma was attributed to being demoted at Wal-Mart. A demotion was once openly discussed by Sam Walton, in front of the demoted associate, at a Saturday morning meeting. It turns out the associate had been promoted, demoted, promoted, promoted, and then demoted again. It was not a badge of dishonor to get demoted at Wal-Mart. "Stepping down" was simply attributed to being "picked green."

Wal-Mart didn't always have the talent to promote from within to fill every position, so at times it recruited experienced professionals from outside the company. I was involved in recruiting a store manager from a Florida grocery chain called Publix for a specialized grocery role we were trying to fill during the early stages of the development of the "Hypermart" concept—an R&D version of the current Supercenter. Grocery-store managers are some of the hardest-working people on the planet; all of them work at least a six-day work week. For this reason, we had to fly this Publix recruit in on a Saturday night so he'd be ready to be interviewed on his day off, Sunday, bright and early. I picked him up at his hotel and ushered him into the Home Office at seven that Sunday morning. When we walked through the executive area, to my surprise, a light was on in the corner office and guess who was sitting at his desk . . . Sam Walton. After I had dropped the recruit off at his first interview I stopped back to talk to Sam.

I asked the question that enquiring minds want to know. . . Why are you here on a Sunday morning and what time did you get here? Sam told me that he often came in to work on Sundays at three or four in the morning with the intent of working until about ten after which he'd head for church. He explained that Sunday mornings provided quiet private time for him to get real work done with few interruptions. He asked me what I was doing and I told him about the Publix recruit who was interviewing for a job. Sam asked if I would bring the recruit by for him to interview for a few minutes.

Our recruit was in for a memorable experience. I sat in on the interview, watching Sam's interviewing style closely. After they exchanged pleasantries Sam proceeded to use this impromptu opportunity to learn as much as he could about Publix. The question that really stands out in my mind was his opening question. He said, "Publix is a grocery retailer I have the greatest respect for, what do you think is the key to their merchandising strategies?" He had used the same type of question when he interviewed me. It was apparent that he used interviews as a way to gain intelligence he could use to improve Wal-Mart. He was dumb as a fox, using these interview opportunities to suck the recruit's brain dry. I learned from Sam Walton that if you ask well-thought-out questions, interviews can be a great way to find out what is going on inside your competitor's businesses, whether you intend to hire the recruit or not.

In every area of the business, in every store, and in every department, Wal-Mart is seeking competitive advantage. With over a million associates working for the company, the staffing of talented people is yet another pivotal competitive advantage. Wal-Mart is the largest private employer in the USA, second only to the federal government in sheer number of people employed. With some stores experiencing turnover as high as 300 percent annually, it's a real problem simply filling work schedules with qualified associates. People are Wal-Mart's greatest asset but because of turnover may also be its greatest liability. The ability to staff open positions with quality people may be the Achilles heel of the Wal-Mart strategy.

Imagine trying to staff stores 24/7/365 paying at or just above minimum wage. In many job markets it's tough for any company to find talented people willing to work the day shift, let alone the second and third shifts. Add to that the churning of retail employees at all levels due to the availability of good jobs, quickly exhausts the pool of talented people. What I've heard called "retail rat syndrome" drives nomadic retail employees to accept employment elsewhere for another 15 to 20 cents per hour.

In some markets, retailers are forced to hire anyone who walks in the door. Staffing at the low end of the wage food chain is a nightmare! That is one of Wal-Mart's greatest challenges. I believe for this reason that it may be one of its competitors' greatest opportunities. Because of its size and the turnover of staff, Wal-Mart must hire huge numbers of people. Under those circumstances maintaining quality is almost impossible. Hopefully, you have the advantage of being much more selective in your choice of employees.

To understand the Wal-Mart staffing strategy it is important to also understand its self-professed blueprint for people. The human-resources function at Wal-Mart is actually called "People." The people strategy at Wal-Mart has three components: Hire the best, provide the best training, and be the best place to work. In the days of Sam Walton, these goals were highly regarded. Back in those days Wal-Mart was also perceived as one of *Fortune* magazine's "100 Best Companies to Work for in America." Wal-Mart believes in hiring a diverse associate staff and the stores reflect a decent cross-section of the demographics of American society. It is at the management level that Wal-Mart finds it challenging to maintain diversity.

I think experienced professionals outside of Wal-Mart who are considering going to work for the retail giant do so when they get emotionally caught up in the myth and cultural folklore of the company. The company story is so compelling that people, just as I did, go there to gain the experience of working at one of the most unusual companies on the planet. I know that at the moment I made my decision to work there, I lost sight of the fact that Wal-Mart managers in the stores and the headquarters on average work harder and longer hours (a six-day work week) than employees at other companies. I think many recruits are so enamored with the idea of being part of the Wal-Mart success story that they lose sight of the long hours and hard work associated with being on the team. Some have a rude awakening after joining the company.

A *USA Today* article titled "While hiring at most firms chills, Wal-Mart's heats up," says, "Coleman Peterson is facing a mission that's almost impossible. As executive vice president of Wal-Mart Stores' "people" division, he will oversee the hiring of more than 1 million employees over the next five years. That's like hiring the entire population of Rhode Island or San Antonio. About 800,000 global new hires will be added, and other hires will take the place of current employees expected to leave because of natural turnover. That will bring Wal-Mart's total global workforce—already the largest private labor force in the United States—to more than 2 million, from 1.3 million. That would eclipse the population of the U.S. Armed Forces, which was about 1.4 million in 2000." Peterson who recently left Wal-Mart, describes the People Division's priorities as "getting, keeping, and growing great associates."[1]

When I worked at Wal-Mart, we went to great lengths to recruit entry-level management talent into the stores. One strategy I personally developed involved the use of a satellite broadcast targeted at over 30 business schools at colleges across the country. The broadcast was called a "satellite business symposium" but in reality it was a recruiting event. Sam Walton was interviewed, in the Wal-Mart broadcasting studio, by a panel of college students who asked his views about retailing careers, his own career, Wal-Mart's culture, and what it takes to be successful in business. The symposium was beamed live to colleges across the country and even accommodated live telephone call-ins from several colleges and universities. The event provided a rare glimpse into the Wal-Mart culture and the mind of its leader. The use of satellite broadcasts to recruit new employees may seem extreme, but when you are trying to hire literally hundreds of talented entry-level managers, using a variety of creative means is essential.

When I first reviewed the satellite-symposium concept with Sam he was truly excited about it. Sam was a college graduate, having attended the University of Missouri. He had majored in economics. He saw the value of using young college students as a way to build company bench strength quickly to insure a pool of trained home-grown leaders was available to fill store management openings from within. It didn't really matter to the company what major or degree a college student received because of the company's belief in cross-pollination of associates between functions. Regardless of the job you started working in you were likely to end up in another area of the business. Cross-functional movement of people happens all the time. Sam encouraged associates to be entrepreneurial in their thinking and not to limit themselves to one functional area. There are no career barriers at Wal-Mart for those who are hardworking and who can get along with people.

I remember that as excited as Sam was with college campus recruiting, he was equally concerned with promoting internal hourly associates who worked for us while they attended college. Wal-Mart aggressively hires college students to work for the company in part-time jobs with the hope that they will be interested in staying with the company upon graduation. He wanted us to be sure to take care of those loyal students, who currently worked for us and knew our culture and work ethic, by offering them management jobs when they graduated.

Wal-Mart's appetite for quality people is virtually insatiable. Just one of the large Supercenters may have sales in excess of 100 million dollars and employ as many as 600 associates. To supervise that large a store requires as many as nine assistant managers, two co-managers and the store manager. With turnover in some metropolitan areas as high as 300 percent, Wal-Mart is always in the business of hiring quality people. Company leaders spend an enormous amount of time trying to hold on to the people they have, because experienced and loyal employees are far more likely to create positive customer-service experiences, which in turn leads to satisfied and happy customers.

For retention purposes, each year Wal-Mart does what it calls "grassroots surveys" of its current associates' opinions. Most companies call this type of survey an "employee opinion survey." According to a Wal-Mart manager I talked to who worked in the stores for 16 years the same associate issues had a tendency to bubble up year after year: "Pay, training, benefits, unequal treatment of the associates, and scheduling. These issues also are some of the reasons why associates quit their jobs." The results of grassroots surveys are taken very seriously by company leaders and individual management careers have been made and destroyed based on them.

Steve Sheetz says that at his company retention is one of Sheetz Convenience Stores competitive advantages. "We think it is important if you are going to emphasize customer service. The thought of constantly training people is crazy and the costs involved are staggering when you lose people. From a customer-service standpoint the customers really want to know the people when they go in there. They hate when Susie serves them every day and Susie is gone tomorrow."

Turnover of employees is also expensive. If you have low turnover, count yourself among the lucky. If you have high turnover you're paying the price in lost productivity, lost sales, and lower service. If you want to develop a retention strategy, a starting point is to gain a thorough understanding of the reasons employees are leaving in the first place. You also need to understand why your long-term employees have decided to stay.

I think we would all agree that there are cases where some turnover is actually advantageous. Did you ever experience relief when one of your employees quit? So there are cases where targeted turnover can actually be a good thing. But, remember, you are in the business of employing people, not "unemploying" people. Your goal in life is not to be the trainer of quality people so that your competitors or other companies can reap the benefits of your labor. Your goal has to be to hire great people and hold on to them. If you can keep your turnover at a manageable level you will do a better job of servicing your customers. You could actually turn retention into your own competitive customer-service advantage.

There is a point when too much turnover becomes a disruption to any business. That point arrives when not having someone in place disrupts the continuity of service to customers. I've heard statistics on the high cost of turnover that range from 3,000 dollars per occurrence to half of the departing employee's first year's salary. Regardless of the exact dollar amount, we're talking about big bucks. You can bet Wal-Mart is aggressively pursuing turnover control, especially when you realize the costs associated with it—though some would argue that employee turnover actually saves the company money in wages and because fewer associates are eligible for company benefits.

I believe excessive turnover negatively affects everything retailers are trying to accomplish. Imagine how much easier your job would be if you were able to stem the tide of turnover. You'd have a well-trained, highly productive team of qualified people. Your time would be yours with which to handle all of those management aspects of your job that are now neglected. And yes, you'd have the time to be proactive in your employee relations. Life would be so good you wouldn't be able to stand it!

In a high-turnover environment managers are thrown into a vicious cycle of hiring and turnover. They have precious little time to address training, employee issues, setting promotions, staying in stock, or serving customers as they desperately scramble to fill those open positions. More often than not, managers figure out a way to magically pull rabbits out of their hats. It is difficult to find quality people in the first place and it is an equally difficult challenge to hold on to them once they are on board.

Unfortunately, when retailers are in financial trouble, it's their best people who jump ship first. By the time a company declares bankruptcy there are pretty slim pickings for competitors to recruit and hire. In a failing company, the best people kind of subscribe to that old Woody Allen line, "It's not that I'm afraid to die. I just don't want to be there when it happens." They jump ship early and, by doing so, cause the decline to occur more rapidly than it would have otherwise. For this reason it is important for retailers to take steps to retain their best talent through the good times and the bad times.

Performing an exit interview is a good way for you as a manager to discover the reasons your employees are leaving. Over a period of time, trends will become evident and you can develop strategies to counteract your turnover. Consistently interviewing all departing employees will help you to clarify the trends in your turnover, and to make the business case for your turnover-reduction strategies. People quit jobs for all kinds of reasons. They also stay with companies for very specific reasons. The goal of exit interviewing is to learn from the past so that you don't repeat mistakes in the future.

Additionally, people who leave a company are often unhappy. If separations are managed poorly, departing employees have a tendency to poison the well, by sharing with anyone who will listen the specific reasons for their unhappiness. Don't let departing employees have a detrimental effect on the morale of your entire team. Understand your turnover problems but focus your time, energy, and effort on retaining the good employees who work for you.

The retailing industry has more than its share of staffing paradigms. A significant problem for recruiters is the perception that retail jobs aren't for those oriented towards a career. Because of this misconception, the industry doesn't attract the brightest and best people who are looking for career opportunities. For this reason, staffing is a struggle for Wal-Mart and will continue to be a struggle as it attempts to staff its growth in the future.

If you are experiencing a similar problem with attracting talented career-oriented employees, I recommend you hire summer interns from colleges in your area. In addition, hire year-round high school or college students to work in part-time jobs. Some of the students may be interested in full-time work upon graduation. Even if you don't hire any of those students who worked for you, they may end up helping you spread the word about retailing careers on campus through their discussions with other students and educators.

Wal-Mart uses pre-employment testing in addition to drug screening to assist interviewers in making proper selections. According to Orion PE, the testing company that performs the pre-employment attitude tests on behalf of Wal-Mart, "the tests are computer scored and evaluate things like:

- how willing the applicant is to accept direction from supervisors and follow policies and procedures
- how likely the applicant is to be absent or tardy
- how well the applicant values working in a team
- how permissive the applicant's attitudes are toward illegal workplace drug use
- how likely the applicant is to rationalize workplace theft and cheating
- how likely the applicant is to frequently change jobs
- how willing the applicant is to be helpful and courteous to customers
- how likely the applicant is to take safety risks that will endanger himself/herself and others
- how eager the applicant is to accept challenges, meet goals and succeed on the job"[2]

The post-survey interview questions generated in the scoring process help interviewers explore areas of concern with the applicant so they can make more effective hiring decisions. They also allow interviewers to counsel the applicant about what is expected should he or she be hired. Testing of applicants being considered for hire is a major expense but I can assure you it has paid back big dividends to Wal-Mart or it would have discontinued the practice long ago. Drug screening and pre-employment testing are pivotal to Wal-Mart's staffing strategy.

Managers who work in retailing companies have their own set of unique staffing beliefs. In my own experience I've found retail leaders often believe that people from outside the retail industry can't possibly understand what we do in retailing. That's not the case at Wal-Mart. It figured out long ago that if you want to be a world-class company you have to hire a blend of people from other retailers and bring world-class people from outside the industry into key management positions. It also understands that retail companies generally aren't known for having people who have had exposure to world-class best practices. It really doesn't take bright talented people hired from other industries that long to learn the retail business and start adding value.

It is my belief that if you challenge your internal staffing beliefs and begin to seed talent from world-class companies outside of retailing, your organization can achieve more of its true potential faster. Outsiders will quickly and accurately challenge old ways of doing things, helping you reach new levels of performance and uncover hidden capabilities. By doing so, you can substantially differentiate your company and brand within the retailing industry and strive to become the best that you can be.

With unemployment the way it is, there is really no reason for you to attempt to "train your way to prosperity" for some of your key open positions. Training for key positions almost always takes too long. Remember, more often than not it is easier to hire a skill off the street than it is to try to train it later.

I was schooled to be an aggressive recruiter of talented people. When I worked in specialty retailing, I hired a recruiter based in Columbus, Ohio, who recruited talented people for me out of the various Columbus-based Limited Divisions constantly. We were very successful. I tried the same strategy in San Francisco, where the Gap is headquartered. I was completely unsuccessful in recruiting highly desirable Gap employees. I used to tell retail headhunters who wanted my business to recruit three buyers or merchandise planners for me out of the Gap headquarters and that I would jump on a plane tomorrow to interview them. Not one of the many recruiters was ever able to meet that challenge! I later found out that the reason for my failure was a direct result of the strong culture at Gap and the perception of living in San Francisco. A recruiter told me that the CEO of the Gap, Milliard "Mickie" Drexler, simply refused to allow employees of the company to leave! He reportedly said, "We will never lose a current employee simply because another company offers them more money." I was at American Eagle Outfitters for nine years and during that time, as hard as we tried, we were never able to recruit a single employee directly out of the Gap's headquarters; at the same time we recruited many talented people out of the Limited. This story illustrates that it is possible to retain key people in a retailing company if the CEO makes retention a priority.

I learned that there are some great companies in the retail industry who train their people well, from whom you can steal talented people. The department stores have always been a great source of talent, especially buying talent. I was taught to walk into the cosmetics area of department stores and recruit because that's where they slot their brightest people with the strongest interpersonal selling skills. I was also taught to walk the mall an hour before stores were scheduled to open in search of the aggressive store managers who opened their doors early to grab more business. I often walked into competitor's stores to view product merchandising firsthand in my efforts to recruit the truly exceptional merchants.

The same technique worked when I was recruiting private-label product developers/buyers. What better way to evaluate a recruit than by looking at his or her actual product assortment in the stores today? If we were recruiting a sweater buyer we'd shop sweaters. If we needed an outerwear buyer we'd shop for coats. Once we identified great product it was a pretty simple task to identify and make contact with the buyer responsible for it.

In his book *Topgrading* (Prentice Hall, Inc. 1999), Bradford Smart defines "A," "B," and "C" talent. He describes an A Player as an individual who is considered in the top 10 percent of the available talent pool in the marketplace, at that level or in that job category; they are paid a premium for their skill and knowledge. A B player is considered an individual in the 65th to 89th percentile and they, too, receive above-average compensation. A C player is below the 65th percentile. It stands to reason that C players in any job or job category receive significantly lower compensation than that earned by A and B talent. Bradford Smart doesn't define a talent level below the C player level because in my estimation the assumption is that companies can't expect to beat the competition without the brightest and best people. They avoid hiring lower-caliber talent at all costs.

Using these definitions, I believe Wal-Mart has a few topnotch A player leaders spread sparingly around the organization, primarily at the Home Office. These A players serve as a brain trust for the organization, as they are responsible for developing key short- and long-term strategies. The company has a solid group of B players primarily in its management ranks. Many, but not all of their store managers fall into the B player category. The vast majority of Wal-Mart's store managers, department managers, and associates are C-caliber talent. Based on my observations, it was apparent that their store's staffing strategy focuses on hiring very average C talent. Most of us would be appalled if our managers went out of their way to hire C players but Wal-Mart taps into that mostly untapped labor pool every day.

According to Smart, "topgrading" is the practice of packing the team with A players and clearing out C players, a practice followed by companies like GE and PepsiCo. In my opinion, Wal-Mart does just the opposite, foregoing higher-level, higher-priced talent in favor of lower-skilled and lower-paid C players. This is another example of Wal-Mart challenging conventional business practices.

There are lessons to be learned from Wal-Mart's staffing strategy. I believe that because of the cookie-cutter nature of Wal-Mart's stores the intellectual horsepower of the organization—for strategy development purposes—is centered in the hands of a few very smart people at the top. Everyone else is counted on to tactically implement those strategies with lockstep execution.

What is hard for outsiders to understand and hard to duplicate is that Wal-Mart takes this army of average and some below-average people and gets them to perform at above-average levels of performance. They pay them at low levels of compensation and are still able to get them to perform at above-average levels. That level of productivity drops billions of dollars to the bottom line and it's one of the primary reasons for the unbelievable success of the company. It is also the reason the Walton family has amassed a 100-billion-dollar fortune!

By contrast, many competitors hire higher-quality talent than Wal-Mart. They also pay a wage premium for that talent. Interestingly enough, due to a lack of consistent standards many extract average to below-average performance levels out of their above-average workforce. Simply put, they pay more and get less out of the talent they've hired; in other words, they get "less from more." Wal-Mart, however, focuses more on the cost of payroll when they hire. They hire for attitude and focus less on the skills and experience of the individuals they hire. This is an example of Sam's "picking 'em green" staffing strategy. By hiring C talent Wal-Mart has tapped into a readily available pool of people generally overlooked by competitors. By training them the "Wal-Mart Way," paying them at the lowest levels possible and holding associates to above-average standards, the company in essence gets "more from less." Wal-Mart's approach to staffing challenges the conventional wisdom taught in every "how to hire" training class and business school in this country!

Whether you agree or not, most companies don't have more than a handful of true A players, although they falsely self-identify the existence of large numbers of A-quality talent in their company. Some companies don't have any true A talent. You are fooling yourself if you believe you have a staff of the brightest and best people in industry employed at your company because I'd be willing to bet you don't. The A players you identify are simply the best you have, but in all likelihood they aren't the best in class when compared across the industry. If they were as good as you believe they are you'd have them protected by a contract so your competitors couldn't steal them from you. Retail is a tight industry with respect to knowing who the most talented people are; if you had a bench loaded with true A players you would be getting pounded by headhunters stealing your talented bench strength out from under you.

When most executives inventory the top-performing people within their own organizations they develop lists against internal benchmarks, which is what headhunters call identifying the "tallest midget." The better way to do this is to compare your A talent against that of world-class companies. You'll quickly find that your talent pool doesn't always measure up. I am not suggesting you hire A players for every position because the fact is you couldn't hold on to them if you could do it. Simply sprinkle some highly talented people throughout your organization and you'll have internal benchmarks to point to as a standard for staffing within your own company.

Let's talk about human nature with respect to perceptions about people for just a moment. In a psychological study by the College Board a group of people was asked to rank themselves on "their ability to get along with others." All of the participants, 100 percent of them, put themselves in the top half of the population! A whopping 60 percent rated themselves in the top 10 percent of the population and a full 25 percent thought they were in the top one percent of the population. In a parallel finding, 70 percent rated themselves in the top quartile in leadership. We all think we are the best; we're wildly irrational about ourselves and the people who work around us![3]

Challenge your own beliefs about the quality of your own staff. Try to be objective. Your familiarity with and loyalty to your own people may mask the true quality of the individual members of your own team. You may be accepting less than satisfactory performance. Wal-Mart recognizes its best people and it deals with those who aren't performing. When you as a supervisor accept less than satisfactory performance, you have become part of the problem!

Another secret to successful staffing is the idea of finding one or two executive-level "franchise players" who can help lead your team to become the best that it can be. The term "franchise player" originated in the National Hockey League. The first true "franchise player" in professional sports was Gilbert Perreault. Perreault, nicknamed "the franchise," was drafted by the Buffalo Sabres who built their organization around him in 1970. The concept of "the franchise player" is now commonplace in professional baseball, football, basketball, hockey, and soccer.

At American Eagle Outfitters, the specialty apparel retailer, we used this technique effectively. The top leadership team was staffed with solid and experienced executives, but we lacked a catalyst. Jay Schottenstein, the company's CEO, strategically placed a 26-year-old brand marketing expert in a key turnaround leadership position as vice president of the marketing department. His expertise was instrumental in focusing the private-label brand strategy, identifying the targeted customer and their values, and designing the remodel of the stores, fixtures, signage, and advertising. With his marketing leadership and vision, American Eagle Outfitters was "pulled out of the ditch and the wheels were put back on." The company later executed a successful IPO and the stock subsequently split four times!

A smart CEO can use the franchise-player staffing concept to catapult his or her company to the next level. Sam Walton leaned on two executives who were best in class in the retailing industry. David Glass (CEO) and Don Soderquist (COO) were both talented executives qualified to be chairman of the board at any number of Fortune 500 companies. David was a financial wizard and business strategist while Don was a charismatic leader like Sam Walton. When Sam died he left the company in their capable hands and under their direction the company never missed a beat, continuing to grow and flourish around the world.

The key for retailers is to recruit more and more-talented people into the company pipeline. Retailers have to stop settling for less than the best talent in the marketplace by seeding future leaders at every level. Hiring people who, as they say in sports, are stronger, are faster, and can jump higher than you can drives everyone on the team to higher levels of performance. Better people yield better results. Constantly ask yourself the question each time you make a hiring decision, "would a world-class company hire this individual?" If the answer is "no" you should not hire that recruit either. A good rule of thumb is, "Don't hire people from the other half of the class that made the top half possible."

Staffing management positions correctly from the start is the ball game. I'm often surprised by the limited attention given to the selection of front-line managers and supervisors. If you think about it, all the business standards are set and executed at that level and poor leadership has to equal a poor business outcome. Not to be harsh, but in staffing positions it's kind of like the old technology saying, "garbage in, garbage out."

I'll share with you one of the greatest secrets of staffing an organization to insure qualified and quality promotables are in place at every level of an organization. First, the management-selection process should include no less than three interviews with current members of the leadership team. Now, here's the secret: Establishing the requirement for an interview with a manager two levels above the position. Why is this important? Human nature is the answer.

How do you think managers answer the question, "Do you think it is important to hire people who are better than you are?" You probably guessed right, they all answer affirmatively. But that is not the correct question to ask. The correct question is, "Do you hire people who are better than you are?" Many managers will openly admit they don't out of fear of hiring their own replacements. Knowing human nature it's important to use a staffing safety net to insure that high-quality managers are consistently hired.

Thus the secret to building bench is this: Require the manager two levels above the open position to interview and approve all new hires. You'll see the quality of your staff quickly begin to improve. Managers two levels above a position clearly want people who are better than the current crop of managers and employees on their staff. At this level there is a vested interest in building bench strength. This strategy works equally well for headquarters, store, distribution, fleet, and office jobs.

One of the keys to turning staffing into a competitive advantage is to cast a wider net. What I mean by this is to recruit talented people using non-traditional methods. Here is a list of additional recruiting sources for you to consider using, most of which Wal-Mart already uses:

- State and local employment agencies
- Employee referrals
- Active applications on file
- Local military bases
- Walk-ins
- High schools and colleges
- Classified advertising
- Mobile advertising signs near landfills
- DECA students
- SIFE students
- The Urban League
- VA job-placement programs
- State job-training programs
- Local cable television stations
- Community action groups (disabled)
- Area churches
- Radio stations
- Internet

Colleges are an extremely important source of talent at Wal-Mart. The company recruits at over 80 campuses around the country, literally hiring hundreds of management trainees for the stores every year. I can remember our dissatisfaction with the turnover rate of college hires within their first three years of employment. I personally think that turnover was a result of culture shock—it's not easy for students to go from the laid-back lifestyle of a college campus to warp speed in the competitive world of retailing. Additionally, it is difficult to pair new hires up with management mentors who in every case value college recruits. Many of the managers responsible for training newly hired college graduates are themselves non-degreed. They came up in retailing the hard way and for this reason some of them believe everyone else should too. The majority of young people today don't buy into that type of thinking. Unless they sense they are being treated as valued partners the long hours and workload become more than the recruit bargained for. Turnover becomes the inevitable outcome.

To solve this problem, Wal-Mart hires lots of college students to work in the stores in hourly paid positions while they are still attending college. This way students get to know and understand the inner workings of the company and the culture. They get to know the managers and gain an appreciation for what it takes to be successful in the company. When they are about to graduate, Wal-Mart gives priority to currently employed college students for the available management-trainee opportunities. This approach has proven to be much more successful from a retention standpoint than that of recruiting students directly off the college campus without previous Wal-Mart work experience.

Wal-Mart is a big supporter of the retailing institutes at Texas A&M, Brigham Young, James Madison, the University of South Carolina, the University of Arkansas, Purdue, and Florida State. We used to bring our interns in from those schools to work in Bentonville, in office jobs, for the summer. Our goal for our summer interns was twofold: first, to convert them to full-time employment when they graduated, and second, to have them return to campus as ambassadors for the company. To achieve the second goal the company used a "campus manager" program, staffed by interns returning to college in the fall. Student campus managers helped to promote Wal-Mart careers on campus. Supplied with company business cards, campus managers were official representatives at their schools. They would speak at campus meetings and support company recruiters in setting up interview schedules. This program gave Wal-Mart an advantage in attracting students to interview with the company.

An important part of the recruiting efforts involved the realization that developing relationships with professors at the colleges and universities where Wal-Mart recruited was extremely important. The professors represented continuity as they would be teaching at those schools for years to come. Their recommendations were highly regarded by students. Influential professors were invited to attend the annual shareholders' meeting held in Fayetteville, Arkansas, at the University of Arkansas basketball pavilion. Sam went out of his way to spend time with each professor in attendance, especially those representing schools with retailing institutes.

The professors invited to attend the Wal-Mart shareholders' meeting when Sam Walton was running them got a once-in-a-lifetime experience. The shareholders' meeting itself is like no other held in America. It really showcases the company and its culture for all to see. Associates from across the country would arrive in that huge basketball arena representing stores from every state in the union. Over 10,000 would show up for a combination old time revival meeting/shareholders meeting. It was one part theater and one part circus and Sam was the ringleader. Lee Greenwood kicked off one such meeting with a stirring performance of "I'm Proud to Be an American." It turned into a big sing-along involving everyone in attendance. Even associates got the chance to perform on the stage. You couldn't help but walk away motivated from the sight of fellow employees performing as a barbershop quartet or a country-western band so professional they looked and sounded as if they belonged at Nashville's Grand Ole Opry!

Another avenue of attracting talent to Wal-Mart is through an organization called Students in Free Enterprise (SIFE). According to the SIFE web site,

> "SIFE is a global, non-profit organization that is literally changing the world through highly dedicated student teams on more than 1600 university campuses in 40 countries. SIFE offers these students the opportunity to develop leadership, teamwork and communication skills through learning, practicing and teaching the principles of free enterprise, thereby improving the standard of living for millions in the process. Guided by distinguished faculty advisors and supported by businesses around the globe, SIFE Teams teach important concepts through educational outreach projects, including market economics, entrepreneurship, personal and financial success and business ethics to better themselves, their communities and their countries. Each year, SIFE competitions are held worldwide, drawing together thousands of students and business leaders to pay tribute to these extraordinary educational outreach projects."

In 1985, Jack Shewmaker, who was formerly vice chairman and CFO of Wal-Mart Stores, Inc., became SIFE's Chairman, adding significant credibility to the organization and resulting in rapid growth of fundraising. Because of Wal-Mart's involvement in SIFE, corporate membership in the organization is a veritable "who's who" of retail manufacturers. Companies represented include many of Wal-Mart's suppliers, including Black and Decker, Hormel, Gillette, Pepsi, Frito-Lay, 3M, Tyson's, Campbell's, Cargill, Elmer's, Coca-Cola, and BIC. The SIFE organization is truly global with branches in Africa, Asia, Europe, Latin America, North America, Australia, and New Zealand. (See this Web link for more information on SIFE: http://www.sife.org/home/dream_team2.asp)

Wal-Mart provides stipends to faculty advisors who are named Sam M. Walton Free Enterprise Fellows, in honor of the founder of Wal-Mart. Under Jack's leadership, the number of regional competitions grew, the number of participating teams hit an all-time high, and SIFE's board of directors grew to more than 100 members strong. Wal-Mart's affiliation with SIFE has proven to be an excellent source for recruiting talented entrepreneurial-minded individuals. The relationship with SIFE is so important to Wal-Mart that the company's vice chairman, Tom Coughlin, is on their board of directors. Jack Shewmaker, now retired, remains a SIFE board member as well. Today, corporate membership on SIFE's board of directors totals more than 200 big name organizations.

Another key source for retailers to recruit talented entrepreneurial people into their retail stores is an organization called Distributive Education Clubs of America (DECA). DECA's slogan is "Developing Future Leaders in Marketing, Management, and Entreprenuership." According to the DECA Web site, "today 170,000 marketing students, 4,500 marketing teachers, and 14,000 postsecondary Delta Epsilon Chi members enjoy the benefits of membership in DECA, the association for students and teachers of marketing, management, and entrepreneurship." K-Mart is on the advisory Board of DECA. Participating schools in DECA include high schools, technical schools, and two- and four-year colleges and universities across the United States (see this link for more information on DECA: http://www.deca.org/nab/). The board of directors of DECA includes an impressive list of retailers. Wal-Mart has recruited DECA students in the past but they are not active in the organization today.

I have had the opportunity to recruit talented students from both DECA and SIFE and I personally believe these are two of the best sources of finding management talent and future buyers for retail companies. Their students are some of the brightest, most well-rounded, and most highly motivated I've ever met. Both organizations have local, state, and national meetings mentoring high school and college students. Both organizations have grown to be international in scope. Developing contacts with the local chapters of DECA and SIFE ensures a full pipeline of motivated, entrepreneurial recruits for your company. Here's an easy-to-replicate strategy which you can use immediately to upgrade the quality of talent in your own organization.

At Wal-Mart, a newly hired college recruit could work his or her way up to store manager in less than three years. Opportunities are offered based on merit, not on how long you've been with the company. With base and bonus it is quite possible for a 25-year-old college graduate to run a big-volume store and earn over $100,000 per year. Word on college campuses concerning Wal-Mart is generally positive and we had little difficulty filling our interviewing schedules.

But generally speaking, whether we care to admit it or not, retailers—even Wal-Mart—do not attract the top students on campus. Many other companies court the best college students throughout their college years, even offering them summer internships. I've found that unless a student is actually attending a retailing institute or majoring in retail, merchandising, or design, he or she probably didn't enter college with the expectation of joining a retail company upon graduation. Most settle for retail jobs as a last resort if they haven't had a better offer from another non-retail company. If you don't believe me, have an open conversation with a group of college students about retailing careers. I've even talked to retailing executives over the years and very few went into retail straight out of college.

A major factor affecting and shaping student's opinions about retailing careers—believe it or not—is the parents of the college students themselves. Picture this: Mom and Dad just paid a small fortune to put Johnny or Mary through school and the idea of their joining a retail company upon graduation wasn't what they had envisioned. The thought of seeing your college-educated son or daughter trading in their graduation cap and gown for one of those blue smock–type vests with an "everyday low price" embroidery and a "Hi, my name is Johnny or Mary" name tag on it is more than many parents can stand.

When I worked at Frito-Lay one of our sister companies, Taco Bell, experienced this same phenomenon. The difference was that it was recruiting MBAs into financially lucrative management-training programs. If the parents and students could look beyond the initial assignment Johnny or Mary could quickly be in a multi-site leadership position at Taco Bell managing an army of people and pulling down a six-figure income. But the thought of their children peddling tacos wearing those striped shirts and funny little hats, or pushing a broom during the training period, was downright embarrassing for the parents. It seems the parents would rather their children work in office buildings, in cubicles, wearing business attire and earning half of what they could in retail careers at companies like Wal-Mart or Taco Bell. I wish someone had sat me down when I was 21 years old and explained the career paths in retailing to me the way I've just described them to you. If more students understood the career and financial potential of retail I think we'd see more of the brightest and best people intentionally entering retail as a career directly from college.

When I was sent to interview on campus for Wal-Mart at Penn State University, two of us were assigned to interview a total of six interview schedules. That's a lot of interviewing. Anyone who was interested in signing up to be interviewed could put his or her name on one of our schedules. We weren't particular and really couldn't afford to be. We each interviewed one schedule of 13 students per day for three days straight, and at the end offered half of those we had interviewed the opportunity for a second interview. Many were called and many were chosen. This gives you a sense for the tremendous appetite Wal-Mart has for hiring inexperienced college students in an effort to build the company's bench strength. In contrast, when I interviewed on college campuses representing Frito-Lay we were extremely selective. We might offer one top-notch student off a handpicked interview schedule of 13 a second interview: Few were called and even fewer were chosen.

Military recruiting is still another source of talented and experienced leaders for Wal-Mart. Junior military officers are trained, mature, and disciplined leaders. Many have pensions as a result of their years of service. From a pay standpoint former military leaders are very reasonably priced and successful at making the transition into the disciplined leadership roles offered in retail. If you have military bases in your area, check out one of their career fairs. In some cases, those leaving the military are interested in staying in the local area, but in my experience, I have found most want to relocate. The good news for employers is that those leaving the military are provided with a generous relocation package paid for by the federal government.

There is an old saying in recruiting circles that perceived good companies have some bad people and perceived bad companies have some good people. You shouldn't assume that just because someone has worked for a particular company that he or she is good or bad as a result of that affiliation. Don't assume that people who have worked at Wal-Mart are all talented or that people from K-Mart are less talented. That type of thinking leads to staffing mistakes. You find great people by interviewing a lot of people in order to find that one to whom you offer the job.

The assumption that your competitors have better people than you do may also be a flawed one. Take the time to thoroughly interview applicants and check their industry references. I've always found that retailing is a small tight community when it comes to supplying references. Remember, to find the brightest and the best talent you must recruit constantly. Highly skilled people who can make a difference in your business are out there; you just have to find them one at a time.

All in all, talent is one of the areas in which you should always be able to outperform Wal-Mart. Its philosophy is to hire average people in the hopes of motivating them to perform at average or even above-average performance levels. Walk into a Target store and a Wal-Mart store and compare and contrast the quality of people; you'll see that the two companies have very different hiring standards. I believe that Target hires higher-caliber people in every position. You'll see a similar difference when you compare and contrast Wal-Mart's associates with K-Mart's employees. I believe that K-Mart has lower staffing standards and that its stores reflect that fact. Remember, the kinds of people you hire are a direct reflection on your brand.

What is your standard for staffing employees? How do your people compare to those of your competitors? Are you selective in choosing very bright, high-potential people for your business, or do you settle for whoever applies? When you evaluate the quality and caliber of your current team are your A players really B- or C-quality when objectively compared to the talent in the marketplace? The selection and retention of quality employees is the foundation upon which every one of your other strategies is based. Your own standards for quality can be your best friend or your worst enemy.

But where do you find great people? One of the keys is to change the way you go about sourcing a pool of candidates. Hiring a diverse workforce is a great way to increase the pool of qualified and talented applicants for your open positions. Wal-Mart is the leading employer of people of color in the United States. More than 160,000 African Americans and more than 105,000 Latinos work at Wal-Mart and Sam's Club stores and distribution centers nationwide. Additionally, Wal-Mart Stores, Inc. is one of the leading employers of senior citizens in the United States, employing more than 164,000 associates ages 55 and older. Wal-Mart has been recognized as one of the leading employers of disabled people in the nation. In the 2002 annual poll by *Careers for the Disabled* magazine, Wal-Mart was named first among all U.S. companies in providing opportunities and a positive working environment for people with disabilities.[4] Because of growth, turnover, and necessity, Wal-Mart aggressively recruits people of all varieties:

> "President and CEO Lee Scott challenges new associates this way: We employ people from all walks of life, from every educational level—people who have many different talents and ambitions. Our founder, Sam Walton, proved that people can make a difference. If you have a vision, with dedication and hard work you can realize your greatest dreams...Our company is not just bricks and mortar, cash registers and signs—it's people working together to serve our customers and each other. That is our philosophy. And while our company hardly resembles our first small store in Rogers, Arkansas, our early values remain with us."[5]

I have often noticed that companies experiencing difficulties finding qualified people have one thing in common. They often use the same methods of staffing that they have always used and eventually come to the realization that those methods are no longer working. This is like fishing in the same small pond for a long time. You tend to catch fish from the same species and eventually you catch all the desirable fish. The solution is simple: Cast a wider recruiting net into different and bigger un-fished ponds. Go after new people who are not like the people you currently employ. Your stores should reflect the diversity of the communities where you do business.

Staffing should be one of your most important competitive advantages. It will be if that is the way you view the importance of staffing great people. Challenge your own staffing beliefs. Your customers expect to see diversity when they shop in your stores and your employees expect to work in a diverse workforce. You will attract an ethnically broader customer base when your store reflects a cross-section of society; this includes old, young, disabled, African American, Hispanic, Asian, American Indian, male and female employees.

Performance feedback is a powerful motivator. Wal-Mart managers receive feedback constantly on how they are performing, some of it positive and some of it not so positive. A Fortune 500 company CEO once said, "If you want to recognize someone do it publicly, if you want to give them performance feedback do it privately." The message is "Catch employees doing things right." Accentuate the positive behavior of individuals or your team publicly and eliminate negative behavior privately, behind closed doors. Be a fact-finder, not a fault-finder. Learn one of the simple non-monetary recognition techniques used by Wal-Mart by taking a look at the vests worn by cashiers at a store near you. You'll see lots of lapel pins recognizing stellar sales and service accomplishments.

We all spend an inordinate amount of time, energy, and effort on the employees who are sucking the vitality out of an organization, rather than on the top performers who are working with us to create synergy. My opinion is that you should spend more time on the top-performing 80 percent of your workgroup and aggressively upgrade the lowest 10 to 20 percent of the deadwood, systematically. That's exactly what some of the most respected companies do each and every year.

As you begin to catch people doing things right you will also simultaneously need to continue to deal with the nonperformers. I can tell you that Wal-Mart leaders don't have much patience for nonperforming or low-performing associates. Over time they will quietly eliminate poor-performing employees by providing them with feedback, which either moves their performance up or moves them out of the company. By systematically dealing with the lowest performers, and replacing them with employees with higher potential, managers improve the performance of the entire team.

In my career, I've always been amazed at the inability of good leaders to deal with employee job-performance problems systematically. Ask managers in any organization for a list of perceived poor performers and most can provide a list with little effort. If identifying underperforming people is so easy, then why don't company leaders deal with those offenders quickly and directly? The short list is because of legal concerns, lack of time to pin the issue down, no replacement, and out-and-out fear of confrontation.

If you show me an employee job-performance problem, I'll show you how it falls into one of four performance "buckets." Once you've pinned the issue down to the root cause, dealing with it becomes much easier. The first performance "bucket" is Dkh, which symbolizes a performance problem caused by an employee who is "devoid of know-how" (a coaching/training issue). The second "bucket" is De, symbolizing an employee whose performance problem is "devoid of effort" indicated by the fact they know what to do but aren't doing it—that is, nonperformance (a counseling issue). The third performance "bucket" is Da, which is an individual who is "devoid of ability" (bad hire), and the fourth performance "bucket" is Di, which symbolizes an employee who is "devoid of integrity" (dishonest). Every employee job-related performance problem falls into one of these four performance "buckets." In my business coaching practice, I teach company managers specific techniques for developing a "human inventory" of their staff through a "9-box" forced ranking process I learned from PepsiCo, designed to provide clarification of performance issues.

In my experience I've found that by coaching or counseling poor performing employees a full 90 percent of them can become solid performers. Employees identified as Da or Di need to be moved out of the company quickly. There is no faster way to raise your organization's performance level than by dealing with performance issues every day. Another thing you can do immediately to raise the bar going forward is simply to provide a comprehensive orientation or indoctrination to new employees coming into your company. Wal-Mart deals with its non-performing employees each and every day and thoroughly orients its new hires. You should, too.

Building bench strength takes incredible organizational discipline, which many companies and executives, when you get right down to it, really lack. I witnessed high standards of staffing discipline at Frito-Lay. Let me illustrate the concept of staffing discipline with a true story. One of Frito-Lay's divisional vice presidents of route sales, with whom I worked closely, had a regional manager opening we needed to fill in New Orleans, Louisiana. At that time, Frito-Lay had what it called the "Twenty-Percent Rule" to ensure adequate bench strength. The Twenty-Percent Rule meant that at least one out of the five regional manager positions always had to have a high-potential, "bulletproof promotable" in place. This meant that one of the five incumbents had to be ready to be promoted instantaneously. The company used the Twenty-Percent Rule in all departments across all jobs. At the time of this search four of the five regional managers were considered pros in position and were unlikely to be promoted to the next level. This put pressure on us to fill the open position with a bulletproof promotable.

Here's where the organizational discipline came into play. We interviewed a regional candidate from another consumer-packaged-goods company who had all of the prerequisite experience to be a great regional manager for us. In fact, he was a stronger manager than the other four regional managers we already had in place. The problem was that he wasn't promotable to the next level. Many companies without discipline would have hired him on the spot, but not Frito-Lay. We turned him down and continued searching until we found a high-potential, promotable regional manager for New Orleans. That's organizational discipline!

If you objectively take a mental inventory of your staff, how does it stack up to the best talent available in the marketplace? If it doesn't stack up, it is time for you to systematically upgrade the quality of your team. As turnover occurs it is up to you to raise the bar and have the discipline in staffing to hire better employees than currently exist to fill every open position. Over a short period of time you will surprise yourself with the quality transformation occurring within your own team. There truly is no better way to bring your organizational culture to a higher level faster than through the aggressive day-in-day-out staffing of quality talent.

Finding talent is more than simply hiring people. It is hard work; it takes a year-round dedicated effort. Also, it takes the ability of the interviewer to see the hidden potential a recruit brings to the organization. Past performance is generally an excellent predictor of future performance. Talented people are impact players who can make a difference in the company. "Every day is draft day" must become your recruiting philosophy if you want to find them. Unfortunately, truly talented people are few and far between. To find them you must diversify your recruiting strategy. The good news is that talented people come in all colors, shapes, and sizes. Whether they work full-time or part-time, the standards are the same. Don't overlook the fact that one of the greatest sources of talented new employees may be the referrals of your current top-notch employees, because birds of a feather flock together.

Imagine how your company would improve if you had positive and highly talented employees in every job, trying to help you hit your performance goals every day. Yes, that is possible and yes, that is the goal company leaders are supposed to be trying to achieve now. Chester Cadieux, chairman of QuikTrip Corporation, said, "We're very selective.

We go through five people to hire one part-time employee, through ten people to hire one full-time employee. Most of the people who run our company started at the entry level." When you hire great people, staffing becomes a competitive advantage because the employees you hire are pivotal to your success. You can have the best product and store location around but if your staff is weak or poorly trained you will experience mediocre results.

There is no more important asset to the success of your company than those employees you hire and put in direct face-to-face contact with your customers. Be known in your community for having great people and you'll become an "employer of choice." Remember, applicants will evaluate your organization by walking into your store and meeting your employees. By sizing up your team the best potential applicants will make their decision to apply or not apply. Make certain your team reflects the high standards of quality for which you want to be known. Follow the lead of the world's largest retailer by subscribing to the belief that "It's our people that make the difference!"

Talent Checklist

Review this talent checklist of success strategies and tactics designed to help you compete with big-box retailers like Wal-Mart and not only survive, but thrive.

Staffing
- ✓ Recruit constantly; establish a belief that every day is draft day
- ✓ Realize that bright, motivated people are interviewing you while you're interviewing them
- ✓ Remove recruiting obstacles and increase the speed of filling open positions
- ✓ Hire people who are better than you are—smarter, better educated, and with more potential
- ✓ Hire experienced people over less experienced whenever possible
- ✓ Seed some talented people from a respected competitor to learn from its experience
- ✓ Cast your hiring net wide and hire from a diverse pool of people
- ✓ Hold managers accountable for retention/turnover
- ✓ Exit-interview departing employees
- ✓ Actively address employee-performance problems and replace nonperformers
- ✓ Set goals for having qualified people on your bench to ensure promotion from within
- ✓ Establish a mission and vision statement and clarify your organization's core competencies

Bringing Out the Best in Your Employees
- ✓ Believe in people more than they believe in themselves; expect the best
- ✓ Try to understand what makes each individual tick
- ✓ Establish, and personally practice, high standards of productivity and quality
- ✓ Create an environment where making a mistake is not fatal
- ✓ Recognize role models to encourage others
- ✓ Create performance heroes by applauding achievement
- ✓ Employ a mixture of positive reinforcement and performance feedback
- ✓ Encourage teamwork and cooperation over competition
- ✓ Lead by example—walk the talk by modeling the right behaviors yourself

Employee Retention Ideas
- ✓ Thoroughly orient newly hired employees
- ✓ Provide employees with training and development opportunities
- ✓ Empower people and enable them to take ownership of their customer-service responsibilities
- ✓ Show tolerance of people who make mistakes
- ✓ Communicate to employees the competitiveness of your pay and benefits programs
- ✓ Provide performance feedback to employees periodically
- ✓ Balance internal promotions and external hiring
- ✓ Have an open mind and an open door
- ✓ Identify and leverage each individual's special skills and abilities, which that person alone brings to your team
- ✓ Enable employees to act as mentors for new employees
- ✓ Set the course for your team and have the courage to stay with it
- ✓ Try to have fun at work. Be a pressure-relief valve for your people

How Managers and Supervisors Can Avoid Causing Employee Turnover
- ✓ Take care in screening job applicants
- ✓ Establish effective employee-communication programs
- ✓ Deal with problem employees, preferably during the orientation period
- ✓ Show respect for employees and treat people fairly
- ✓ Listen to employees before making decisions that affect them
- ✓ Clean and maintain—bathrooms, locker rooms, eating areas, and parking areas
- ✓ Give employees a sense of job security by demonstrating fair treatment of everyone
- ✓ Communicate with employees about the company and their jobs
- ✓ Promptly respond to employee questions, problems, and complaints
- ✓ Monitor and respond to employee complaints
- ✓ Develop and administer consistent policies and procedures

7

Service Strategies and Tactics

"Wal-Mart's internal customer-service standards reminded me of the motto of the Three Musketeers: 'All for one, one for all!'"

From Wal-Mart and Sam Walton I learned an employee and customer-recognition secret that I'd like to share with you. Sam had learned from his managers in the New Orleans area a French Creole customer-service concept called "lagniappe" (pronounced *lan*-yap). Lagniappe is a little something extra given as a gift of appreciation, like the thirteenth donut in a baker's dozen—a gratuity. At Wal-Mart, it's a way of translating the concept of exceeding customer expectations into action on the part of associates. The idea for Wal-Mart's now famous people greeters, which in itself is a form of lagniappe, came from the New Orleans area.

In employee-relations terms lagniappe might be a note of appreciation sent to an employee's home, a performance lapel pin or simply a kind word of appreciation for a job well done. In customer service, lagniappe might be free samples for the customer, rolled-back prices, or two-for-one specials. Thanking the customers for their purchases is yet another example.

The people-greeter at every Wal-Mart store is lagniappe personified. You don't find greeters in any other store and they give you a big smile and a friendly "Hello, welcome to Wal-Mart." They even give you a shopping cart to hurry you along on your shopping adventure. The people-greeters give you the feeling that you are part of the Wal-Mart family and they are glad you stopped by. They are trained to treat you like a neighbor because they want you to think of Wal-Mart as your neighborhood store. Sam called this approach to customer service "aggressive hospitality." He found that going the extra yard for the customers and showing concern for their needs increased the likelihood of their returning again and again to shop his stores. Interestingly enough, a secondary responsibility of a people-greeter is to watch people coming and going to prevent theft—or in retail terms, shrinkage.

It's great customer psychology if you think about it. The customers are in a positive frame of mind from the moment they cross the threshold of the store. I'm sure studies would bear out the fact that people who feel good about the shopping experience have a tendency to shop longer and buy more products. From smiley-faced signage to brightly colored rollback signs, around every corner awaits a surprise for the customer of Wal-Mart's stores. It turns the mundane task of shopping the store into an adventure. It drives impulse buying and encourages full shopping carts at the register. Lagniappe is just a little bit more of something you were never expecting, but that Wal-Mart knows you're going to enjoy.

Lagniappe is a way to add customer-perceived value to the shopping experience at very little cost to the company. As an example, Sam Walton used to encourage store associates to smile at customers. He said that smiling costs nothing but shows you care and enriches the receiver. He wanted associates to treat customers like their friends, neighbors, or guests. Lagniappe breeds goodwill, positive customer relations, and most importantly higher sales. Sam Walton was a very smart man. He figured out a powerful way to build relationships with customers and a simple way to communicate that concept to his management team. The use of lagniappe by Wal-Mart's store teams provides competitors with a customer-service challenge to be reckoned with. So from an employee-relations standpoint lagniappe costs nothing but pays big dividends.

The customer-service tactics at Wal-Mart are full of opportunities for lagniappe. They include: a greeting, a smile, the offer of a shopping cart, eye contact, enthusiastically asking "may I help you," using good active listening skills, knowing the store and where product is located, taking customers to the product requested, quickly getting customers through the registers, and thanking customers for their business. Lagniappe is also meticulously threaded through and through the surprising array of products and prices offered throughout the store. The resulting customer shopping frenzy is something to behold!

Unless you've personally observed and experienced shopping at a Wal-Mart Supercenter during the Christmas season, you can't truly appreciate the fanaticism of its shoppers. The experience begins stressfully as you approach the store in search of the most elusive commodity of all . . . a parking space. You find yourself in a battle with experienced drivers piloting minivans and pickup trucks of every type whose owners are bound and determined to race around the lot to get a parking space before you do. New York commuters would blush at the rudeness experienced in rural towns across America as normally friendly small-town folk become ravenous shoppers in a feeding frenzy. They are prepared to risk it all to get into the store as fast as they can, and you are taking your life into your own hands if you get between them and their parking spaces. The excitement doesn't end there.

Watching customers shop in a Wal-Mart store is like watching a search for buried treasure. You'd think they'd never shopped the store before as they scour the aisles searching for new products or lower prices on existing ones. They are armed with their wobbly wheeled shopping carts, and God have mercy on fellow shoppers who venture into a crosswalk without looking both ways. If that happens to you, you're likely to get run down by wild-eyed, deal-seeking shopping fanatics intent on filling their carts with products produced in exotic places like India, China, and Malaysia. By the time their discount-induced trances are over they are pulling into their driveways at home, wondering where all the time went. Spouses will ask them later why they bought this or that and the reply will be, "Because I couldn't pass it up at that price."

I believe the entire shopping experience at Wal-Mart is a form of lagniappe. Everywhere you turn in the store there is a little something extra: a lowered price, a bin of too-good-to-be-true bargains that you have never seen before. Shopping in a Supercenter, for some, is a 200,000-square-foot escape from reality adventure. It's not as much a shopping trip as it is some sort of Neanderthal hunter-gatherer exercise after which customers arrive home triumphant with their bounty. The hunt rarely ends until the shopping cart is filled to the brim with bargains the family just can't live without. Stories of the trials and tribulations of the hunt are shared within the family enclave as if the provider had some sort of Darwinian near-death experience. The stories and trophies of the successful hunt for bargains are talked about with pride long after the shopping adventure and these stories are the stuff that family folklore is made of.

I think that much of the customer-service experience in the store can be traced back to Sam's belief in the importance of lagniappe. You see, lagniappe is Wal-Mart's way of bringing the concept of exceeding the customer's expectations to life. When questioned about Wal-Mart's secrets of success, Sam Walton has been quoted as saying, "It has to do with our desire to exceed our customers' expectations every hour of every day."[1] So imbedded within the concept of lagniappe is the foundation of one of the great secrets of Wal-Mart's success in customer service. Sam was careful to never over-promise and under-deliver to the customers, erring instead on the side of under-promising and over-delivering. This is another one of Wal-Mart's simple ideas that you can immediately implement in your business. I will tell you in advance that like much of what Wal-Mart does this simple technique is easy to understand yet hard to duplicate.

Sam Walton studied the teachings of W. Edwards Deming, one of the gurus of the total-quality movement, who taught the Japanese the ways and means of improving their productivity and competitiveness through focusing on continuous improvement. Sam even traveled to Japan where he learned many valuable customer-service lessons from Deming.[2] I believe his beliefs about lagniappe and exceeding customer expectations were also influenced by his exposure to Japanese businesspeople.

The Japanese believe in and practice a concept quite similar to lagniappe called *kikubari*. Kikubari is defined as the ability to anticipate the needs of others. For businesses it represents a cultural quest for world-class excellence in products, employees, and service. Kikubari, as a customer-service concept, gives Japanese consumers the comfort of knowing that someone back at the manufacturing plant producing the products is looking out for them. Kikubari is one of the most important skills Japanese workers must learn to be successful in their business lives. Kikubari represents an outside-in approach to outstanding employee relations, quality product development, and exceptional customer service. It might sound funny that a backwoods retailer from the Ozark mountains would embrace the business philosophies of the Japanese and Deming, but I believe that's exactly what happened.

Whether or not you embrace the concepts of lagniappe and kikubari, the point is that you need to focus on anticipating, meeting, and exceeding your customer's expectations. The only way I know to get that done is through a motivated staff of employees. How can you expect your employees to look out for the needs of customers if your company managers don't look out for the needs of the people tasked with serving those customers? If you can culturally capture the spirit of lagniappe or kikubari in your own company you'll be embracing one of the greatest secrets of the Wal-Mart culture, which is: If you take care of your people, your people will take care of the customer and the business will take care of itself. Sam Walton knew that sales will follow if the focus is properly placed on proper treatment of employees who in turn will treat the customers right.

Retailers that are public companies have always been haunted by the periodic reporting of their same-store sales or comparable-store (comp-store) sales numbers, which are published for all to see each month. Same-store sales measure the results of stores open for more than a year and are an indicator of how the company itself is performing as well as how it is faring against its competition. Comp-store sales provide company investors and company leaders with an apples-to-apples comparison of this month's sales with the same month's sales from a year ago. Data across the industry are then used to compare each retailer's comp-store sales growth against competitive trends. Companies' stocks rise and fall on the periodic reporting of their comp-store sales figures.

When Wal-Mart comes into a market and begins generating sales it is the comp-store numbers of local competitors that suffer. Mom-and-Pop retailers are impacted more so than chain store operators. Chain stores are better able to absorb the impact of lost sales in their total sales across the company.

I can remember the emotional roller-coaster ride at American Eagle Outfitters following our IPO. As a public retail company we were thrown into Wall Street's fishbowl for the first time along with companies like Gap, Abercrombie and Fitch, Eddie Bauer, and others. Our headquarters developed an emotional personality, which was upbeat and optimistic when our comp numbers were positive and downright pessimistic when the comp numbers fell.

Our company executives became paranoid, sweating bullets each time the numbers were about to be reported. Panicked by the possibility of a falling stock price, company executives participating in investor conference calls resorted to telling our investors about future growth plans and strategies. Months later when comp-store performance levels weren't achieved the stock price would drop precipitously, more than our poor performance warranted, because of lost confidence on the part of investors.

We learned an important lesson the hard way. When it came to Wall Street we needed to let our numbers speak for themselves. Over-promising and under-delivering to Wall Street is the sure path to financial misery. As I recall, our company stock had a value of sixteen dollars a share on the day of the IPO and rose quickly to around twenty-seven dollars. As our comp-store numbers began to falter the stock dropped in a short period of time to about five dollars a share. We quickly learned to take a long-term perspective and began to under-promise and over-deliver. Our executives had learned that there is a relationship between company performance and stock value that "is what it is." We didn't need to talk a good game, we needed to play a good game and let the results speak for themselves. Back-to-back-to-back quarters of steady and profitable sales growth are the only necessary things to build confidence in a company's stock. In the following years American Eagle Outfitters stock rose steadily, splitting four times. In the process, I learned that fear of failure is an excellent motivator of leaders to achieve financial results.

I was always impressed at Wal-Mart with the long-term perspective company leaders took on the performance of the company and its stock. The focus is placed on the things the company can control and efforts are made to do whatever possible to manage costs and increase product sales. Wal-Mart reports domestic comp-store sales increases for the past ten years: five percent in 2002, six percent in 2001, five percent in 2000, eight percent in 1999, nine percent in 1998, six percent in 1997, five percent in 1996, four percent in 1995, seven percent in 1994, and six percent in 1993. This is the kind of consistent performance Wall Street investors want to see and the 11 two-for-one stock splits are evidence of investor confidence.[3]

Sam Walton built Wal-Mart into the company it is by living the following philosophy: Sam said, "There is only one boss—the customer—and he or she can fire everybody in the company from the chairman down, simply by spending his or her money elsewhere." In reality, in any business, you need your customers much more than those customers need you. Repeat business is the key to increasing sales consistently, quarter after quarter, year after year. Great service is a key component in achieving great sales.

In a *Time Europe* article entitled "Inside the World's Biggest Store," Bill Saporito writes, " 'We (Wal-Mart) could write a training manual about our experiences in Germany,' Lee Scott [Wal-Mart CEO] says. 'We really did more things wrong than right.' German consumers love low grocery prices, which would make them the perfect clientele for Wal-Mart, but they, too, experienced culture shock when confronted by Southern hospitality. Germans found Wal-Mart's famous door greeters appalling, and they don't want to be approached by ever-helpful clerks in the stores— it's considered an intrusion."[4] As Wal-Mart has learned internationally, when it comes to customer service one size doesn't fit all!

Globally, business competition is changing rapidly and not just in retailing. I remember an anecdote about the book *In Search of Excellence*,[5] which was written over twenty years ago. Eighty percent of the companies highlighted in that book have merged, failed, or gone out of business! As you think about your own business, ask yourself the question, "What strategies and tactics are we implementing today to insure our success in the future?" If your initial thought in response to that question is, "We intend to do things the same way we have always have done them," then think again. The retail paradigm has shifted and past success is no guarantee of future success.

Recently I was personally confronted by a global business change in retailing as I ordered my wife a gift from the Franklin Mint gift catalogue. Franklin Mint has brick-and-mortar stores located in shopping malls and it sells collectibles for the mass market. On this particular day I called its 800 number to place an order. I found out that the woman who processed my order worked in a call center halfway around the world in New Delhi. I was calling at three in the afternoon East Coast time and the phone was answered in India at 1:30 A.M. Because of the time-zone difference I was literally making a telephone call to place an order "today" and that order was being instantaneously processed "tomorrow"! The order was processed flawlessly and I quickly received an e-mail confirmation.

I was a bit surprised that a specialty retailer the size of Franklin Mint would have the call volume to justify setting up a phone center in India. I decided to call Wal-Mart's toll-free number to check out its Wal-Mart Connect® $9.94-per-month Internet service and at the same time check out how it handles phone traffic. As it turns out I was instantaneously connected to a call center in Bangalore, the Silicon Valley of India. The call-center employee spoke perfect English and handled my questions concerning setting up an Internet account without fanfare.

These two examples illustrate how the world we live in is shrinking. With the evolution of satellite-communication technologies for phone and computer evolving rapidly, businesses are able to leverage lower costs around the world. The cost savings associated with setting up call centers in places like India are substantial. The unfortunate byproduct of global expansion is of course the loss of American jobs. You could say that our loss is their gain in standard of living.

Advances in technology have also allowed significant improvements to services provided to technologically savvy consumers. Here's an example of one such customer-service technology advance from the con-venience-store industry. A little over a decade ago all customers who pur-chased gasoline at a convenience store had to walk inside to pay, creating impulse-purchase opportunities. Today, with credit-card-scanning tech-nology, gasoline customers may never walk inside the store again. Steve Sheetz said;

> "About 60 percent of gasoline purchasers at convenience stores pay with cash inside the store versus 40 percent who swipe a credit card at the pump. "About one-third of those who come inside make a purchase and two-thirds don't. It costs $8,000 per card reader and dispenser per pump to put it in. We put an average of eight of those in, so it's like $64,000 per store. So let's see now, I get to spend $64,000 and for that I get less cus-tomers coming inside. Well a lot of people in the convenience-store indus-try didn't embrace it, they said that's crazy, we're not spending that, but that's what the customer wants. It doesn't matter how far you analyze it, the customer doesn't want to come in. It's really about whether you are truly customer-driven and willing to spend the money. I'll tell you it's a

lot of money to put in those card readers but it is a customer expectation and you're either going to have them or go out of business."

As the industry changes and existing customer-service expectations change, retailers have to adapt their service philosophies accordingly. Failing to do so is a certain path to a slow and lingering death for your business. Chester Cadieux, chairman of Quik Trip Corporation, put it this way: "There is still tremendous growth possible. You have to push categories, give people selection and price. I believe in execution, doing the basics right over and over and over again, besting the competition in service, value, and price. If you're thirsty, that's an immediate need with immediate gratification. It's the kind of society we live in. Give people what they want."

A study was published by Coopers and Lybrand capturing the beliefs of 407 of the CEOs of the fastest-growing U.S. companies. Those CEOs are taking the mantra "the customer is king" to heart. Eight in ten cite quality of customer service as very important to the growth of their businesses. Among other things, the CEOs were asked the question, "What is most important to sustaining growth?" According to the results of the Coopers and Lybrand study, "84 percent agreed quality customer service outweighs everything including new products, advertising and sales promotion, technology, strategic alliances and business acquisitions."[6] This is good news for retail companies. There is no single component of the customer experience over which they have more control than service. Unfortunately, this is also the area where many retailers fall short of their customers' expectations.

Wal-Mart's 2001 Annual Report discusses a renewed focus on customer service through a concept called "retailtainment:"

> "Wal-Mart understands that today's consumers have an incredible array of shopping choices from which to choose. Not only do they want the best value for their hard-earned dollar, but they also demand outstanding customer service. We realized early on that we must take care of Customers and that part of doing so is creating a fun, dynamic shopping environment. At Wal-Mart, we call the concept retailtainment and our goal is to add excitement to the shopping experience. The result is a fun environment for the Customers and our Associates, but other benefits include increased customer traffic and loyalty because that Customer looks forward to their trip to Wal-Mart. Every store is encouraged to create its own 'wild and crazy' retailtainment events specifically designed for its individual community."

Retailtainment is another form of customer-service lagniappe. Wal-Mart's executives obviously know the importance of customer service to increasing company sales and profitability. Wal-Mart is known as a place where prices are low and value and service are high.

The customer-service standards at Wal-Mart have an internal-customer component and an external-customer component. The definition of external-customer service is what you'd expect—the care and feeding of the customers crossing the thresholds of Wal-Mart stores. The definition of internal-customer service is using the same high standards for treating fellow employees that companies use to treat their external customers. The concept of setting high internal-customer service standards is somewhat foreign to many organizations. Some in actuality have a double standard of treating customers well and fellow employees just so-so. Not at Wal-Mart.

The philosophy of internal and external customer service at Wal-Mart could be boiled down to one action which is to drop everything for the customer. This drop-everything philosophy is the cornerstone of the customer service in Wal-Mart stores. However, the drop everything philosophy also pertains to internal customer service between associates, departments, and even vendor partners. I was always surprised by the friendly and cooperative nature of the people working in other departments in the headquarters who would drop what they were doing to help you. Keep in mind that every associate in the Home Office, distribution centers, and stores has more to do in a given day than will ever get done. That makes it all the more amazing that other associates stop what they are doing to help you; but that's what internal customer service is all about. In their internal-customer service relationships with one another, Wal-Mart employees operate with integrity. Internal customer service wasn't something they just talked about, it was something I saw happening every day.

In most companies, if you ask another department for help with solving a problem or assistance that only it can provide, you are likely to hear a litany of excuses as to why it can't help you. This does not happen at Wal-Mart. Its internal customer-service standards remind me of the philosophy of the Three Musketeers, "All for one, one for all." If you need help from another department or function all you have to do is ask and the associates from that department will immediately drop everything regardless of how busy they are. As I grew to understand and embrace the cultural values of Wal-Mart, I found I did everything I could to reciprocate when requests were made of me by others, even when those requests caused me to take time away from other important work for which I would personally be held accountable. The cultural adaptive measure for everyone was to work more hours in an effort to catch up.

Now why does internal customer service happen at Wal-Mart and not at many other companies? It all comes down to customer-service standards. At Wal-Mart it's not okay to tell one of your internal customers you don't have time to help, just as it would be unacceptable to say that to a customer in the store. I know from my own firsthand experiences working in other Fortune 500 companies how unusual Wal-Mart's internal customer-service standards truly are. It's not a "program du jour;" associates embrace internal and external customer-service standards enthusiastically each and every day.

So how do you get your own people to commit to serving your internal and external customers to this level? Wal-Mart measures customer service and ties rewards to it. All performance reviews are tied to customer-service indicators. Both internal customer service and external customer service are measured in these reviews. Wal-Mart was one of the first companies to implement 360-degree performance reviews including internal customer-service feedback from supervisors, subordinates and cross-functional internal customers. What you measure is what gets done. That managers are expected to model good customer-service behaviors for the associates reporting to them is an example of Wal-Mart's servant-leadership philosophy.

The key to customer service are those one-on-one transactions out on the floor between your customers and your employees. They happen hundreds of times every week, and at those moments of truth do your employees clearly understand your expectations for service? What have you done to program service into the DNA of your culture? Here's a customer-service cultural-integration idea I learned from the Foodland grocery chain. It took the word "customer" and turned it into an employee-communication acronym:

- Courtesy—Customers want to be treated like invited guests. Welcome them to the store
- Understand—You make a difference, you create the store personality
- Smile—It takes more effort to frown
- Talk—Converse as if the customer were your friend
- Offer a greeting if you are within ten feet of a customer
- Make it easy for the customer; be positive
- Enjoy what you are doing and it will show
- Remember—We treat the customer like gold. The customer is the most important person in the store!

Regardless of how you do it, communicating your customer-service standards to your employees and executing them has to become a way of life in your stores. The entire shopping experience is the store's customer-service experience. The quality of service should make a statement about your brand. Everything should be choreographed to work in harmony to create a seamless service experience for each and every customer.

When customers are in your store, make your service standards like those in the theater. When the curtain goes up, it's showtime. It's time to meet and exceed expectations. Your audience is the customers who keep you in business. If you don't do a good job of meeting their needs they'll vote with their feet. Customers expect to be treated well and will go elsewhere if they aren't. Unfortunately, one customer with a bad experience will tell lots of other people how he or she was treated, whereas a customer who receives good service probably won't tell a lot of people about the experience. But if you truly exceed the customers' expectations, they may toot your horn to everyone they meet.

I asked Kerley LeBoeuf from NACS about the importance of valuing employees to the creation of a service culture and he said,

> "I think it is important to have a human-resource program that is superior. You can go into a McDonalds and you can say if they are wearing that little outfit and that cap it doesn't make any difference who is there but that's not totally true. It could be the person running the register changes from shift to shift or from day to day but the right human-resource program will get you clean restrooms, it will get your product fronted, it will keep your parking lot clean and that sort of thing. If I was coaching folks I'd say you need to look at payroll as an investment not an expense. If you have the best people and the best service and the friendliest folks you don't have to have the best price. A lot of people will go out of their way a little bit to go into a place, kind of like Cheers, where everybody knows your name. Convenience stores must 'out-convenience and out-friendly' competitors like Wal-Mart."

Wal-Mart is known for its folksy southern hospitality. Everybody's on a first-name basis. All the associates at Wal-Mart wear name badges with their first names proudly displayed for the world to see. Every hourly associate, manager, and executive wears one. Sam Walton's badge simply said "Sam." Associates are also encouraged to use the names of their regular customers in order to personalize their customer service. Sam's Club associates are able to thank each and every customer by name since the Sam's Club membership card includes the member's picture and name. It's also easy to find the customer's name on his or her credit card or check. Again the goal is to treat the customer like a neighbor or to create the perception that Wal-Mart is the customer's neighborhood store. Customer-service training at Wal-Mart is also quite folksy, focusing on smiling at and being friendly to all the customers.

One of the culturally ingrained service standards of Wal-Mart is the Ten-Foot Rule or Ten-Foot Attitude. The Ten-Foot Rule simply means that whenever an associate comes within ten feet of a customer the associate is to smile and make eye contact, greet that customer, and ask if he or she can help the customer find anything. The associate is supposed to drop everything in order to focus on the customer.

Another customer-service mainstay of the Wal-Mart culture is the Sundown Rule, which is another way of saying, "Don't put off until tomorrow what you can do today." It demands that all associates respond to requests from internal and external customers on the same day on which they are received. I had a Sundown Rule poster prominently displayed in my office as a constant reminder to me to follow through on my commitments to get back to my customers that day. It is a difficult standard to achieve and impossible in an eight to five workday. It did create a tremendous sense of urgency around every request, whether it was an A priority or a C priority. This standard made the end of every workday as focused and frenetic as the beginning. People had a tendency to come to work early and stay late. A seven to seven work day wasn't all that unusual for salaried employees intent on living up to the lofty standards of the Sundown Rule.

One of the most important cultural anchors of Wal-Mart's customer-service standards is the company cheer. The first place I personally heard and participated in the Wal-Mart Cheer was at a Saturday morning meeting. Imagine bringing together your leadership team on a Saturday morning at the crack of dawn and asking them to do a company cheer. I don't think you'd find the managers at most companies too receptive. At Wal-Mart they cheer enthusiastically at the top of their lungs, often while standing on their chairs!

In describing the point of the Wal-Mart Cheer, Sam Walton is quoted on the Wal-Mart web site as saying, "My feeling is that just because we work so hard, we don't have to go around with long faces all the time— while we're doing all of this work, we like to have a good time. It's sort of a 'whistle while you work' philosophy, and we not only have a heck of a good time with it, we work better because of it. We love to have fun, we do work hard, and we always remember whom we're doing it for—the customer." The cheer always ends with the question, Who is number one? to which every Wal-Mart Associate hollers "THE CUSTOMER...ALWAYS!"

If you walk into a Wal-Mart store anywhere in the world you have a chance of experiencing a Wal-Mart cheer in any of eight different languages. Because of the 24/7/365 operating standards of most stores, the manager has no choice but to conduct a team meeting, every day, in the front of the store while customers are milling around. The cheer is a public celebration and demonstration of Wal-Mart's commitment to service for all to see. To this day, the cheer provides communication of the service philosophies as new associates are added to the team. There is no confusion as to who is number one at Wal-Mart... the CUSTOMER!

Wal-Mart and Sam Walton were influenced years ago by a Norwalk, Connecticut, grocery store called Stew Leonard's. Advertised as the worlds largest dairy store, Stew Leonard's is known for its innovative practices with respect to customer service: It was an early innovator of customer focus-group meetings and customer-suggestion programs. Today, Stew Leonard's conducts two-hour public seminars on customer service, sharing its innovative customer and employee practices to outsiders for $295 per participant.[7]

Sam often quoted a customer-service saying he learned from Stew Leonard's that goes like this: "Rule number one is that the customer is always right, rule number two is that if the customer is wrong refer to rule number one." This saying is taught to all managers during the Walton Institute training program and forms the basis of Wal-Mart's aggressive product guarantees and customer-service philosophies. How often do you conduct meetings with your employees to reinforce your service standards? I'll bet you don't do it every day. Do you hold meetings once a week? Wal-Mart is reinforcing its service culture every day. That's how the company keeps service the foremost priority and the responsibility of everyone in the store, even when it has as much as 300 percent turnover!

Customer Satisfaction is guaranteed at Wal-Mart. The company believes that the majority of customers are fair. So to satisfy complaints, associates are trained to ask the customer, "What would you like us to do to fix the problem?"... and then the associates are empowered to fix it. They use the golden rule to satisfy their customers.

In life and in business, what you think about most of the time is what you become. Allow me to illustrate this point with a real-life example. My wife, Sheryl, and I made a decision to send our daughter, Heather, to Sylvan Learning Centers to focus on developing strong mathematical skills. Heather started going to Sylvan for math training in the fifth grade and continued going all the way through high school. When she took the Scholastic Aptitude Test (SAT) she scored 610 on math as a junior! Her score in math placed her in the 80th percentile of college bound seniors nationwide! What she focused on and thought about was becoming a math wizard and that's exactly what she has become.

The same singularity of focus works just as well in business. At Wal-Mart they constantly think about providing low prices, superior service, and satisfied customers, and that's what they deliver. I believe a large portion of the success achieved in life and in business is a direct result of starting your thought process with the end—a successful outcome—in mind. If you believe you can do something, you can do it and if you believe you can't, you can't. Competitors of Wal-Mart have to believe that they can compete effectively to have the best chance of being successful. Anything less than that level of belief and commitment has to lead to a bad outcome.

Focusing on providing the right products and outstanding customer service to your targeted customer is really the key to the retail ballgame. The small retailer actually has an advantage over the big-box stores in their community in their ability to provide locally-tailored products and personalized service. The bread and butter of the local merchant is and always has been their knowledge of each and every customer and with that knowledge comes the ability to exceed their customers' expectations. By doing so and providing a diverse, broader array of products and services, a competitor of Wal-Mart cannot only survive but thrive.

I asked John Morrison, the state director of the Missouri Grocers Association, about customer shopping preferences and he said, "There are some people who don't mind shopping in a 200,000-square-foot store; there are others who don't want to shop in a 200,000-square-foot store. I think there is a lot of education that needs to go out so the consumer can make up their mind where they want to shop and how often they want to shop." But smaller competitors need to beware!

Wal-Mart is coming to a neighborhood near you with a smaller, more convenient, 40,000- to 55,000-square foot store called Neighborhood Market. 75 percent smaller than a Supercenter, these stores are designed to grab market share from traditional grocery stores and convenience stores. The stores carry 28,000 items including: fresh meat, produce, dairy products, deli foods, fresh fruits, and vegetables.

In a *Wall Street Journal* article, Louise Lee writes, "In building smaller stores, Wal-Mart is also acknowledging that giant stores require a commitment of time and energy that shoppers don't always have."[8] "We lost a lot of customers because the Supercenter is too busy and not convenient," says Wal-Mart Senior Vice President Jay Fitzsimmons. "Where we're losing sales is to the grocery stores" and other small stores.

Wal-Mart hopes that the strategy shift will help it move into new areas, from very small towns to metropolitan areas, that are too small for a Supercenter or couldn't support another large store." We want to address those markets where we couldn't get a Supercenter in," Mr. Fitzsimmons says.

Wal-Mart has toyed with the idea of building smaller "neighbor-hood stores" for several years, trying to design an outlet that would fit somewhere between a Supercenter, which lacks convenience, and an old-fashioned convenience store, which doesn't stock enough to allow low prices."

More than fifty Neighborhood Market Stores have already been opened in seven states, including Utah, Florida, Texas, Arkansas, Tennessee, Oklahoma, and Alabama. Half of the stores are located in Texas. Wal-Mart has approached the design and rollout of this new concept store very carefully, taking over five years to test various store designs.

Mike Troy reports in *DSN Retailing Today*, "The prototype Neighborhood Market store Wal-Mart opened a year ago in Rogers, Arkansas, was lauded as an improvement over earlier versions because of its reduced construction and operating costs and improved merchandising. And most aspects of the store design, construction materials, product mix, and service offerings remain intact. For example, the Dallas and Oviedo stores retained the industrial appearance of the Rogers prototype, including bare concrete floors, exposed and unpainted ceilings, and galvanized refrigerated fixtures. They also offer one-hour photo processing, a drive-through pharmacy and the unique Grab 'n Go department inside the store's entrance where customers pay for coffee, doughnuts, and newspapers on the honor system."[9]

Using Supercenter and convenience together has always been an oxymoron. For customers, shopping a 200,000-square-foot store is both time-consuming and physically exhausting. The Neighborhood Market, however, is designed with customer convenience in mind. Easy access close to home, small enough to get in and out of quickly, enhanced service, and low Wal-Mart prices create a convenient shopping experience for the time-strapped consumer. With its Neighborhood Market concept Wal-Mart will capture a larger share of the local urban grocery store and convenience store market close to where the customers live.

Whether it's a discount store, Supercenter, Sam's Club, or Neighborhood Market you can bet Wal-Mart is working on ways to take customers away from you. In an NHPR broadcast entitled, "Plymouth Adapts to Wal-Mart," Shannon Mullen described how one small New England town was forever changed when Wal-Mart came to town.

Steve Rand owns a hardware store that's been on Main Street in downtown Plymouth for more than one hundred years. The store weathered two World Wars and the Great Depression. But Rand has found himself on a new front—this time he's up against the world's largest retailer and the convenience of one-stop shopping. It's another war, it's a different war, Wal-Mart is a big outfit, very efficient, tough competitors. They're a little on the predatory side.

Wal-Mart opened a Supercenter in Plymouth almost one year ago, a few miles outside of town, on the Tenney Mountain Highway. The store's managers make sure their prices are always lower than Rand's. That means competition for customers comes down to service. We've been changing our business to make it Wal-Mart-proof by segmenting our business, the kinds of things that are not duplicable. Our plumbing department is famous. If you have a plumbing problem, you see us. Our rental department is a very strong part of our business. We rent everything from backhoes to bolt-cutters. From tents to fountains for your wedding. So it's a very complete, service-oriented business. It takes good people and it's not something Wal-Mart can do.

Clare Moorhead is executive director of the Plymouth Chamber of Commerce. She says the competition from Wal-Mart has several downtown businesses looking for a niche. They're trying to get the same group of customers but that's kind of what being in business is all about, you know free enterprise.[10]

If Wal-Mart's arrival in town is the catalyst for your business to start improving customer service, it is in all likelihood too late. A good merchant by definition should have been providing great service to customers already. Once the big box arrives it is too late to atone for past service sins and you will experience payback from customers who are well aware that they have been historically slighted. When you were the only store in town your customers were forced to shop there, but not anymore. In small towns across America, and the world for that matter, Mom-and-Pop operators who failed to serve their customers have been forced to close their doors upon the arrival of Wal-Mart. In many cases they didn't have to shut down as they had a viable retail concept that could have survived. But higher prices coupled with lackluster customer service causes customers to seek other alternatives. Not serving the customer is a fatal flaw in retailing that will cause your business to fail. That's a basic lesson taught in Marketing 101!

Customers who have a positive experience with a business are likely to continue shopping there, even if the prices are a bit higher. Providing terrific service may be the single most important element to retaining your customers when Wal-Mart arrives. One loyal customer is worth big bucks to any company. My wife Sheryl's weekly $200 grocery receipt is a good indication of the value of one good grocery customer. Over a year's time she spends over $10,000 at the local grocery store to feed our family of four. When the construction of the Wal-Mart Supercenter is completed about six miles from our home, she plans to begin shopping there. Over the next ten years, the business she is taking from the low-service, overpriced grocery store where she currently shops will be worth over $100,000! If she can save ten percent on our groceries at the Supercenter, that represents a potential savings to our family of $10,000 cash over the next ten years. Good service and lower prices is a hard combination to beat.

What are the values of the Wal-Mart customer? Fred Martels, president of People Solutions Strategies, recently published the results of his January 2003 Wal-Mart Supercenter Customer Loyalty Study and was kind enough to send me a copy. In his survey, he focused on critical variables that have an impact on the customer's decision to continue shopping at Wal-Mart. Table 7-1 shows the results of the customers' values in order of priority:

"A customer's consistent total shopping experience drives loyalty," says Martels. "Customers become loyal and feel compelled to shop with a particular store when they consistently receive exceptional value, and have consistent experiences."[11]

There are a number of lessons every retailer can learn from this survey. The top five customer-ranked values are price, in-stock products, product quality, product variety, and treating customers with respect. If you take each of the values from this survey and honestly evaluate the perception of your own customers about your organization you have the framework for developing a focused and competitive customer-service

Table 7-1

Customer Values	Extremely Important (%)	Neutral (%)	Extremely Unimportant (%)
#1 Competitive prices	96	3	1
#2 In-stock products	94	6	0
#3 Product quality/Freshness	92	6	2
#4 Product variety	89	9	2
#5 Treat customers with respect	89	8	3
#6 Enough staff to serve	87	11	2
#7 Store conditions	87	12	1
#8 Pleasant place to shop	87	12	1
#9 Friendly employees	89	8	3
#10 Capable employees	84	13	3
#11 Helpful managers	80	16	4
#12 Advertised specials	81	12	7
#13 Close to my home	75	20	5
#14 Customer recognition	67%	28%	5%

strategy. Within each of these elements lies an opportunity for you to establish standards to compete more effectively.

Competitive prices—Not too hard to believe that this was ranked number one by Wal-Mart's customers. As a competitor, you can't afford to get into a price war. You will lose trying to play that game. Do whatever you can to control expenses and negotiate well with your suppliers. Differentiate your product lines to avoid direct competition on the same or similar products. Understand how your customers view your prices and service in terms of why they continue to shop your store. Do shopping-cart comparisons of your competitors' pricing structures to stay competitive. Stay in touch with how satisfied your customers are with the perceived value your products provide.

In-stock products—Nothing is more frustrating for the customer than for you to be out of stock on a given item. One of Wal-Mart's towering strengths is product replenishment. Because of its sophisticated technology, vendor partnerships, and strategically located distribution centers it is good at backfilling the shelves. The breakdown at Wal-Mart typically occurs at the local level when department managers or store associates are slow to remerchandise product. As good as it is, just walk around a Wal-Mart store and you will see holes in its merchandising. You can't afford to be out of stock due to back-ordered product. You also need to remerchandise your shelves throughout the sales day. Nothing else matters if you are out of stock, because being out of stock is equal to being out of business.

Product quality—Wal-Mart's low-price strategy has also led to lower-quality products. In groceries you have a real opportunity to consistently provide products that are fresher and of a higher quality. Customers perceive value in higher quality products and for that reason are willing to pay premium prices. That has been the key to the success of high-priced brands like Frito-Lay. There are cheaper potato chips but premium-priced Frito-Lay products continue to garner 50 percent market shares in many cities across the country. Herein lies an opportunity for you to offer a selection of low-, medium- and higher-end products to satisfy a cross-section of consumer expectations. Whether you are selling potato chips or vacuum cleaners there are consumers willing to pay a premium for higher-quality merchandise that just isn't available at Wal-Mart.

Product variety—Cater to local tastes and consider expanding the products within a category so that you have products not offered at Wal-Mart. Customers like variety and selection. Wal-Mart has space limitations within specific categories and because of sheer size can't identify and buy to local preferences. If you sell T-shirts, offer a wide selection including low, medium, and high price points. Carry unique designs and purchase the technology required to create custom designs. Create your niche and become known as the destination store for T-shirts in your community. This type of strategy also gets you out of direct competition on price.

Treat customers with respect—One of the key competitive advantages of a small business has always been its ability to provide personalized service to the customer. This is the ball game. If a retailer has to begin treating its customers with respect after Wal-Mart arrives it shouldn't have been in the retail business in the first place. Steal a page from Wal-Mart's playbook by treating your customers like guests when they cross your threshold. Each customer presents you with a unique customer-service moment of truth. Capitalize on every opportunity to show your customers you care.

Enough staff to serve the customer—Wandering around a retail store searching for help is a frustrating experience for retail customers. This is an area in which you need to excel. Teach your team to approach customers enthusiastically. Indifference toward customers is a sure way to lose business. You have the opportunity to be more selective than Wal-Mart in hiring your employees. Capitalize on that advantage by selecting higher-quality people.

Store conditions—Bathrooms need to be clean for your customer's use. Lighting should be bright and bulbs all in working order. Floors need to be noticeably clean. Aisles must be clear of carts of restock merchandise. Make sure aisles are wide enough for easy navigation. If you meet the wheelchair-accessibility standards your aisles are going to be satisfactory.

Pleasant place to shop—Music to match the tastes of your targeted customer provides a welcome feeling. The majority of shelf restocking should be done when customer traffic is lowest, preferably before or after store hours. Well-priced merchandise with clear signage reduces customer stress. Appropriately dressed employees with a professional demeanor add credibility to the store.

Friendly employees—Your employees need to sincerely welcome and smile at all the customers as they enter the store and mention in-store promotional merchandise to them. Approach customers and provide assistance if they need it. Require all of your employees to understand your store layout so that they can help customers find products. Train them to walk customers directly to requested products wherever those products may be in your store. Thank your customers for shopping whether they make a purchase or not.

Capable employees—How do your employees stack up? Provide employee sales and service training each and every week. Before the store opens is a great time to teach employees, when their energy is at its peak.

Throughout the sales day there are always slack periods of time when few customers venture in. Use slack sales times to your advantage by providing your employees with product knowledge, so they can meet and even exceed your customer's expectations. It only takes a couple of minutes to conduct a standup sales clinic on an individual product. Make it fun for your employees to learn the features and benefits of your unique products. Teach basic retail selling skills to all your employees. One technique, "tactile involvement," is about getting products into the hands of your customers. When customers actually touch your products, the chances of them purchasing those products goes up geometrically. Sunglasses in a display case won't sell unless your employees get those customers who peer into the case to try a pair on and look in the mirror. When that occurs magical things begin to happen; products sell like hotcakes.

Another great retail selling technique is add-on selling. Teach your employees to suggest compatible or complimentary product to one already in the cart of the customer. Suggest socks to the customer to go with the shoes they've already selected or a belt with pants. At the register employees should always review the customer's purchases and in a helpful way suggest another item that the customer may have missed. I am always impressed with McDonald's drive-through window employees from San Francisco to Sanibel who consistently use suggestive selling techniques, asking every customer, "Would you like a cherry pie with your order today?"

Helpful managers—The store management team needs to constantly model customer-service behaviors for the employees. In some stores, managers are held directly accountable for executing a significant percentage of the total daily sales themselves. In small stores the merchant does it all, from cleaning up spills to selling and cashiering. Your managers should walk the customer-service talk by actively participating in customer-service activity throughout the day. Show me a manager who is above customer service and I'll show you a manager ill-suited for retailing.

Advertised specials—Nothing attracts customers and creates store traffic like advertising promotional product. Coupons, bag stuffers, mail-outs, and newspaper ads are all great means of creating retail excitement. Customers love advertised specials, so buy deep. Work with your suppliers to develop a calendar of promotional product events throughout the year.

Close to my home—Wal-Mart's customers are willing to drive a considerable distance to shop. Your advantage may be that you are located closer to your customers' homes. That's called convenience. If you are near a Wal-Mart, try to leverage the additional customer traffic that comes to town from outlying areas.

Customer recognition—Do what you can to personalize the relationship with your customers. Get to know your repeat customers by name and use their names. Creating a friendly neighborhood-store environment is something you can do. Familiarity builds customer loyalty.

Most of these fourteen customer-ranked values are tactical-execution issues easily within the control of the local store team. Develop your own customer-service strategies around them. With that thought in mind you need to be prepared to make changes well ahead of Wal-Mart's arrival. Shop one of its current stores and compare and contrast the product offerings with those of your business. Develop a product-differentiation strategy and begin to implement changes immediately. Find a niche or develop a pocket that is uniquely yours. Form strong supplier partnerships and together with those suppliers develop a promotional-product calendar. Of course, shore up your customer service and really focus on controlling costs. You may find you are able to actually leverage the increased traffic coming into your area, as Wal-Marts draw customers from long distances away.

Wal-Mart provides outstanding service to its customers in so many different ways. They focus on executing the basics: Clean floors, clear signage, clean bathrooms, people greeters, supplying shopping carts, being in stock, smiling at the customers, and taking customers right to what they need. They use an "outside in" approach to product and service by finding out what the customer wants and then they go out and meet those needs. Buyers travel to the stores constantly to visit with associates and customers to determine how they might buy product to best suit the needs they uncover. This fanatical focus on customer service is the foundation of Sam Walton's incredible success.

The good news is that providing great service is and always has been one of the hallmarks of professional retail merchants. The bad news is that many retailers have lost sight of the importance of good old-fashioned service to their own bottom lines. You and your team of employees have the opportunity and the responsibility to invest the effort every day into capturing the hearts and minds of each and every one of your customers. You can't afford to have an off day. John Morrison, the state director of the Missouri Grocers Association, said, "Our businesses believe in balanced business growth and we believe in maintaining the center of the city and the social and economic culture of the city. Money that is spent at local retailers is circulated and recirculated three to five times but money that is spent on out-of-town ownership usually leaves [town] in a matter of hours, never to return. Routinely, our businesses donate quite a lot of money to high-school bands, fire departments, you name it. We've been community supporters and financial supporters, routinely supporting the local economy."

The formula for successful service isn't as simple as smiling at your customers and saying, "May I help you?" That's not customer service. With that canned greeting 99 percent of the time the customer will give you a canned response, "No thank you, I'm just looking." When that happens you have effectively blocked yourself from further discussions with that customer. Avoid overused greetings like the plague. A better way to address customer service is through the use of suggestive selling techniques intended to point out current specials or product promotions. By observing customer behavior you may be able to ask a question that gets the customer to talk and provide insights into his or her wants and needs. When it comes to customer service, customers today are looking for "less sizzle and more steak."

The success formula for customer service starts with providing product-knowledge training to managers and employees. Service strategies require bright, assertive employees who enjoy engaging customers in conversation. They take training by store managers and vendors on the features and benefits of products and services offered. Armed with product knowledge, employees can positively and directly affect store sales. Without it your employees don't add any value from a customer's perspective.

Every customer must be greeted and approached and helped if necessary. If the customer is receptive your employee should engage the customer in conversation and attempt to determine through good listening what he or she needs. By observing carefully, your employees can suggest other products that match those already in a customer's arms or shopping cart. The net effect of approaching every customer and using suggestive selling techniques will be increased store sales as well as increased average units per transaction.

Customer service is generally so poor in this day and age that you don't necessarily have to strive to exceed your customers' expectations; to impress them, simply meet those expectations. That may sound strange but it is true. Customers have been conditioned over the years to expect less than satisfactory treatment, so when you provide good service you have in essence exceeded their expectations. Set a goal to satisfy your customers, treat them well every time they come into your store, and your service standards will be perceived to be head and shoulders above those of most retailers.

Service Checklist

Review this service checklist of success strategies and tactics designed to help you compete with big-box retailers like Wal-Mart and not only survive, but thrive.

Customer Service
- ✓ Hold a standup meeting with employees each day before the doors open
- ✓ Realize your employee's attitudes affect customer attitudes, which affect store performance
- ✓ Teach employees to approach and greet every customer
- ✓ Make customer service a core competency and a competitive advantage
- ✓ Provide product benefits and features training to employees in slack periods
- ✓ Train employees to point out current sales and promotions for customers
- ✓ Make certain that when a customer asks for help your employees are responsive
- ✓ Establish a philosophy to drop everything else to serve your customers
- ✓ Teach employees to look for opportunities to suggest additional items
- ✓ Empower employees to resolve customer complaints without supervision

Guarantee
- ✓ Exceed expectations by accepting merchandise returns with no questions asked
- ✓ Make sure employee body language and attitudes are positive when employees accept returns
- ✓ Satisfy a dissatisfied customer on the spot
- ✓ Adopt the philosophy that the customer is always right
- ✓ Hold your suppliers accountable for product-quality issues
- ✓ Become known for standing behind your products and services
- ✓ Attempt to satisfy every customer who has a problem with merchandise

Convenience
- ✓ Do whatever you can to help customers in and out of your store quickly

✓ Train employees to be uniformly helpful, knowledgeable, and polite
✓ Make you store layout make sense to ensure it is easy to shop
✓ Make sure shopping carts and baskets are always readily available
✓ Open additional registers quickly as customer volume dictates the need
✓ Ask customers how they perceive the ease of shopping your store

CONCLUSION

> "The key to competing and surviving against Wal-Mart is to focus your business into a niche or pocket where you can leverage your strengths in the local marketplace."

If you are one of Wal-Mart's direct competitors, I hope you agree that competing with them requires an understanding of the company's inner workings. What is readily apparent by external observation of the company provides little competitive insight into what is actually happening behind the scenes. For uninformed competitors, it's analogous to the captain of a ship attempting to navigate around an iceberg by only observing and being concerned about the 10 percent of the ice mass protruding above the water's surface when 90 percent of the danger is actually hidden from view below the surface. Through my experiences working in Bentonville with Sam Walton, I hope you are gaining a better understanding of the "Wal-Mart Way" to help you to be better able to successfully compete, survive, and thrive in the dangerous and turbulent "retailing waters" of a Wal-Mart world!

As I travel, I have found that people are fascinated and want to know all about the inner workings of the culture of the world's largest retailer. Many have heard about Sam Walton and are interested in hearing stories about the myth and folklore of the company. The power of Wal-Mart is communicated to the associates and brought to life through storytelling. Illustrative stories, used in their training programs, make the complicated understandable and the mundane more interesting. Company folklore is fascinating to hear and the stories are easily told and retold as new employees join the company. Rich stories of the company's history put a human face on its company culture in an otherwise cookie-cutter, big-box work environment.

One of the great Wal-Mart stories I heard when I worked there was about Sam Walton visiting stores while piloting his own aircraft. He'd take off from Rogers, Arkansas, and fly over many different towns on his way to some distant destination. As he came upon a small town with a Wal-Mart and a K-Mart he would fly over the parking lots of both stores, and if after carefully observing both he felt uncomfortable with the number of cars in the parking lot at K-Mart versus Wal-Mart, he was known to drop out of the sky unannounced. Once he had landed he would make his way over to the local Wal-Mart and have a talk with the store manager. The two of them might go over and visit the K-Mart to observe firsthand what was going on.

This wasn't a show to impress the troops, this was Sam Walton leading by example by visiting stores every week of the year. (In the early days, he prided himself on the fact that he visited every store in the chain at least once per year, though as the company grew it became logistically impossible for him to do that.) The logic behind the store visits was twofold: First, he valued firsthand observation of competitors' strategies and tactics in the marketplace, and second, visits provided an opportunity for him to spend time reinforcing the company culture with the associates.

To this day, Wal-Mart executives and operations regional VPs travel to the stores every week of the year. They are all based in Bentonville and travel out on Monday mornings, returning on Thursdays with fresh intelligence about markets and competitors from across the country. They visit their own stores and they visit competitors' stores. They keep their eyes open for new ideas, which they bring back for discussion and implementation across the chain. By traveling to the stores constantly, they keep their finger on the competitive pulse all the time. This allows company leaders to know more about what is going on out in the market than any of Wal-Mart's competitors.

I believe that Wal-Mart's knowledge of the marketplace continues to provide it with a significant competitive advantage. Company leaders have always subscribed to the philosophy that the best defense is a good offense. By traveling in the field and visiting stores every week the executives, buyers, and operations leadership of Wal-Mart are able to gather fresh, firsthand intelligence about what is really going on out there. Knowledge is power.

The executives of many of Wal-Mart's competitors' stores sit in their ivory towers and must rely on secondhand and dated information about the ever-changing retail landscape. I think secondhand information is often filtered by those providing it in order to ensure that top executives don't shoot the messenger. Without knowing it, executives are often told what they want to hear, and end up making important decisions with bad data; garbage in equals garbage out. The current marketplace knowledge that Wal-Mart executives base their decisions on is a more powerful competitive weapon than the dated and inaccurate intelligence many competitors are often forced to use. I hate to say this, but Wal-Mart executives know more about what is going on in some of the competitors' stores then the executives of those companies.

Retail is and always has been hard mental and physical work. If you want to avoid being crushed by your competition you have to outthink, out-plan, outwork, and out-execute them, 52 weeks a year. That's the ongoing commitment you have to make to the strategy and tactics you have to have to win at retail. Imagine coupling the power of the economies of scale of a company like Wal-Mart with better marketplace intelligence than anyone else. Add to that Wal-Mart's ability to change directions like a nimble PT boat, instantaneously, forcing competitors to attempt the impossible task of turning their aircraft carriers on a dime. Wal-Mart is in shape, focused, and ready to compete at the big-league level. It is winning the marketplace battle for competitive information each and every day. By the time competitors discover Wal-Mart's latest tactics, the nimble giant has already moved on to another even better strategy.

You would think a company the size of Wal-Mart would begin to lose its ability to focus on local competition simply because of its size. The belief most of us have about large companies is that they become slow on their feet. Because of the store-within-a-store strategy and empowerment of local managers and associates Wal-Mart can effectively and rapidly adjust to changes in local markets. Local Wal-Mart store managers have the freedom to adjust pricing, merchandising, and product to best meet the ever-changing needs of their hometown customers and local competitors. Big companies aren't supposed to be able to do that and most can't. Wal-Mart thinks small, one store at a time, one department at a time, one customer at a time. By thinking in this way Wal-Mart simplifies everything that they do. They avoid trying to consume the entire pie by simply carving it up into smaller consumable pieces.

Unlike the managers of other large retail companies, Wal-Mart managers can make important decisions at the local level that directly affect sales and profitability today. No need to go up the bureaucratic chain of command and wait for a decision from someone who is too far from the action to make an informed decision anyhow. At Wal-Mart, managers are truly "intrapreneurial" merchants who are given the decision-making authority necessary to run a mega-million-dollar business. They are encouraged and empowered to think like business owners. That's not the case in every company.

When a Supercenter comes to the outskirts of town it affects every retailer around. Some will realize sales increases by simply drafting off the increased traffic. However, most businesses will experience lost sales that will never return. If you are in the path of the retail giant there is one thing you can count on: Business as you know it has forever changed. Once you come to grips with that reality you must muster the energy to quickly adapt or perish.

There are so many business areas in which Wal-Mart puts pressure on its competition: Price, Operations, Culture, Key-item promotion, Expenses, Talent, and Service. Every waking hour of every day Wal-Mart executives are trying to figure out ways to improve their business. They don't value maintaining the status quo as much as they value innovation for the benefit of the customer. All of Wal-Mart's competitive advantages boil down to lower prices, being in stock with the right product, and great service. Wal-Mart buyers, store managers, and associates are loyal to their ultimate boss, the customer.

To be successful in any business it is important to understand and embrace the basic building blocks of business. In response to the ever-present question, "What is Wal-Mart's secret to success?" Sam Walton compiled a list of ten key factors that unlock the mystery. These factors are known as "Sam's Rules for Building a Business":

Rule #1: Commit to your business.

Rule #2: Share your profits with all your associates, and treat them as partners.

Rule #3: Motivate your partners.

Rule #4: Communicate everything you possibly can to your partners.

Rule #5: Appreciate everything your associates do for the business.

Rule #6: Celebrate your successes.

Rule #7: Listen to everyone in your company.

Rule #8: Exceed your customers' expectations.

Rule #9: Control your expenses better than your competition.

Rule #10: Swim upstream.[1]

Each of Sam's ten rules is easy to understand but I can assure you they take a real commitment to implement. In a way these rules represent Sam Walton's secret cultural formula for Wal-Mart's success. Six of the rules are about ways to treat employees, and one each is about cost control, customer service, focused business commitment, and blazing your own trail. Sam's rules are a combination of getting back to business basics and embracing golden-rule principles. As I read the list I imagine the reader mentally checking off each rule and saying, "I do that." There is no doubt that intellectually all of Sam's rules make sense to anyone reading them, but like so many things in business good ideas are often lost in the act of being put into action. I can simplify his list of ten rules to five that capture more concisely what he was trying to say:

1. Commit to and communicate a clear business strategy.

2. Take care of your people.

3. Control costs.

4. Take care of your customers.

5. Take calculated risks to set your business apart.

You need to understand these rules of successful engagement if you want to successfully compete in any business, no matter who your competition is. Taking Sam's ideas a step further, the key to competing and surviving against Wal-Mart is also to focus your business into a niche or pocket where you can leverage your strengths in the local marketplace. It won't be easy, as so many failed retail companies across the world can attest, but it can be and has been done in every market into which Wal-Mart has entered. When Wal-Mart comes to town retailers that sell goods or services different from those sold by Wal-Mart may actually experience sales increases due to the increased customer traffic coming to town from outlying areas. By contrast, those retailers that have failed to differentiate their product offerings from Wal-Mart's experience losses in sales. The key is to work with your vendors to develop a competitive strategy and to then have the competitive courage to stay the course.

Steve Sheetz, chairman of the 300-convenience-store chain Sheetz, has both good news and bad news about Wal-Mart's impact on his business. On the positive side he says, "When a Wal-Mart comes to town, especially in the past, it was always good for us if we were close by, it brought more traffic, their customers may need gas or something in a hurry and stop by. We are right beside Wal-Mart at many locations and in the past the impact has, no question, been positive." The bad news is, "With the gasoline offer [at Wal-Mart] that's now beginning to change, because a lot of their gasoline operations now really emphasize cigarettes and cigarette pricing. So those little outposts out on the parking lots of the Wal-Marts are really pushing gasoline and cigarettes and now that's beginning to change the model and that's going to impact us." The point here is, once again, that past success is no guarantee of future success in the dynamic and ever-changing world of retailing. Change is inevitable and if you're standing still you will get run over.

Chester Cadieux, chairman of Quik Trip convenience stores, put it this way, "The dynamics of retail... it's a war... just kill or be killed!"

Here is a summary of my thoughts on what you can do to compete and survive in a big-box world:

Price—Don't try to compete on price; differentiate your product selection. Shop the competition and become an expert on competitive pricing. Find your niche or pocket and offer unique products and services. Always price staples within ten to fifteen percent of Wal-Mart's price.

Operations—Break the "ready, shoot, aim" tactical orientation by developing an actual strategy to compete. Once your strategy is in place, have the courage to remain committed to your plan. Set high standards and strive to become operationally excellent. Try to simplify rather than complicate your business, but sweat the important operational details. Take the necessary steps to insure you have clean floors and windows, a clean parking lot and bathrooms, clear signage, filled shelves, customers moving through the registers quickly, and team spirit.

Culture—Communicate your values and beliefs over and over again to your employees. Focus them on meeting the needs of your customers. Reinforce the fact that change is a way of life and that unless we embrace it, we will fail. Long hours and hard work are a retail way of life. Build a can-do culture with a strong sense of urgency. Capture the hearts and minds of employees and get everybody thinking of good business-improvement ideas.

Key-item promotion/Product—Determine who you are and uniformly communicate your brand message to your entire team. If necessary, pit vendors against one another to get the best price, products, and promotions. Buy and display merchandise as if you are serious about being in business. Invest in local advertising and promote products and services. Offer private-label products that are exclusively yours. Innovate, don't always follow the trends, blaze your own trails, and set some trends yourself.

Expenses—Become obsessed with controlling costs. Make sure executives model those behaviors for employees. Tightly manage labor costs, overtime, and work schedules. Negotiate and renegotiate everything. Communicate expense-control standards to everyone and hold everyone accountable. Teach your managers and employees to approach cost control as if they owned the business and were responsible for writing the checks. Make certain your executives aren't saying one thing while doing another by requiring them to model penny-pinching behaviors for employees.

Talent—Recruit constantly and hire people who have both experience and high potential, what I call "using sledgehammers to drive thumb tacks." Build bench strength so promotional opportunities can be filled from within whenever possible. Recognize performers and deal with non-performers. Understand the reasons for turnover but focus on retention.

Service—Never take your customers for granted. Empower your employees to make decisions involving customer concerns. Form a benchmarking group of successful retailers and learn from one another. Reward employees who demonstrate the correct customer-service behaviors. Shop your own store as if you were a customer walking in for the first time.

So where do you start as you develop your responsive competitive strategy to compete and survive? There are three very important areas within which I think you should concentrate your initial strategy: building customer loyalty, controlling your costs, and increasing the sales of your business. All three are easy to understand yet hard to implement without a concentrated and focused commitment to changing or modifying the way you currently do business. Wal-Mart has turned retailing into an extreme sport and has rewritten the rules of the competition. Competitors must develop new skills and relearn ways of doing things in order to compete.

In the appendix of this book I have included a self-assessment check-off list you can use to evaluate your management practices and your business across a wide array of important criteria: pricing, accessibility, operations, staying in stock, visual merchandising, technology, retail-team synergy, "branding" your service culture, your management team, vendor partnerships, product merchandising, product assortment, private-label product, promotional activity, expense control, talent, bringing out the best in people, retention, management impact on turnover, customer service, product and service guarantees, convenience, survival strategies, vision and values.

Also in the appendix is a list of 50 key business questions you can use to stir up creative thinking. The self-assessment checklist and the 50 questions are a great means of kicking off an open discussion at a cross-functional management retreat. At times this type of self-discovery process leads to heated discussion as passionate and caring leaders give their opinions on critical business issues. This should be encouraged. As a business coach and experienced turnaround team member, I have worked with companies to develop an objective self-evaluation and have facilitated discussions of the findings. I've found that if the participants feel comfortable giving their opinions, important insights into real business issues will come out that need to be addressed. Your own team will come up with some breakthrough strategies which could help catapult your business to a new level. Contact me if you'd like for me to run a self-assessment exercise at your company.

By going through the business self-assessment process with your entire leadership team you ensure that everyone hears the same thing at the same time and strategies can be developed to strengthen areas of weakness. A side benefit is improved communication and a better understanding of cross-functional and -cultural issues. Repeating the process periodically provides an opportunity to measure progress towards established goals and you can make sure everyone is on the same page.

The bar has risen on what it takes to be successful in customer service, cost control, and building your business. Customer expectations have changed and so have retailing standards. What it took to be successful in retail in the past doesn't work today and it definitely won't work in the future. Success today takes a solid strategy, hard work, longer hours, organizational discipline, a lot of courage, and sweating the details. You can't just build a store and expect that customers will flock to it. You have to create your own niche with differentiated products that your targeted customer wants and needs. To compete with the big box you have to think out of the box.

Using "loyalty" and "customers" in the same sentence, in this day and age, almost seems like an oxymoron! Customers are fickle, willing to shift their loyalties in response to the best advertised price or the latest marketed promotion. They'll even drive twenty miles to save a dollar. With this in mind, local retailers need to provide a higher level of service to stand out against big-box competitors. There are real opportunities to leverage your local-market knowledge, buy to local preferences, and design more effective targeted advertising and promotional programs to meet the specific needs of local consumers.

You can realize another advantage by going back to the basic lessons of Marketing 101 and simply taking the time to get to know your customers on a more personal level. Re-court your current customers and invest time in every customer who takes the time to cross your threshold. Turn the customer-service experience in your store into a local advantage. There is no reason your service levels shouldn't exceed the service that customers receive at Wal-Mart. You don't have many areas of competitive advantage against Wal-Mart so don't squander the chance to leverage and build customer loyalty.

The pressures on pricing make it more important than ever before for you to control your costs wherever you can. Stop being sentimental about spending money and get tough about saving it. Selfishly look at ways you can reduce or renegotiate costs in every area. Look at it this way: If there is an expense there is a way to either lower or eliminate it. Push hard on suppliers and distributors for price concessions. I guarantee you'll have success more often than not. Pit vendors against one another to ensure you get the best prices. Don't simply accept price increases that are passed along to you. Send a clear message to your suppliers that you aren't a pushover when it comes to negotiating prices. Let them take it out of some other retailer's hide!

Develop strategies to control all the costs within your control, including utilities, wages and schedules, overtime, recycling, telephones, shipping, paper, printing, fixtures, and leases/rent. Take a page out of the Wal-Mart playbook—squeeze nickels and you'll save dollars. Send a message to your employees that waste won't be tolerated and that controlling costs is an important priority. Control your labor costs each and every day and you'll drop big-time dollars to the bottom line.

Remember, Wal-Mart's cost of sales for payroll is somewhere in the six- to eight-percent range and I'll bet yours is in the 9 to 12 percent range or even higher than that. Do something about modifying your work schedules now and shift the burden onto managers to carry a bigger share of the workload themselves. Set goals and reduce your store overtime as much as you can. Managers faced with cutting payroll and overtime get very efficient very quickly at getting the work done through others given the option of doing it themselves. I know your first thought is that this is impossible but that's exactly the strategy that Wal-Mart employs. Remember that if one can do it all can do it!

Finally, you have to figure out ways to build your business. One of the fastest ways to reduce expenses as a percentage of sales is to increase revenue by generating more dollars per square foot of selling space. I've heard it said that volume solves the sins of the world in retailing. Expenses as a percentage of total sales fall when sales rise. Loss of sales volume exposes an already weak expense structure faster than anything. Years of comp-store increases may lull a successful retailer into a false sense of security, if it has taken the position that its expenses are in line with its current volume. Expense corrections must be a daily activity, not one for the end of the quarter or the end of the month. Establish the discipline necessary to control expenses constantly, whether sales are up or down. Company leaders need to get alarmed when expenses are out of line so that everyone feels and understands the importance of controlling costs.

For those who have experienced the arrival of a big-box competitor, you already know about the loss of revenue caused by its market entry. Intense price competition is inevitable. Local retailers have to quickly find a niche or pocket for themselves by expanding their product and service offerings and promote products to increase customer traffic to their stores.

Real partnerships with vendors are pivotal. Make your vendors understand that helping you to be successful helps them to be successful.

With over 260 billion dollars in sales, and store operations in ten countries around the world, Wal-Mart is a big-box predator on the prowl. No retail sector can escape its insatiable appetite for more customers as it gobbles up market share with its everyday low prices and bites heartily into the economies of small towns and entire countries.

Leveraging its economies of scale and superior execution, it devastates contenders with a massive one-two punch of formidable buying power and unprecedented cost-control discipline. One can only imagine the CEOs and directors of competitors shaking their heads in wonder as they see themselves caught up in an unfair fight as the traditional rules of retail engagement deteriorate along with their market share.

High expectations are one of the keys to Wal-Mart's success. Holding its managers and associates to high standards leads to higher productivity, which reduces costs. With lower operating costs the company can afford to offer lower prices, which in turn build sales and profitability. Greater sales and profitability allow the company to open more stores. With more stores come greater economies of scale. Greater economies of scale further lower costs. This awesome spiral is evidence of a never-ending mission to drive cost out of the system, which in turn allows the company to pass the savings along to the customer.

Where there are retail customers to be had and money to be made Wal-Mart will aggressively go after the business. Company leaders plan to double the size of the company by 2005 to almost 500 billion dollars. Currently 1.3 million employees are working for the company, and if current growth targets are accurate the number of employees will grow to over two million in that time. Sales growth will come from a combination of international and domestic Supercenter expansion and the opening of new concept stores like the Neighborhood Market.

Those who already compete directly with Wal-Mart know the difficulties of simply surviving in the shadow of the retail behemoth. Some retailers, caught in the expansion path of the 800-pound gorilla, don't even realize that they are about to take a beating if they don't prepare themselves for the onslaught.

Every business has an Achilles heel, even Wal-Mart. Some think its biggest weakness may be the size of the company itself. In the history of the world, no other business has ever grown to the same gargantuan proportions. Few other companies have the wherewithal to be all of the following: a retailer and a manufacturer, a seller and a supplier, an internal distribution company and a back hauler for manufacturers. At this point, as it continues to grow, everything it does is trailblazing. No one else has ever faced the challenges it is facing as it spreads its operations further and further around the world.

My goal in writing was to give you a glimpse inside the company and the culture so you can see for yourself what you're up against. As I stated in the introductory chapter, it is much easier to tell you why it is difficult to compete with Wal-Mart than it is to tell you how to compete with it. Its strengths as a company far outweigh its weaknesses.

Throughout this book I've talked about the many strengths of Wal-Mart, what I have often referred to as its competitive advantages. I went back through this book and counted the number of times I used the phrase, "competitive advantage(s)" and found I'd used it 50 different times. When I think about Wal-Mart I think about the overwhelming competitive advantages it has in so many different areas including merchandising, store operations, customer service, technology, distribution, cost control, and culture. Coupled with those strengths it is one of the most innovative companies you'll ever find. It is rare for a single organization to have so many strengths and so few weaknesses. Most companies rely on one competency or towering strength and work constantly to shore up their weaknesses.

To help you to understand what it takes to compete with Wal-Mart and survive I'll share with you a final glimpse into the mind of former CEO David Glass. On the wall of his office, in front of his desk, David had a plaque staring him squarely in the face each and every day as he prepared to do retail battle. He even ended some of the talks I heard him give with this quotation. I think the words capture Wal-Mart's competitive nature, behaviors, and beliefs about winning and survival better than anything else. This quotation provides competitors with a glimpse into the minds and competitive psyche of Wal-Mart's leaders. Here's what it said:

> "Every morning in Africa, a gazelle wakes up. It knows it must run faster than the fastest lion or it will be killed. Every morning a lion wakes up. It knows it must outrun the slowest gazelle or it will starve to death. It really doesn't matter whether you are a lion or a gazelle . . . when the sun comes up, you'd better be running!"

Appendix

Competitive Business Strategies and Tactics Self-Assessment to Help You Evaluate Your Ability to Compete and Survive Against Wal-Mart

With a critical eye, go through the following assessment of your own company's strategies and tactics, and identify those areas in which you need to improve. The second section provides fifty thought-provoking business questions for your team to review as you develop your competitive game plan.

Once you identify areas in need of improvement, develop competitive strategies around them. Focus your team on those areas to enhance your ability to compete.

Table A.1 Business Strategies and Tactics Self-Assessment Inventory

Are you Prepared to Compete with Wal-Mart? As you respond to each item think about your own current strategy and tactics.

(place an "X" in the appropriate box)

Pricing	Strongly Agree	Tend to Agree	Don't Know	Tend to Disagree	Strongly Disagree
Don't compete by carrying the exact same product as big-box competitors					
Pricing strategy does not attempt to go toe to toe with them on prices					
Asked vendors for competitive product/pricing ideas					
Offer higher-quality products at higher price points					
Perform shopping-cart price comparisons regularly					
Broadened our selection of products and services					
Talked to vendors about partnering on lower prices					
Shopped competitors' stores and thoroughly understand their pricing strategies					
Asked suppliers for special-buy and sale merchandise					
Shelves or products are clearly marked with price labels					
Product guarantees and service after the sale are clearly advertised					
Accessibility					
Store is easily accessible					
Store hours reflect those of our competition					
Customers are easily able to navigate our aisles					
Store maintains competitive hours throughout the year					

	Strongly Agree	Tend to Agree	Don't Know	Tend to Disagree	Strongly Disagree
Accessibility (*continued*)					
Employees park their cars in an assigned area far away from the store entrance					
Parking in front of store is designated for customers only					
Customers perceive store as easily accessible					
Operations					
Floors are clean and shiny. Rugs are vacuumed each and every day					
Bathrooms are kept clean and someone is assigned to regularly maintain them					
Displays are well lit and shelving and fixtures are clean and dust-free					
Store windows are kept clean					
Stock is kept clean and rotated if necessary					
Aisles are kept clear and free of restock merchandise					
Employees are focused on shrinkage control					
Staying in Stock					
Employees are trained on the importance of constantly being in stock					
Employees are required to police the aisles to fill in inventory holes					
Employees restock merchandise without management direction					
Aggressive reorder processes are in place to avoid being out of stock					
A positive brand statement is made to customers by the first-class manner with which promotional product is merchandised					

Table A.1 (*Continued*)

(place an "X" in the appropriate box)

	Strongly Agree	Tend to Agree	Don't Know	Tend to Disagree	Strongly Disagree
Staying in Stock (*continued*)					
Promotional inventory is bought deep enough to ensure enough product to meet customer demand					
Inventory is organized so products are easy to find and accessible when restocking is needed					
Remerchandising occurs throughout the sales day during slack customer-traffic periods					
Cashiers proactively communicate restocking needs					
Suppliers clearly understand their role and your expectations about timely product deliveries					
New merchandise flows in seamlessly to replace sold-out or poor-selling product					
Visual merchandising					
The store and displays are well signed and appealing to customers					
Vendors supply attractive graphics and provide new ones as promotional strategies change					
Signage reflects current promotional activity					
Graphics and signage make a clear and uniform statement about the brand image you intend to convey					
Signage is prominently displayed on promotional product and in-store specials					
Signage is of high quality, reflecting the values of your store brand					

	Strongly Agree	Tend to Agree	Don't Know	Tend to Disagree	Strongly Disagree
Visual merchandising (*continued*)					
Signage and graphics uniformly reflect quality and continuity of the store's theme					
Technology					
Scanning technology is in place to improve service and lower costs of managing inventory					
Store physical inventory is never managed at the expense of serving customers					
Shelf price labeling is used to minimize the need for employees to individually price-sticker each unit of product					
Suppliers are leveraged for support in managing inventory via technology					
UPC bar codes are used to manage inventory					
Retail-team synergy					
Employees enthusiastically work together toward a common set of goals					
Individuals and groups receive sales, product knowledge, and service training					
The time and talents of individual employees are known and understood so they can be leveraged effectively to improve the business					
Employees are empowered to serve the customers					
Fact-finding, not fault-finding is the way performance feedback is given					

Table A.1 (*Continued*)

(place an "X" in the appropriate box)

Retail-team synergy (*continued*)	Strongly Agree	Tend to Agree	Don't Know	Tend to Disagree	Strongly Disagree
Managers embrace diversity and that is reflected in their current staff					
All store managers are visible on the floor and know employees, by name, on sight					
The company is committed to quality, innovation, continuous learning, and continuous improvement					
Morale is high and employees like to work here					
Employees often refer friends and relatives for consideration for open positions					
Goals are understood and employees are driven to produce results					
Feedback in the form of praise and criticism is being given all the time					
Employees manage company resources as if they were their own					
Communication is active and open and new ideas are solicited from all employees					
When conflict does arise issues are resolved quickly					
Employees take on new challenges with enthusiasm					
"Branding" your service culture					
Your brand story has been clearly and uniformly communicated to employees and customers					

"Branding" your service culture (*continued*)	Strongly Agree	Tend to Agree	Don't Know	Tend to Disagree	Strongly Disagree
If you were to ask individual employees to explain your brand story to you, you are confident you will hear the same correct version from each and every one					
Rich stories and folklore of your own company are used to proliferate your service-culture expectations and define your brand					
Key openings are filled from within in order to maintain continuity of company standards and culture					
The performance contributions of each employee are measured each and every day					
Performance standards have been clearly established and have been communicated to employees					
Employee-reward systems are tied to productivity goals (monetary or non-monetary)					
Service standards are reinforced by managers who model appropriate service behaviors themselves					
Employees are empowered to serve the customer without management intervention					
Your management team					
Managers are held accountable to high standards and excuses for nonperformance aren't accepted					
Managers are hiring the brightest and best people available in the market and not settling for less than the best talent					
Turnover of people is at a manageable level					
Quality internal talent is already in place and trained, allowing internal promotions to fill management vacancies					

Table A.1 (*Continued*)

(place an "X" in the appropriate box)

	Strongly Agree	Tend to Agree	Don't Know	Tend to Disagree	Strongly Disagree
Your management team (*continued*)					
Employees are well trained					
Managers value the contributions of employees and morale is good					
Star performers are recognized and nonperformers are dealt with					
Managers demonstrate the ability to proactively drive sales and control costs					
Vendor partnerships					
True vendor partnerships have been formed to improve your ability to compete					
You have clearly communicated your sense of urgency to your suppliers					
Suppliers work with you to develop promotional-product strategies					
Constantly evaluate the quality of service provided by suppliers and replace unresponsive vendors					
Suppliers have been asked for successful strategies other retailers are currently using effectively					
In-store product training has been requested for employees at the vendor's cost					
Requested discounted, close-out, sale, or special-deal merchandise for your customers					
Vendors have been asked for product-assortment-differentiation ideas					

	Strongly Agree	Tend to Agree	Don't Know	Tend to Disagree	Strongly Disagree
Vendor partnerships (*continued*)					
You have verified that current product mix is differentiated from big-box competitors'					
Suppliers have been asked to help you develop an annual product-promotional-calendar strategy					
Suppliers have been asked about their opinion on what you can do to improve the competitive position of your business					
Product merchandising					
You have communicated to employees that out of stock is out of business					
Shelves look full, sending the message you're serious about the business					
There are no holes in inventory merchandising					
Vendor-supplied temporary modular promotional displays are utilized					
Products are merchandised and promoted together where it makes sense (tortilla chips and salsa, shoes and socks, batteries and battery cables, wiper blades and window-cleaning fluid, etc.)					
Effective point-of-sale merchandising is used to drive impulse purchases at the register					
Product assortment					
You have developed a product mix that appeals to local tastes and interests					
Selection of products and services is clearly differentiated from competitors, creating a competitive niche					

Table A.1 (*Continued*)

(place an "X" in the appropriate box)

	Strongly Agree	Tend to Agree	Don't Know	Tend to Disagree	Strongly Disagree
Product assortment (*continued*)					
Higher-quality, higher-priced products are offered in the product mix					
Promotional products are used to attract customer traffic					
You use customer input in product selection					
Current product mix avoids carrying the exact same merchandise as Wal-Mart					
Private-label product					
You have developed a private label program with suppliers					
You have shopped competitors' stores specifically to view their private-label offerings					
You have talked to managers of stores with successful private-label programs for advice					
You have asked your customers if they would purchase generic or private-label products and if so what their product preferences are					
Promotional activity					
You promote like you mean it . . . buy deep and merchandise products in a way that makes a statement that you are serious about your business					
A monthly promotional calendar is in place					
Employees are taught to be merchants . . . they create merchandising displays and signage					

	Strongly Agree	Tend to Agree	Don't Know	Tend to Disagree	Strongly Disagree
Promotional activity (*continued*)					
Merchandise contests are in place to get employees excited about merchandising and selling products					
Employees routinely suggest items to customers on the sales floor and at the register					
Promotional strategies, especially current ones, are understood by employees					
Displays are always set up in time to match your promotional-product-calendar commitments and advertising					
"Rain checks" are honored when promoted product runs out					
Signage is clear and properly placed					
Expense control					
Schedules are managed to avoid having employees work overtime					
Everything is recycled to reduce costs					
The appropriate emphasis is placed on shrinkage (theft) control with your staff					
Employees clearly understand that waste reduces company profitability					
Your lease has been renegotiated with the landlord					
A "wastebuster" expense-reduction program is in place, rewarding employees for ideas that control costs					
Work schedules are adjusted to correspond with the peaks and valleys of sales volume					

Table A.1 (*Continued*)

(place an "X" in the appropriate box)

	Strongly Agree	Tend to Agree	Don't Know	Tend to Disagree	Strongly Disagree
Expense control (*continued*)					
The pay week is set up so hours can be frontloaded and necessary labor cuts made on the slowest sales days of the week and not on weekends (Example: Thursday to Wednesday)					
All managers are working at least a forty-eight hour work week					
You ask employees to contribute one good methods-improvement idea per week and reward ideas that are implemented					
Wages and benefit costs are in line with those of direct competitors in the market					
Talent					
You recruit constantly					
You realize bright motivated people are interviewing you while you're interviewing them					
Obstacles to recruiting have been removed to increase the speed of filling open positions					
You try to hire people who are better than you are: smarter, better educated, and with more potential					
Whenever possible, hire people who are experienced over those who are inexperienced					
You have hired talented people from a respected competitor to learn from their experience					
Managers cast their net wide and hire a diverse pool of employees					
Managers are held accountable for turnover and all departing employees are exit-interviewed					

	Strongly Agree	Tend to Agree	Don't Know	Tend to Disagree	Strongly Disagree
Talent (*continued*)					
Employee-performance problems are actively addressed: nonperformers are moved out of the company					
Qualified people are on your bench to ensure your ability to promote from within					
A clear mission and vision statement have been established to clarify your organization's goals					
Bringing out the best in people					
Managers expect the best and hold employees accountable for results					
Managers understand what motivates each employee and leverage employee strengths with that knowledge					
Managers walk the talk by setting and modeling personal standards of excellence					
Risk taking is encouraged and making a mistake is not fatal					
People are recognized for a job well done					
An open-door policy is in place to address employee concerns					
Employees, if asked, would characterize their work environment as fun					
Retention					
Newly hired employees are thoroughly oriented					
Employees are provided with training and development opportunities					

Table A.1 (*Continued*)

(place an "X" in the appropriate box)

	Strongly Agree	Tend to Agree	Don't Know	Tend to Disagree	Strongly Disagree
Retention (*continued*)					
Employees are encouraged to take ownership of their job responsibilities					
Managers show tolerance for employees who make mistakes					
Pay and benefits are competitive and employees know it					
Performance feedback is given to employees periodically					
Promotional opportunities are filled with the best candidates; internally promoted or externally hired					
Current employees are asked to act as mentors for newly hired employees					
Management impact on turnover					
Care is taken in screening job applicants					
Employment references of applicants considered for hire are always called					
Employee concerns are dealt with promptly					
Managers show respect in their treatment of all employees					
Employee bathrooms and eating areas are kept clean and neat					
Commitments on hours promised to employees are lived up to					
No favoritism is shown to any individual employee					
Managers respond to employee questions, problems, and complaints					
Policies and procedures are thoroughly communicated to employees					

	Strongly Agree	Tend to Agree	Don't Know	Tend to Disagree	Strongly Disagree
Customer service					
A standup meeting with employees is held each day before the doors open to discuss sales, service, and expenses					
Managers realize that employees' attitudes affect customer attitudes and store performance					
Employees are taught to approach and greet every customer					
During slack sales periods employees are taught product benefits and features					
Employees are trained to point out current sales and promotions to customers					
When a customer asks for help your employees are always responsive					
Add-on selling is taught and employees look for opportunities to suggest additional items					
Employees are required to drop everything else to serve customers					
Employees have the responsibility and the authority to resolve customer complaints without supervision					
Product and service guarantees					
Merchandise returns are accepted with no questions asked					
Employee body language and attitudes are positive when employees accept returns					
Dissatisfied customers are satisfied on the spot					
The "customer is always right" philosophy is in place					
Suppliers are held accountable for product-quality issues					

Table A.1 (*Continued*)

(place an "X" in the appropriate box)

Product and service guarantees (*continued*)	Strongly Agree	Tend to Agree	Don't Know	Tend to Disagree	Strongly Disagree
Your business is known for standing behind its products and services					
Convenience					
Store layout makes shopping easy for customers					
Employees are trained to be uniformly helpful, knowledgeable, and polite					
Cashiers do whatever they can to help customers get in and out of the store quickly					
Additional registers are opened quickly as customer volume dictates the need					
Managers jump in to help wherever they can to speed customers through the registers					
Customers perceive shopping your store as a positive and convenient experience					
Survival strategies					
A well thought-out strategy, has been developed to stop the ready, shoot, aim mentality of retailing					
The products in our store are clearly differentiated from big-box competitors'					
Brand messages are well defined and uniformly communicated					

Survival strategies (continued)	Strongly Agree	Tend to Agree	Don't Know	Tend to Disagree	Strongly Disagree
Merchandise is bought and displayed as if you are serious about being in business					
Company values and beliefs are communicated over and over again to employees					
Products are promoted and advertising is considered an investment rather than an expense					
Managers and employees sweat the details and constantly strive to become operationally excellent					
Change is viewed as a way of life—it must be positively embraced or failure will occur					
Managers and employees are obsessed about controlling costs					
Company culture includes a strong sense of urgency					
Don't always follow the trends; blaze your own trails and set some trends yourselves					
Encourage people to simplify things rather than complicate the business					
Sweat the details—majoring in the minors because retail is detail					
As strategies are developed there is an understanding that ninety percent of strategy is execution					
Continuously learn about our competition by shopping the competition periodically					
Participation in local benchmarking groups is viewed as important in order to learn from the successes of others					

Table A.1 (*Continued*)

(place an "X" in the appropriate box)

Survival strategies (*continued*)	Strongly Agree	Tend to Agree	Don't Know	Tend to Disagree	Strongly Disagree
Managers periodically shop your own store as if they were a customer walking in for the first time					
Decisions are made and there is a willingness to take risks and sometimes make mistakes					
Establishing vendor partnerships is a priority					
There is a realization that past success is no guarantee of future success					
Vision and values					
Company managers and employees have been provided the opportunity to provide input into the creation of the company vision and values					
A clearly defined company vision has been developed in writing and distributed for all to see					
Training of managers and employees about the vision and company values are ongoing					
Company communications discuss the company's vision and values to reinforce them					
Copies of the company vision and values are posted on company bulletin boards					
Storytelling is used to reinforce and support the communication of the company vision and values					

Table A.2   Competitive Business Strategy and Tactics Questionnaire

Fifty Key Business Questions to Stay Competitive in a Wal-Mart World

1. What differentiates your business, product, or service from your competitors'?

2. What obvious weakness(es) does your business have that could cause serious damage or problems if competitors capitalized on them?

3. If you wanted to build your business what great idea(s), product(s), or service(s) do you have to drive that growth?

4. What are the core vision and beliefs of your organization and do your employees all know and understand them?

5. What are the five things your employees like least about your company and what are you doing to address those concerns?

6. What are the five things your employees like best about your company?

7. If you could talk to your former customers what would they tell you was the reason they took their business elsewhere?

8. What are the core competencies of your business versus what they need to be? Are you relying on outdated competencies rather than adapting to the rapidly changing market?

9. What department(s) in your company do you regularly hear griping or complaining about and why? What are you doing about it?

10. Who are your competitors and what are they doing really well that you can learn from or adopt outright?

11. If you could change one thing about your company that would improve your competitive position what would it be?

12. If your company were in trouble and had to file for bankruptcy what would you point to as the probable reason? What can you do to prevent that from ever happening?

13. Why do people like to work for your company and what are the things they tell you they don't like when they leave? How are you perceived as an employer by potential recruits?

14. What are some examples of things you are doing differently today from a year ago and what are some things you intend to do differently a year from today?

15. If you had a round-table meeting with your customers what kind of things would they tell you they like about your company and what would they tell you they don't like?

16. What new ideas are you working on today that will set your business apart from your competitors a year from today? Five years from today?

17. What is it about your business that clearly sets you apart and gives you the upper hand versus your competitors?

18. If your employees were honest with you, which of your current processes would they tell you are antiquated or overly bureaucratic?

19. What aspect of your culture thoroughly frustrates you and your employees and why aren't you doing anything about it?

20. If a layoff were announced tomorrow and you were required to reduce your workforce by ten percent, how difficult would it be to come up with a list of underperforming or poorly performing employees? If it isn't difficult, why aren't you dealing with that lowest ten percent systematically now?

21. Do you have the caliber of people on your bench to staff your own growth?

22. Have you lost or gained market share in the past year? If so, why? To whom have you lost market share and why?

23. How does your cost structure compare to the industry standards? What is your target?

24. What are your turnover rates for people and what is acceptable to you?

25. Why are employees leaving the company and is there anything you can do about it?

26. What is your pay strategy and does it allow you to recruit the quality of people you need to drive the business?

27. Are systems in place to recognize performance and deal with non-performers?

28. What are your competitors doing in the marketplace that is head and shoulders above what you are currently doing? Why aren't you copying that strategy?

29. What are the five things your customers like least about your company and what are you actively doing to address those concerns?

30. What are the five things your customers like best about your company and why?

31. If your boss were to come to you tomorrow to terminate your employment what aspect of your work would likely be the reason? What can you do today to strengthen that area?

32. Do your employees feel overwhelmed by the amount of paperwork sent to them? Are managers pencil-whipping problems rather than getting out to actually solve them?

33. Are your managers doing everything they possibly can to simplify every area of operation or does your culture have a tendency to overly complicate things?

34. When was the last time a brilliant idea bubbled up from your employees? Do you have a great-idea-generation program?

35. On a scale of one-to-ten, how well does your organization adapt to change? Do you deal with resistance to change head-on?

36. Do you have any franchise players who are invaluable to your organization and, if they left for a competitor, could clearly damage you?

37. What kind of ongoing employee-communication strategies are in place?

38. Do employees feel free to bring their concerns forward to management or are they punished for stating their opinions?

39. If asked, what ideas would your senior leaders give to improve the business?

40. Are there any weak links on your team keeping you from achieving your goals?

41. Do people in your organization make excuses for missing deadlines, and if so, what are their typical excuses? Do you let them get away with those excuses?

42. Do your employees show genuine interest in your customers or are they indifferent? What about your managers?

43. Are there cultural barriers or bureaucratic requirements in your company that prevent your employees from serving your customers to the fullest extent possible?

44. On a scale of one-to-ten, what would your employees tell you is their level of empowerment to meet the needs of your customers without asking permission from someone else?

45. Do managers use e-mail as a replacement for face-to-face communication and the supervision of employees?

46. When was the last time you surveyed your employees' opinions?

47. Do you view your vendor relationships as adversarial or are they true partnerships?

48. When was the last time you surveyed your customers' opinions?

49. If you could start over from scratch, what would you do differently and why?

50. Name one or two franchise players or four or five A players who work for your company. What are you doing to hold on to them?

Michael Bergdahl is a Speaker and Business Coach and he is available to come to your company and make a presentation or to facilitate a strategy session with your leadership team.

Notes

Introduction

1. Kaiser, Emily. "Can $250 Billion Wal-Mart Think Small?" *Reuters*, 21 June 2003.
2. Wal-Mart official web site. http://www.walmart.com.
3. Dicker, John. "Union Blues at Wal-Mart." *The Nation*, 28 June 2002.
4. Saporito, Bill. "Inside the World's Biggest Store." *Time Europe*, 20 January 2003.
5. Grant, Lorrie. *An Unstoppable Marketing Force: Wal-Mart Aims for Domination of the Retail Industry—Worldwide.* 6 November 1998; p. 01.B.
6. Carl, Traci. *The Arizona Republic Online*, "Wal-Mart's expansion going global." *USA TODAY*, 5 April 2003.
7. Rossingh, Danielle. "Wal-Mart: A Retail Titan." *BBC News World Edition*, 14 January 2003.
8. Potvin, Kevin. *The Republic*, 19 April 2002.
9. Editors. "Steel Versus Silicon." *Forbes.com*, 7 July 1997. http://www.forbes.com/free_forbes/1997/0707/6001129a.html

Chapter 1

1. Giuliani, W. Rudolph, *Leadership*. New York: Miramax Books, 2002, p. 164
2. Callahan, Patricia and Ann Zimmerman. "Wal-Mart, After Remaking Discount Retailing, Now Nation's Largest Grocery Chain." *The Wall Street Journal*, 31 May 2003.
3. Achua, Christopher F. "Small-town merchants are not using the recommended strategies to compete against national discount chains: A prescriptive versus descriptive study." 2001.
4. Walton, Sam. *Made in America*. New York: Doubleday, 1992, pp 32–33.
5. Cullen, Jim. "'Category Killers' Stalk Small Towns; U.S. regulators shrug at 'free-market' consolidation." *The Progressive Populist*. February 1997.
6. Stone, Kenneth E. "The Impact of Wal-Mart Stores." 1993.
7. Cullen, Jim. "Category Killers" Stalk Small Towns; U.S. regulators shrug at 'free-market' consolidation." *The Progressive Populist*. February 1997.
8. Walton, Sam. *Made in America*. New York: Doubleday, 1992. pp. 235–236.
9. Achua, Christoper F. "Small-town merchants are not using the recommended strategies to compete against national discount chains: A prescriptive versus descriptive study." 2001.

Chapter 2

1. Walton, Sam. *Made in America.* New York: Doubleday, 1992, p. 261.
2. Ibid. pp. 140–141.
3. Ibid. pp. 116–117.
4. Ibid., p. 263.
5. http://www.morningnewsbeat.com/archives/2003/03/25.html
6. Lindeman, Theresa, "New Wal-Mart Distribution Center Covers A Lot Of Ground." *Pittsburgh Post-Gazette,* 16 July 2003.
7. Lundberg, Abbie. "The I.T. Inside the World's Biggest Company" *CIO magazine,* 1 July 2002.
8. Koprowski, Gene."RFID Emerges to Threaten the Bar Code." *TechNewsWorld,* 29 July 2003.
9. http://www.morningnewsbeat.com/archives/2003/03/25.html
10. http://www.bentoncountyrepublicans.org/labor.html

Chapter 3

1. Sidey, Hugh. "The Two Sides of the Sam Walton Legacy." *Time magazine,* 20 April 1992.
2. Roosevelt, Theodore. "Citizenship in a Republic." Speech, 1910.
3. Eisner, Michael and Tony Schwartz. *Work in Progress.* New York: Random House, 1998. p. 245.
4. Burke, W.W. and Litwin, G. *A Causal Model of Organizational Performance,* in Pfeiffer, J.W. (ed). The 1989 annual: Developing Human Resources. San Diego: University Associates, 1989.

Chapter 4

1. Baron, Kelly. "Spamouflage and Cajun Crawtators." *Forbes.com.* 29 October 2001.
2. Achua, Christopher F. "Small-town merchants are not using the recommended strategies to compete against national discount chains: A prescriptive versus descriptive study." 2001.
3. Walton, Sam. *Made in America.* New York: Doubleday, 1992, p. 79.
4. Useem, Jerry. "One Nation Under Wal-Mart." *Fortune,* 18 February 2003.
5. Dick's Sporting Goods web site.
6. Eisner, Michael and Tony Schwartz. *Work in Progress.* New York: Random House, 1998, p. xi.
7. Boyle, Matthew. "Brand Killers." *Fortune,* 21 July 2003.
8 Daniels, Alex. "Wal-Mart counsels vendors to embrace new technology." *Arkansas Democrat Gazette,* Northwest Arkansas edition, 10 October 2003.
9 Whiting, Rick and Beth Bacheldor, "Wal-Mart To Brief Top Suppliers On RFID Plans." *InformationWeek, Internetweek.com.* 6 October 2003.
10. Bowers, Katherine. "The Bentonville Boom" *Women's Wear Daily,* 25 June 2003.
11. Useem, Jerry. "One Nation Under Wal-Mart." *Fortune,* 18 February 2003.
12. Kaiser, Emily. "Can $250 Billion Wal-Mart Think Small?" Reuters, 21 January 2003.

Chapter 5

1. Eisner, Michael and Tony Schwartz. *Work in Progress.* New York: Random House, 1998, pp. 362–363.

2. Wal-Mart official web site. http://www.walmart.com
3. Guest, Greta. "Execs' frills bled Kmart, lawsuit says." *The Detroit Free Press,* 19 November 2003.
4. Greene, Robert. "The Wal-Mart Equation." *LA Weekly,* 3–9 October 2003.
5. Wal-Mart official web site. http://www.walmart.com
6. Walton, Sam. *Made in America.* New York: Doubleday, 1992. pp. 284–285.
7. Quinn, Bill. *How Wal-Mart is Destroying America and the World and What You Can Do About It.* Berkeley: Ten Speed Press, 2000.
8. "Carrefour vs. Wal-Mart: The Battle for Global Retail Dominance." http://www.agsm.edu.au/~timdev research/cases/Carrefour.pdf
9. Ibid.
10. *The California Space Authority Newsletter,* Vol 4, Spring 1999.

Chapter 6

1. Armour, Stephanie. "While hiring at most firms chills, Wal-Mart heats up." *USA Today,* 25 August 2002.
2. http://www.employeeselect.com/needIntegrityTest.htm "The Orion PE System is a computer or Scoring Center based integrity and work attitude assessment that provides reliable, valid, objective information on job related attitudes an applicant brings to the workplace."
3. http://www.religion-online.org/cgibin/ relsearchd.dll/showarticle?item_id=1356
4. Wal-Mart official web site. http://www.walmart.com
5. Ibid.

Chapter 7

1 Wal-Mart annual report. 1995. p. 5.
2. Walton, Sam. *Made in America.* New York: Doubleday, 1992, p. 289.
3. Wal-Mart official web site. http://www.walmart.com
4. Saporito, Bill. "Inside the World's Biggest Store." *TIME Europe,* 20 January 2003.
5. Peters, Thomas J. and Robert H. Waterman. *In Search of Excellence.* Warner Books: New York. 1982.
6. "Quality of Customer Service Is Most Important and Cost-Effective Source of Growth For Fast-Growth Firms." PricewaterhouseCoopers' "Trendsetter Barometer." 11 June 1998.
7. Stew Leonard's website. http://www.stewleonards.com
8. Lee, Louise. "Facing Superstore Saturation, Wal-Mart Decides to Think Small." *The Wall Street Journal Interactive Edition,* 25 March 1998.
9. Troy, Mike. "Neighborhood Market caps year with round of new market entries." *DSN Retailing Today,* January 27, 2003.
10. Shannon Mullen "Plymouth Adapts to Wal-Mart." NHPR Broadcast. 25 July 2003.
11. Martels, Fred. "The 2003 Wal-Mart Supercenter Customer Loyalty Study," 2003.

Conclusion

1. Wal-Mart official web site. http://www.walmart.com

About the Author

Michael Bergdahl has over twenty-five years of business experience working in a variety of business environments with outstanding business leaders. He has worked for three Fortune 500 companies and has been involved in two successful business turnarounds. His experiences in the restaurant, publishing, petrochemical, consumer packaged goods, discount retailing, specialty retailing and waste industries provide the foundation for his interest in and knowledge of this topic. His years of retailing experience with companies like Frito-Lay, Wal-Mart and American Eagle Outfitters provided the "business laboratory" for him to fine-tune his understanding of business competition. His knowledge of Wal-Mart comes from firsthand experiences working at its Home Office—working with Mr. Sam himself. Bergdahl is an affiliate of Resource Associates Corporation.

Index

Michael Bergdahl—Speeches and Workshops for U.S.A. and International Audiences

The first president of the National Speakers Bureau, Bill Gove, described Michael Bergdahl as "A storyteller who weaves entertainment into his motivational business messages." Lou Holtz describes him this way: "Michael Bergdahl's speaking ability coupled with his exceptional experience with great leaders gives you something that everyone who wants to succeed needs to hear!" Roger Dow, SVP of sales for Marriott International, describes him this way: "He's a sales and service guy who knows how to motivate people to reach their full potential. Speaking from his hands-on experience, he inspires people to give that extra effort that yields big results. If you haven't heard him speak, you've got to hear him speak!"

Speeches for Domestic and International Audiences

What I Learned from Sam Walton: How to Compete and Thrive in a Wal-Mart World.

Horror stories abound about Wal-Mart's entry into new markets and the subsequent destruction of competitors and downtown areas. In this speech, using the acronym, P.O.C.K.E.T.S., Michael Bergdahl describes several effective strategies competitors can and have used to counteract the inevitable pressure created by big-box retailers. Finding your niche in the market is the key to your survival. The key is to avoid the temptation to compete on price. You've got to make the commitment to differentiate yourself by looking for "P.O.C.K.E.T.S." You will learn some secrets other companies have used to compete with Wal-Mart and survive!

F.I.R.S.T—Secrets to Outperforming the Pack

From his experiences working for world-class best-practice companies like PepsiCo's Frito-Lay Division and Wal-Mart, Michael Bergdahl shares with you some of the secrets of their success. As a turnaround team member at American Eagle Outfitters and Waste Management, he learned what it takes to turn a failing company around. He shares the secrets of outperforming the pack in this speech using the acronym F.I.R.S.T., which stands for Focus on the Customer, Inspirational leadership, Results through people, Succession planning/bench-building, and Tactics for driving the business. Combining energy, storytelling, and humor with his practical experience working with executives like Sam Walton, Bergdahl will entertain and provide practical and actionable business ideas to those in attendance.

For more information or to schedule a keynote address or a workshop:

Michael Bergdahl
mbergdahl@aol.com
www.michaelbergdahl.net
1-800-704-9309 (phone)
1-412-635-2638(phone)
1-421-635-0418 (fax)

Keynote Speaker Testimonials

"Your speaking ability coupled with your exceptional experience with great leaders gives you something that everyone who wants to succeed should hear."

—Lou Holtz, Head Football Coach,
University of Notre Dame 1986–1996

"He's a sales and service guy who knows how to motivate people to reach their full potential. Speaking from his hands-on experience, he inspires people to give that extra effort that yields big results. If you haven't heard him, you've got to hear him speak!"

—Roger Dow, Senior Vice President,
Global and Field Sales, Marriott International

"Michael Bergdahl is not a public speaker—he is a storyteller—ever great speaker is a story teller. He makes a point and tells a story. Whether it's a keynote, a luncheon, or an after-dinner speech, Bergdahl might very well be your man."

—Bill Gove, First President
of the National Speakers Association

A Search for Personal Compete, Survive and Thrive Stories

from you or anyone you know who has or is competing in a Wal-Mart World as a Retailer, Non-Retailer, Manufacturer, Contractor, Real Estate Developer, Shopping Center Executive, Municipal Official, Mainstreet Organization Leader, Labor Union Leader or Member, Vendor, Supplier or a current or former Wal-Mart Employee

Readers around the world are eager to learn about your experience!

For my next book, I am planning to research and write about the competitive experiences of people just like you. I would like to incorporate your stories—whether positive or not so positive—about your experiences trying to compete, survive and thrive, domestically and internationally, in a Wal-Mart World. I am asking readers (and non-readers) to share your unique competitive experiences with me—good or bad. Your story may be about a positive Wal-Mart experience or about one not so positive in which you have been involved personally. Your story may be about successes or failures you've experienced personally in pricing, operations, culture, key item promotion, expenses, talent or service. Share your unique story with readers from around the world!

There are three ways to send me your story in writing:

Via Mail to: Michael Bergdahl
                  P.O. Box 291
                  Ingomar, PA 15127-0291
Via E-Mail to: mbergdahl@aol.com

Via my website:
http://www.michaelbergdahl.net/successstory.shtml

Stories should be 250 to 500 words in length (One to two pages typed double spaced). Please include your name, phone number and e-mail address so I can contact you if necessary. If you'd like, I will be sure that you are credited in the book for your story submission. If you want to submit a story anonymously, I will still need your contact information for my files. Stories submitted without verifiable contact information will not be used.